Table of Contents

© 2006 American Education Publishing The Complete Book of Challenge Math

Table of Contents

The Complete Book of Challenge Math
© 2006 American Education Publishing

Adding and Subtracting Whole Numbers

Name _Sweet_

$= \pi \ \frac{4}{5} \ 2 \div {}^3 A - r^2 + 8 \ 1 \times 6^{mm} \ 7 \ 32°F \ 10 \ 63\% \ 8 \ cm \ \frac{7}{8}$

National Chicken Month

The month of September is dedicated to all the chickens that crossed the road. To all those chickens that made it to the other side—Happy National Chicken Month!

Add the numbers in each egg. Then, write each letter in the blank above the matching answer to solve the riddle.

CHICKENS GET THEIR OWN DAY?

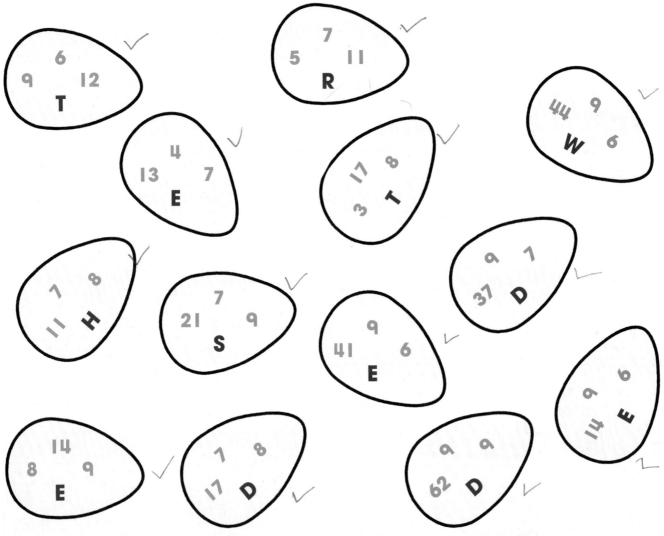

What do mother chickens feed their baby chicks for breakfast?

S H R E D D E D   T W E E T
37 26 23 24 80 53 31 32   27 59 29 56 28

6

The Complete Book of Challenge Math

© 2006 American Education Publishing

= π $\frac{4}{5}$ 2 ÷ ³A − r² + 8 1 × 6ᵐᵐ 7 32°F 10 63% 8 cm $\frac{7}{8}$

Let's Go Bowling

Who won the bowling match? Use the following information to fill out the scoring sheet. The first two frames have been done for you.

- A **frame** consists of two consecutive balls thrown at the same 10 pins.
- Record the score of the first ball to the left of the small top square. Record the score of the second ball in the small square.
- Add the total from both balls to the score of the previous frame to arrive at the total for that frame. The accumulated score is recorded in the lower portion of the frame.
- Draw an **X** in the small square to record a strike. Add 10 points plus the score for the next two balls to that frame.
- Draw a **/** to record a spare. Add 10 points to that frame plus the score of the next ball.

	Name	1	2	3	4	5	6	7	8	9	10	Total
1	Chris	5 4 / 9	7 1 / 17	3 7 / 10	5 0 / 5	10 X / 10	8 1 / 9	4 6 / 10	10 X / 10	6 2 / 8	3 5 / 8	119
2	Jon	3 / / 16	6 1 / 23	9 / / 9	8 0 / 9	7 3 / 10	10 X / 10	10 X / 10	9 0 / 9	8 2 / 10	10 X / 10	166

	Chris			Jon	
Frame	**Ball 1**	**Ball 2**	**Frame**	**Ball 1**	**Ball 2**
1	5 pins down	4 pins down	1	3 pins down	7 pins down (spare)
2	7 pins down	1 pin down	2	6 pins down	1 pin down
3	3 pins down	7 pins down (spare)	3	9 pins down	1 pin down (spare)
4	5 pins down	0 pins down	4	8 pins down	1 pin down
5	10 pins down (strike)		5	7 pins down	3 pins down (spare)
6	8 pins down	1 pin down	6	10 pins down (strike)	
7	4 pins down	6 pins down (spare)	7	10 pins down (strike)	
8	10 pins down (strike)		8	9 pins down	0 pins down
9	6 pins down	2 pins down	9	8 pins down	2 pins down (spare)
10	3 pins down	5 pins down	10	10 pins down (strike)	
11	1	9	11	8 pins down	1 pin down

The Complete Book of Challenge Math

Name _____

$= \pi \ \frac{4}{5} \ 2 \div {}^3A - r^2 + 8 \ 1 \times 6^{mm} \ 7 \ 32°F \ 10 \ 63\% \ 8 \ cm \ \frac{7}{8}$

Angel Games

Ask a friend or family member to play this fun addition game with you.

1. The first player chooses two numbers from the cloud, crosses them out, and adds them using a calculator.

2. The player then uses the Angel Chart below to find the value of the sum and records the score.

3. The second player repeats steps 1 and 2.

4. Continue until all of the numbers in the cloud are used. The highest score wins!

39	107	22
73	53	85
68	117	99
18	136	127
158	46	141

Angel #1	Angel #2
Total:	**Total:**

Angel Chart	
Sum	**Points**
0–60	1
61–120	2
121–180	3
181–240	2
241–300	1

The Complete Book of Challenge Math

$= \pi \; \frac{4}{5} \; 2 \div \; ^3A - r^2 + 8 \; 1 \times 6^{mm} \; 7 \; 32°F \; 10 \; 63\% \; 8\,cm \; \frac{7}{8}$

Adding Whole Numbers

Find the sum of 14,566 and 16,495.

Aberto's Answer:
$$\begin{array}{r} 14{,}566 \\ + 16{,}495 \\ \hline 21{,}051 \end{array}$$

1. Check Aberto's answer. Round each addend to the nearest thousand. Use mental math to add the rounded numbers. How does your answer compare to Aberto's? Do you think his answer is correct? Why or why not?

2. If Aberto's work is wrong, find the correct sum. Explain what mistake he made.

Find the sums.

3. $\begin{array}{r} 431{,}824 \\ + 28{,}249 \\ \hline \end{array}$

4. $\begin{array}{r} 902{,}567 \\ + 379{,}256 \\ \hline \end{array}$

5. $\begin{array}{r} 612{,}173 \\ + 38{,}338 \\ \hline \end{array}$

To check your work, round each addend to the nearest hundred thousand or ten thousand. Use mental math to add the rounded numbers. Put a checkmark next to the answers above that don't match the estimated sums. Look carefully at each answer to find any mistakes.

The Complete Book of Challenge Math

Name _____

More Adding Whole Numbers

Find the sums.

1. $\begin{array}{r} 223{,}416 \\ + \ 21{,}425 \\ \hline \end{array}$

2. $\begin{array}{r} 17{,}627 \\ + \ 428{,}733 \\ \hline \end{array}$

3. $\begin{array}{r} 837{,}354 \\ + \ 415{,}617 \\ \hline \end{array}$

4. $\begin{array}{r} 126{,}478 \\ + \ 31{,}621 \\ \hline \end{array}$

5. $\begin{array}{r} 541{,}439 \\ + \ 21{,}547 \\ \hline \end{array}$

6. $\begin{array}{r} 27{,}438 \\ + \ 411{,}572 \\ \hline \end{array}$

7. $\begin{array}{r} 89{,}526 \\ + \ 911{,}248 \\ \hline \end{array}$

8. $\begin{array}{r} 351{,}237 \\ + \ 72{,}677 \\ \hline \end{array}$

9. $\begin{array}{r} 52{,}375 \\ + \ 76{,}238 \\ \hline \end{array}$

10. $\begin{array}{r} 7{,}182{,}583 \\ + \ 919{,}608 \\ \hline \end{array}$

11. $\begin{array}{r} 173{,}792 \\ + \ 554{,}526 \\ \hline \end{array}$

12. $\begin{array}{r} 652{,}731 \\ + \ 71{,}883 \\ \hline \end{array}$

Use any method to check your work. Be prepared to explain how you know your answers are correct.

The Complete Book of Challenge Math

$= \pi \ \frac{4}{5} \ 2 \div \ ^3 A - r^2 + 8 \ 1 \times 6\text{mm} \ 7 \ 32°F \ 10 \ 63\% \ 8\text{cm} \ \frac{7}{8}$

Plant Those Apple Trees!

Solve each problem. Then, order the sums from least to greatest. Write the letters of the problems in that order on the lines below to answer the question.

1.   4,269,812
              6,922
      + 358,189

J

2.   1,620,803
          2,811,249
      + 4,053,525

P

3.   3,405,000
          1,598,762
      +   46,909

H

4.   985,136
          6,168,523
      +   6,508

H

5.   3,641,805
             56,123
      +   983,057

O

6.   58,921
          7,934,600
      +   846,773

M

7.   1,843,277
          3,462,915
      +   3,610

N

8.   867,426
          1,473,916
      + 7,406,205

N

9.   6,235,403
             62,407
          1,548,522
      +   136,403

A

10.   3,947,601
              89,053
            624,109
      + 4,861,756

A

11.   66,385
          5,281,923
                 801
      +   942,564

C

Which historical character is responsible for planting apple trees across the United States?

___ ___ ___ ___ ___   ___ ___ ___ ___ ___ ___

HIS NICKNAME IS JOHNNY APPLESEED.

The Complete Book of Challenge Math

Name _____

First Flight

Find each sum. Then, follow the directions below.

1.
```
   762,489
     5,628
 6,562,899
+ 2,258,364
```
R

2.
```
 7,986,140
   628,309
 1,421,602
+   26,876
```
A

3.
```
    62,927
 6,291,673
   982,735
+  468,098
```
A

4.
```
 4,634,923
   848,577
     2,698
+ 1,249,864
```
R

5.
```
 1,840,294
   728,166
 5,050,671
+ 3,615,800
```
E

6.
```
 1,650,205
    95,364
 1,079,643
+  346,725
```
T

7.
```
 34,925,635
 55,869,722
+ 9,182,528
```
A

8.
```
 86,624,690
  6,518,315
+4,003,189
```
M

9.
```
 44,649,417
  8,155,627
+ 24,318,243
```
L

10.
```
 2,612,536
   905,428
 4,183,620
+ 1,009,087
```
H

11.
```
 13,421,673
  2,730,948
    457,831
+ 41,173,996
```
I

12.
```
   997,173
 26,321,730
    84,651
+ 1,256,788
```
A

13.
```
 53,601,717
  4,183,552
  8,234,606
+ 13,976,378
```
E

Order the sums from greatest to least. Then, write the letters of the problems in that order on the lines below to answer the question.

Who tried to fly around the world at the equator?

___ ___ ___ ___ ___ ___

___ ___ ___ ___ ___ ___ ___

$= \pi \ \frac{4}{5} \ 2 \div {}^3A - r^2 + 8 \ 1 \times 6$mm $7 \ 32°F \ 10 \ 63\% \ 8$cm $\frac{7}{8}$

The Great Calorie Count

Everyone in Marjorie's family counted calories to maintain a healthy weight. Read about their meals and write the number of calories calculated.

1. Marjorie made a sandwich for her school lunch. She used 2 slices of bread at 58 calories each. She spread 1 tablespoon of margarine on the bread at 101 calories. She added 1 slice of cheese at 101 calories, and a slice of lunch meat at 161 calories. How many calories were in her sandwich?

_____

2. Along with her sandwich, Marjorie ate a pear with 101 calories. She also bought a half-pint of milk with 152 calories. How many calories were in her whole lunch?

_____

3. Marjorie's brother, George, packed his lunch with two chicken legs at 209 calories each, a container of applesauce at 116 calories, a celery stick at 7 calories and a cookie at 96 calories. How many calories were in George's lunch?

_____

4. For breakfast, Marjorie, her brother, and her parents each had a dish of oatmeal at 130 calories, a glass of milk at 150 calories, and a half-cup of raisins at 210 calories. How many breakfast calories did they have all together?

_____

5. For dinner, each family member ate a serving of roast beef at 393 calories, corn on the cob at 242 calories, with margarine at 101 calories. They had green beans at 17 calories, a salad at 52 calories, with dressing at 41 calories. They each had a glass of milk at 150 calories. Their mother said they could have dessert if they each stayed under 1,000 calories for the whole meal. Will they get dessert? Explain.

_____

6. For dessert they each had chocolate ice cream at 220 calories and a slice of cake with 320 calories. How many calories were in each dessert?

_____

The Complete Book of Challenge Math

Name _____

$= \pi \frac{4}{5} \ 2 \div {}^3 A - r^2 + 8 \ 1 \times 6\text{mm} \ 7 \ 32°F \ 10 \ 63\% \ 8\text{cm} \ \frac{7}{8}$

Pig-Out on Math

Solve the subtraction problems. Then, write each letter in the blank above the matching answer to solve the riddle.

1. $\begin{array}{r} 735 \\ -154 \\ \hline \end{array}$ **H**	**2.** $\begin{array}{r} 233 \\ -128 \\ \hline \end{array}$ **S**	**3.** $\begin{array}{r} 571 \\ -316 \\ \hline \end{array}$ **G**	**4.** $\begin{array}{r} 670 \\ -128 \\ \hline \end{array}$ **A**

5. $\begin{array}{r} 586 \\ -369 \\ \hline \end{array}$ **A**	**6.** $\begin{array}{r} 9,141 \\ -1,320 \\ \hline \end{array}$ **E**	**7.** $\begin{array}{r} 1,304 \\ -291 \\ \hline \end{array}$ **B**	**8.** $\begin{array}{r} 5,423 \\ -2,722 \\ \hline \end{array}$ **A**

9. $\begin{array}{r} 4,269 \\ -2,176 \\ \hline \end{array}$ **W**   **10.** $\begin{array}{r} 3,771 \\ -1,860 \\ \hline \end{array}$ **H**

11. $\begin{array}{r} 6,430 \\ -3,429 \\ \hline \end{array}$ **I**   **12.** $\begin{array}{r} 7,621 \\ -4,439 \\ \hline \end{array}$ **M**

Why did the pig act up?

___	___		___	___	___		___	___	___		___	___	___	.
581	7,821		2,093	217	105		542	1,013	3,001	255		1,911	2,701	3,182

14

Subtracting Whole Numbers

Find the difference.

Kimberly's Answer:
$$
\begin{array}{r}
\overset{2\ 1}{\cancel{3}}\overset{}{\cancel{7}}2,5\overset{5\ 1}{\cancel{6}}2 \\
-\quad 81,429 \\
\hline
291,033
\end{array}
$$

1. Melissa checked Kimberly's work by using the inverse operation.
Finish Melissa's work.

$$
\begin{array}{r}
291,033 \\
+\ 81,429 \\
\hline
\end{array}
$$

2. Was Kimberly's answer correct? _____ How do you know?

_____

Find the differences.

3.   521,323
    − 382,417

4.   642,657
    − 148,651

5.   356,274
    − 265,183

6.   407,524
    − 316,257

7.   734,232
    − 682,038

8.   438,285
    − 256,715

The Complete Book of Challenge Math

Name _____

$= \pi \ \frac{4}{5} \ 2 \div {}^5 A - r^2 + 8 \ 1 \times 6 \ mm \ 7 \ 32°F \ 10 \ 63\% \ 8 \ cm \ \frac{7}{8}$

More Subtracting Whole Numbers

Find the differences.

1. 75,132
       − 48,248

2. 32,512
       − 15,788

3. 21,842
       − 20,553

4. 75,615
       − 58,186

5. 369,430
       − 275,768

6. 82,935
       − 74,541

7. 321,423
       − 218,154

8. 43,600
       − 12,243

9. 2,340,642
       −   278,236

Check your answers by using the inverse operation. Look carefully at any wrong answers to find your mistake.

$$= \pi \ \tfrac{4}{5} \ 2 \div {}^{3}A - r^{2} + 8 \ 1 \times 6^{mm} \ 7 \ 32°F \ 10 \ 63\% \ 8\,cm \ \tfrac{7}{8}$$

Scientific Find

In November 1996, scientists in China found something very special that may have proved dinosaurs were the ancestors of birds. Solve each problem. Then, circle the word by each corresponding answer to determine what they found.

1. 6,428,921 − 619,563	The 5,809,358	Cave 6,211,442	65 5,819,441
2. 234,896 − 159,347	paintings 125,551	trillion 75,551	150 75,549
3. 7,640,358 − 3,732,947	million 3,907,411	year 4,112,611	depicting 4,907,511
4. 9,631,400 − 6,298,261	old 3,433,239	year 3,333,139	feathered 3,467,261
5. 4,125,634 − 943,573	DNA 4,822,141	old 3,182,061	dinosaurs 3,882,161
6. 8,341,087 − 2,915,149	fossil 5,425,938	flying 6,634,142	with 5,434,942
7. 1,842,573 − 1,296,499	and 554,074	of 546,074	gene 654,426
8. 3,664,715 − 2,579,806	gliding 1,125,111	strands 1,085,119	feathered 1,084,909
9. 2,671,482 − 843,594	for 1,832,882	Sinosauropteryx 1,827,888	through 2,232,112
10. 5,963,117 − 2,695,528	space 3,332,411	Prima 3,267,589	feathers 3,267,411

The Complete Book of Challenge Math

Name _____

Where's That Locker?

Solve to find each difference. Then, add the digits in each answer and shade the sums in the grid to find the route from the classroom to the lockers. The first one has been done for you.

1. 9,522,519
− 2,893,026
6,629,493 = 39

2. 5,050,671
− 321,263

3. 6,291,673
− 3,186,849

4. 6,291,673
− 826,496

5. 7,986,140
− 92,685

6. 4,634,923
− 2,468,537

7. 3,947,621
− 52,366

8. 5,281,923
− 1,165,737

9. 6,562,899
− 648,920

10. 9,747,507
− 9,269,628

11. 4,235,403
− 536,926

12. 8,485,577
− 6,499,038

13. 4,634,923
− 9,355

14. 7,934,846
− 2,689,572

15. 4,053,803
− 2,144,735

Classroom

35	23	19	45	31	50
42	17	56	48	34	41
29	37	41	21	36	12
49	52	43	30	32	25
28	53	33	46	27	16
51	49	22	44	39	40

Lockers

$= \pi \ \frac{4}{5} \ 2 \div \ ^3A - r^2 + 8 \ 1 \times 6\text{mm} \ 7 \ 32°F \ 10 \ 63\% \ 8\text{cm} \ \frac{7}{8}$

In the Air

What important event occurred on December 17, 1903? Solve each problem. Then, circle the word by each corresponding answer to determine this event.

I.	$\begin{array}{r} 6,846,733 \\ -\ 5,923,788 \\ \hline \end{array}$	Alexander 1,123,055	The 922,945	transcontinental 1,922,985
2.	$\begin{array}{r} 2,811,249 \\ -\quad\ 96,322 \\ \hline \end{array}$	railroad 2,885,127	Graham 2,814,927	Wright 2,714,927
3.	$\begin{array}{r} 9,269,812 \\ -\ 4,674,266 \\ \hline \end{array}$	connects 4,595,544	brothers 4,595,546	Bell 5,215,654
4.	$\begin{array}{r} 3,641,823 \\ -\ 2,327,446 \\ \hline \end{array}$	flew 1,314,377	invents 1,314,423	the 1,326,423
5.	$\begin{array}{r} 5,916,734 \\ -\ 3,625,922 \\ \hline \end{array}$	east 2,311,212	the 2,290,812	a 2,290,242
6.	$\begin{array}{r} 6,381,400 \\ -\quad 576,031 \\ \hline \end{array}$	first 5,805,369	and 3,105,369	second 6,215,431
7.	$\begin{array}{r} 8,926,923 \\ -\ 6,400,697 \\ \hline \end{array}$	wireless 2,526,276	west 2,526,374	powered 2,526,226
8.	$\begin{array}{r} 1,869,187 \\ -\quad\ 67,728 \\ \hline \end{array}$	at 1,701,459	telephone 1,802,661	aircraft 1,801,459
9.	$\begin{array}{r} 5,196,801 \\ -\ 1,961,352 \\ \hline \end{array}$	at 3,235,449	Promontory 4,235,449	in 4,825,449
10.	$\begin{array}{r} 7,410,369 \\ -\quad 815,072 \\ \hline \end{array}$	Point 7,595,217	Kitty 6,595,297	the 7,405,297
11.	$\begin{array}{r} 4,443,924 \\ -\ 4,358,056 \\ \hline \end{array}$	Utah 185,932	United States 185,868	Hawk 85,868

The Complete Book of Challenge Math

Name _____

Meet Me at the Fair

In 1904, the world's fair in St. Louis caused much wonder among people. New inventions, foods, and art sparked interest throughout the world. Read about the fair and calculate the problems.

1. Peanut butter was introduced at the world's fair in 1904. The first commercial peanut butter was produced by a St. Louis doctor in 1890. How long after its production was it introduced at the fair?

_____

2. The largest Ferris wheel was built for the Chicago fair in 1893. The same Ferris wheel was used at the St. Louis World's Fair in 1904. It was torn down and sold for scrap in 1904. How many years did the Ferris wheel run?

_____

3. No one is sure where ice cream was first made, but the ice-cream cone was introduced at the world's fair in 1904. How many years has it been since the first cone was used to hold ice cream?

_____

4. What year was the 100th anniversary of the 1904 world's fair?

_____

5. The hot dog was also introduced at the world's fair in 1904. Carla ate her first hot dog in 1987. How many years after the hot dog was introduced did Carla eat her first one?

_____

6. Approximately 10,984,000 men and approximately 8,927,000 women came to the St. Louis World's Fair. How many more men than women visited the fair?

_____

$= \pi \ \frac{4}{5} \ 2 \div {}^{3}A - r^2 + 8 \ 1 \times 6\text{mm} \ 7 \ 32°\text{F} \ 10 \ 63\% \ 8\,\text{cm} \ \frac{7}{8}$

Oom-pah-pah

Celebrate National Tuba Day. Use the numbers blasting out of the tuba to complete the problems.

1.
```
   105
 +
 -----
   208
```

2.
```
 + 480
 -----
   900
```

3.
```
   369
 +
 -----
   500
```

4.
```
    23
    35
 +
 -----
    84
```

5.
```
    53
 +  48
 -----
   143
```

6.
```
    26
    91
 +
 -----
   163
```

7.
```
 +
 -----
   362
```

8.
```
 +
 -----
    76
```

26

42

217

46

145

40

131

420

36

103

© 2006 American Education Publishing

The Complete Book of Challenge Math

Mixed Addition and Subtraction

Solve the addition and subtraction problems.

1. 721,345
    + 97,275
    _____

2.   19,725
    + 238,324
    _____

3.   405,783
    − 213,277
    _____

4. 514,165
    + 17,829
    _____

5.   43,203
    − 8,364
    _____

6.   752,155
    − 691,196
    _____

7. 72,612
    − 34,458
    _____

8. 532,263
    + 384,517
    _____

9. 2,451,533
    − 987,370
    _____

Check each answer by using the inverse operation. Look carefully at any wrong answers to find your mistake.

Multiplying
Whole Numbers

Name _____

Mr. Clyde's Cursive Cards

It's National Handwriting Day. Mr. Clyde Cursive has his students making a set of cursive cards to help them learn their multiplication facts. Some students are having difficulty writing the numbers on the cards. Help them by writing the missing numbers in cursive on the cards.

$= \pi \ \frac{4}{5} \ 2 \div \ ^3\!\sqrt{A} - r^2 + 8 \ 1 \times 6 \, mm \ 7 \ 32°F \ 10 \ 63\% \ 8 \, cm \ \frac{7}{8}$

Wintertime Wake-Up

The groundhog has awoken from his wintertime nap. Help him move from his cozy den up the tunnel in search of daylight. Follow the multiples of 8 to find his path. You may move horizontally, vertically, or diagonally.

66	60	82	34	26	28	36	8
54	46	62	76	54	44	56	12
14	30	50	36	18	32	42	49
18	54	62	74	38	60	40	34
82	78	48	24	88	54	80	58
49	32	52	34	36	16	28	42
54	28	72	63	54	81	18	14
8	64	36	18	21	27	30	45

YAWN!

The Complete Book of Challenge Math

Name _____

Multiplication Mess

Steve has a messy desk. He also has a messy table. His multiplication table that is. Color the boxes that have incorrect products.

X	0	1	2	3	4	5	6	7	8	9
0	0	0	0	0	0	0	0	0	0	0
1	0	1	2	5	4	5	4	7	8	9
2	0	2	4	7	8	10	11	14	16	18
3	0	3	6	8	12	15	16	21	24	27
4	0	4	8	12	16	20	24	28	32	36
5	0	8	10	15	20	25	30	35	50	45
6	0	5	12	18	24	30	36	42	46	54
7	0	7	13	21	28	35	42	48	56	63
8	0	8	16	26	36	42	49	56	64	72
9	0	9	18	27	36	45	54	63	72	81

Name _____

Looking for Spring

Every year, on February 2, we observe Groundhog's Day. We watch to see if the groundhog will see its shadow when it emerges from its hole. If the groundhog sees its shadow, it is believed there will be six more weeks of winter. If it doesn't, it is believed that Spring will come soon. Use the symbols below to compare each pair of multiplication facts to help coax the groundhog out of its hole.

greater than: >	equal to: =	less than: <

The Complete Book of Challenge Math

Name _____

Tree-mendous Day

Trees provide homes and food for millions of animals, oxygen for breathing, and much, much more.

Circle the hidden multiplication facts in this tree. There are 21 facts in all. You may move vertically or horizontally.

	6	6	36	2		
4	3	3	9	2	1	2
7	16	4	4	4	6	5
28	6	3	5	15	4	6
6	2	12	3	8	24	6
	12	3	6	4	9	36
	7	7	49	32	3	
	21	4	7			
	7	4	28			
	3	2	6			
	9	2	18			

Multiplication Race

Have a partner time you as you race toward the finish line with each car. Use the number above each racing lane as the factor for each equation.

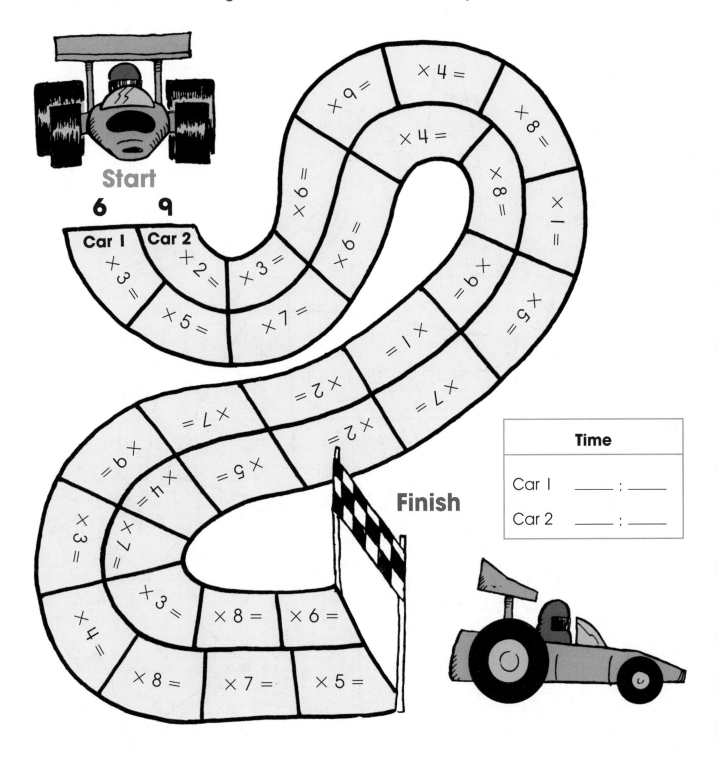

Start

6 **9**

Time		
Car 1	____	: ____
Car 2	____	: ____

Finish

29

The Complete Book of Challenge Math

Name _____

Hip-Hip-Hurray!

Hip-hip-hurray! It's Cheer Day! Today is the day to give a cheer for your favorite team.

Use all of the digits in each megaphone to make a multiplication sentence. Some digits may have more than one answer. The first one has been done for you.

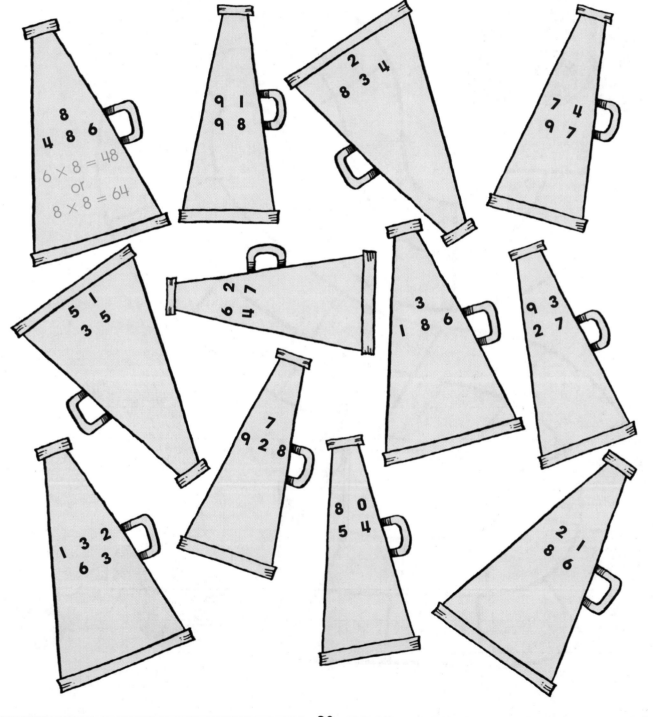

The Complete Book of Challenge Math   © 2006 American Education Publishing

Name _____

$= \pi \ \frac{4}{5} \ 2 \div {}^{3}A - r^{2} + 8 \ 1 \times 6 \text{mm} \ 7 \ 32°F \ 10 \ 63\% \ 8 \text{cm} \ \frac{7}{8}$

Race to the New World!

You are racing the Nina, the Pinta, and the Santa Maria to the new world.
Which ship will be the first to land?

1. Multiply the numbers along each ship's course by the number in the sail.

2. Ask someone to time how long it takes you to sail each course. Your
fastest time will determine which ship wins.

Nina Time: _____

× 3 =	× 5 =	× 8 =	× 1 =	× 0 =	× 9 =	× 6 =	× 4 =	× 2 =	× 7 =

Pinta Time: _____

× 5 =	× 3 =	× 0 =	× 9 =	× 6 =	× 8 =	× 4 =	× 7 =	× 3 =	× 2 =

Santa Maria Time: _____

× 0 =	× 3 =	× 2 =	× 4 =	× 5 =	× 8 =	× 7 =	× 9 =	× 3 =	× 6 =

The Complete Book of Challenge Math

Name _____

Take It Easy

Labor Day signals the end of summer. Many people celebrate by attending picnics or ball games, or by just relaxing with family and friends. This special day is set aside to honor working people.

Here's a number game that you can play for fun. You will need a pair of dice and paper squares to place on the game sheet.

Each player should have a game sheet. Take turns rolling the dice. Multiply the numbers on the dice. Then, use a paper square to cover the product on the game sheet. The first player to cover one row of five squares in any direction is the winner.

1	36	9	24	18
8	6	15	30	25
10	24	18	6	3
12	2	4	12	16
9	12	20	6	10

THE FIRST LABOR DAY WAS IN 1882!

Peanut Scramble

Unscramble the numbers on each of the peanuts. Rearrange the digits on each nut to make a multiplication problem. Write the answer beside each peanut. The first one has been done for you.

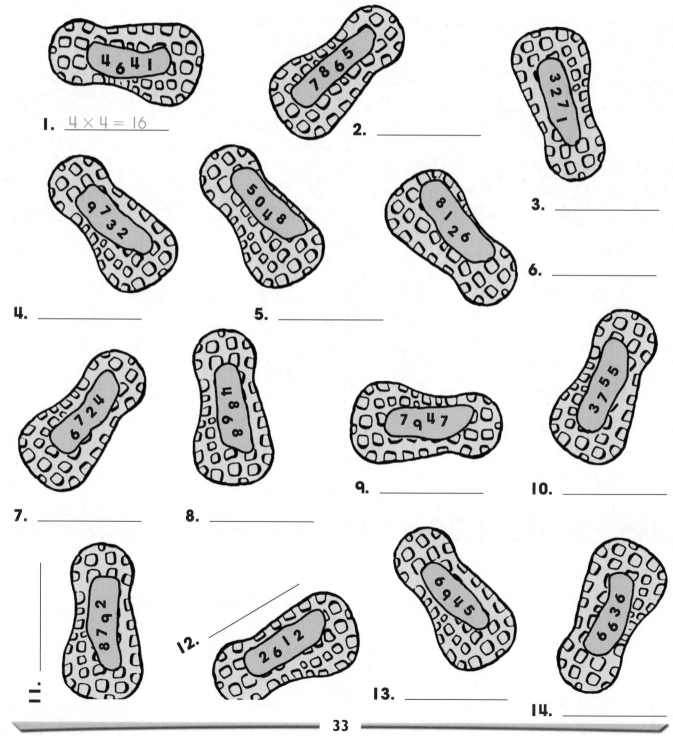

1. $4 \times 4 = 16$

2. _____

3. _____

4. _____

5. _____

6. _____

7. _____

8. _____

9. _____

10. _____

11. _____

12. _____

13. _____

14. _____

The Complete Book of Challenge Math

Name _____

Tickle the Ivories

Tickle the ivories on the piano keyboard to celebrate National Piano Month. Solve the problems on the piano keys. Then, write the letters on the blanks above the matching answers to solve the riddle.

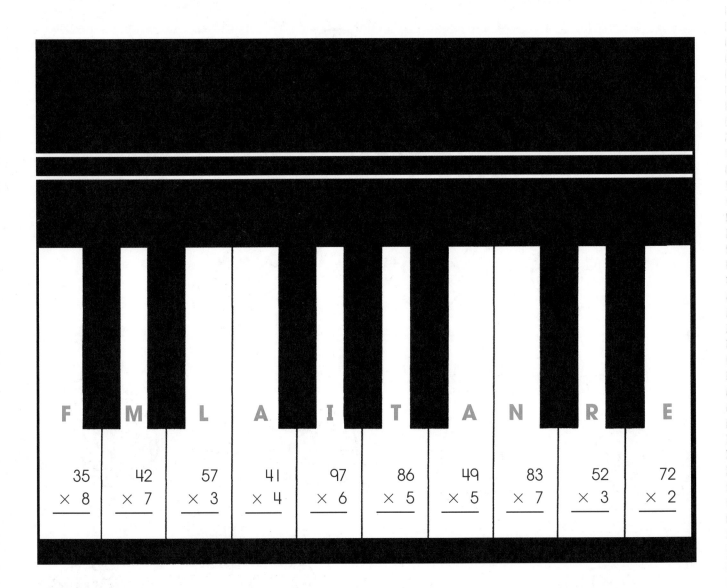

F	M	L	A	I	T	A	N	R	E
35 × 8	42 × 7	57 × 3	41 × 4	97 × 6	86 × 5	49 × 5	83 × 7	52 × 3	72 × 2

What do you get when you drop a grand piano down a mine shaft?

___ ___ ___ ___ ___   ___ ___ ___ ___ ___
164   280 171 245 430   294 582 581 144 156

Name _____

Land Ho!

In 1492, Columbus sailed a fleet of ships across the ocean. Where did Columbus first go ashore? Solve each multiplication problem. Then, connect the dots in the same order to determine the course taken.

1. 46 × 6	**2.** 68 × 4	**3.** 54 × 7	**4.** 83 × 8
5. 67 × 5	**6.** 84 × 4	**7.** 84 × 7	**8.** 93 × 3
9. 32 × 5	**10.** 43 × 8	**11.** 28 × 4	**12.** 37 × 6

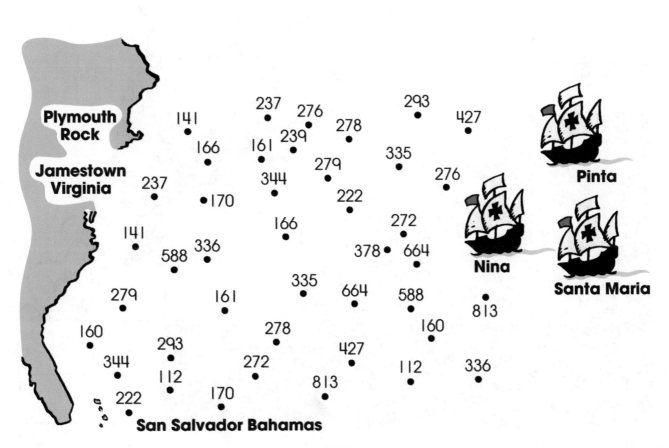

The Complete Book of Challenge Math

Name _____

Building Blocks

It's National Bricklayer's Day. Mr. Mason deserves a day off from the heavy work of laying bricks.

Offer Mr. Mason a hand by filling in the boxes on the brick wall. Solve the problems going across first. Then, check your work by solving the down problems.

Across	Down
A = 253 × 6	**B** = 9 × 2
D = 108 × 8	**C** = 123 × 7
F = 3 × 48	**E** = 63 × 7
H = 14 × 12	**G** = 77 × 6
J = 31 × 8	**I** = 12 × 7
L = 8 × 3	**K** = 92 × 9
N = 41 × 2	**M** = 6 × 7

GEE, THANKS!

$$= \pi \ \frac{4}{5} \ 2 \div \ ^3\!\!/\!\!A \ - \ r^2 + 8 \ 1 \times 6 \ \text{mm} \ 7 \ 32°F \ 10 \ 63\% \ 8 \ \text{cm} \ \frac{7}{8}$$

Check Your Multiplication

Example:

Step 1: Multiply by
the ones.

```
    34
  × 23
  ─────
   102      (34 × 3)
```

Step 2: Multiply by
the tens.

```
    34
  × 23
  ─────
   102      (34 × 3)
 + 680      (34 × 20)
 ─────
```

Step 3: Add the
products.

```
    34
  × 23
  ─────
   102      (34 × 3)
 + 680      (34 × 20)
 ─────
   782      (add)
```

Find the products. Show your work.

1.
```
    52
  × 87
  ─────
```

2.
```
    26
  × 45
  ─────
```

3.
```
    21
  × 31
  ─────
```

4.
```
    41
  × 58
  ─────
```

5.
```
    84
  × 15
  ─────
```

6.
```
   327
  ×  16
  ─────
```

7.
```
   524
  ×  31
  ─────
```

8.
```
   155
  ×  43
  ─────
```

9.
```
   243
  ×  65
  ─────
```

Carefully check each step. Did you perform each multiplication correctly?
Did you multiply by the correct place value? Did you regroup when necessary?

The Complete Book of Challenge Math

Name _____

$= \pi \ \frac{4}{5} \ 2 \div \ ^3A - r^2 + 8 \ 1 \times 6mm \ 7 \ 32°F \ 10 \ 63\% \ 8cm \ \frac{7}{8}$

Let Your Light Shine

Thomas Edison was known as the "Wizard of Menlo Park." One of his greatest inventions was the electric light.

Write the estimated answers in the lightbulbs. Next, solve the problems, showing your work. Then, write the letters on the blanks above the matching answers to solve the riddle.

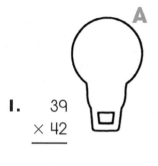

1. 39
× 42

A

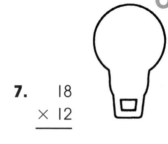

2. 42
× 89

H

3. 68
× 33

E

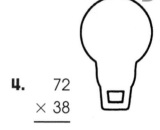

4. 72
× 38

D

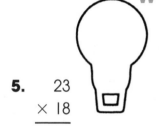

5. 23
× 18

W

6. 49
× 21

S

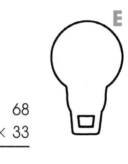

7. 18
× 12

O

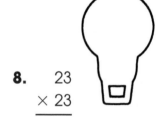

8. 23
× 23

K

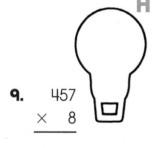

9. 457
×   8

H

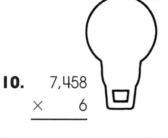

10. 7,458
×   6

C

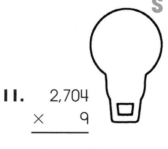

11. 2,704
×   9

S

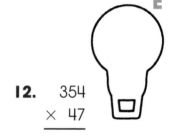

12. 354
× 47

E

How did the man feel when he got a big bill from the electric company?

___ ___ ___   ___ ___ ___
3,738 16,638   414 1,638 1,029

___ ___ ___ ___ ___ ___ ___!
24,336 3,656 216 44,748 529 2,244 2,736

38

Name _____

Multiplying by One Digit

Find each product. Show your work.

1.   649
       ×   8

2.   858
       ×   7

3.   7,642
       ×   5

4.   8,219
       ×   3

5.   5,238
       ×   6

6.   4,623
       ×   9

7.   8,249
       ×   4

8.   8,943
       ×   9

9.   3,268
       ×   5

10.   4,637
        ×   8

11.   8,924
        ×   6

12.   95,201
        ×   5

13.   73,643
        ×   8

14.   51,476
        ×   4

15.   73,629
        ×   5

16.   25,624
        ×   4

17.   63,928
        ×   8

18.   98,215
        ×   6

**Anything's
possible
with practice!**

19.   41,826
        ×   9

20.   53,214
        ×   8

21.   83,265
        ×   4

The Complete Book of Challenge Math

Name _____

Multiplying by Two Digits

Find each product. Show your work.

1. 467
    × 35
    ‾‾‾‾

2. 538
    × 47
    ‾‾‾‾

3. 393
    × 82
    ‾‾‾‾

4. 724
    × 56
    ‾‾‾‾

5. 821
    × 75
    ‾‾‾‾

6. 463
    × 43
    ‾‾‾‾

7. 522
    × 68
    ‾‾‾‾

8. 326
    × 92
    ‾‾‾‾

9. 735
    × 45
    ‾‾‾‾

10. 268
     × 39
     ‾‾‾‾

11. 534
     × 76
     ‾‾‾‾

12. 232
     × 98
     ‾‾‾‾

13. 845
     × 63
     ‾‾‾‾

14. 928
     × 81
     ‾‾‾‾

15. 625
     × 33
     ‾‾‾‾

16. 856
     × 42
     ‾‾‾‾

17. 932
     × 58
     ‾‾‾‾

18. 734
     × 54
     ‾‾‾‾

19. 487
     × 72
     ‾‾‾‾

20. 289
     × 79
     ‾‾‾‾

21. 824
     × 75
     ‾‾‾‾

Practice makes perfect!

22. 936
     × 47
     ‾‾‾‾

23. 365
     × 28
     ‾‾‾‾

24. 573
     × 65
     ‾‾‾‾

25. 792
     × 34
     ‾‾‾‾

The Complete Book of Challenge Math

= π ⁴⁄₅ 2 ÷ ³A − r² + 8 1 × 6mm 7 32°F 10 63% 8 cm ⁷⁄₈

Multiplying by One and Two Digits

Find each product. Show your work.

**Practice hard.
You'll win.**

1. 6,142
× 3

2. 4,921
× 5

3. 3,168
× 8

4. 2,482
× 9

5. 8,142
× 3

6. 4,628
× 7

7. 43,619
× 6

8. 54,613
× 4

9. 86,423
× 9

10. 56,984
× 7

11. 82,412
× 3

12. 46,304
× 8

13. 3,920
× 84

14. 5,549
× 30

15. 6,847
× 27

16. 2,295
× 56

17. 3,240
× 64

18. 6,847
× 92

19. 5,492
× 76

20. 62,003
× 64

21. 81,404
× 76

22. 54,128
× 24

23. 76,132
× 49

24. 59,149
× 26

25. 62,427
× 78

The Complete Book of Challenge Math

Multiplying Whole Numbers

Name _____

It's That Time of Year

Find each product. Then, write the last three digits of each product on the blanks above the matching answers to solve the code.

1. 32,426
   × 63 O

2. 56,841
   × 145 Y

3. 241,650
   × 21 E

4. 45,186
   × 62 A

5. 451,736
   × 57 U

6. 35,086
   × 83 B

7. 47,214
   × 47 M

8. 176,256
   × 172 H

9. 316,520
   × 33 D

10. 160,544
    × 72 N

11. 59,186
    × 112 R

12. 862,411
    × 40 T

13. 72,443
    × 231 L

14. 650,333
    × 29 G

15. 59,627
    × 301 S

What are students saying at the start of the school year?

___ ___ ___ ___ — ___ ___ ___   ___ ___ ___ ___ ___ ___ ...
657 838 838 160   138 945 650   727 952 58 58 650 832

___ ___ ___ ___ ___   ___ ___ ___ ___ ___ ___ .
32 650 333 333 838   532 952 440 952 58 168

Name _____

Multiplying by Three Digits

Find each product. Show your work.

1. 325
      × 614

2. 463
      × 527

3. 265
      × 921

4. 429
      × 304

5. 724
      × 630

6. 512
      × 825

7. 189
      × 432

8. 382
      × 265

9. 361
      × 543

10. 465
       × 734

11. 412
       × 398

12. 252
       × 726

13. 736
       × 413

14. 425
       × 817

15. 832
       × 625

16. 923
       × 542

17. 234
       × 489

18. 564
       × 820

19. 713
       × 256

20. 468
       × 375

The Complete Book of Challenge Math

Name _____

Multiplying by Four Digits

Find each product. Show your work.

1.   5,406
      × 2,142

2.   2,482
      × 4,321

3.   2,042
    × 9,123

4.   2,489
    × 4,300

5.   4,364
    × 5,127

6.   1,481
    × 6,824

7.   1,348
    × 3,421

8.   3,901
    × 4,612

9.   3,842
    × 3,615

10.   3,246
     × 1,482

11.   1,498
     × 8,003

12.   2,514
     × 3,486

13.   3,628
     × 2,749

14.   4,215
     × 1,321

15.   1,347
     × 5,621

16.   1,541
     × 2,824

17.   3,045
     ×9,120

18.   1,423
     × 6,215

19.   2,653
     × 5,214

20.   1,434
     × 8,172

Anything's possible with practice!

$= \pi \frac{4}{5} 2 \div \overset{3}{\_} A - r^2 + 8 \; 1 \times 6 \, mm \; 7 \; 32°F \; 10 \; 63\% \; 8 \, cm \; \frac{7}{8}$

Teamwork

Mr. Muscles, the physical education teacher, asked his class to help organize the equipment after gym class. Use multiplication to answer the following questions. Show your work.

1. There were eight stations in the gym. Each station had six small rubber balls and four large ones. How many balls were there all together?

_____

2. Mr. Muscles stores the jump ropes in boxes. The students collected six boxes with seven ropes, nine boxes with four, and 12 boxes with three. How many jump ropes were there all together?

_____

3. The class used 68 cones during gym. The students put away the cones in several places. There were four stacks of seven in one spot, three stacks of nine in another, and six stacks of two in yet another place. _____

Did the students find all 68 cones? _____

How many, if any, were missing? _____

4. Mr. Muscles divided the class into groups of five. He wanted to see which group could collect the most baseballs. In Group A, two students collected three, one collected five, and the other two collected two. In Group B, four students collected four and one collected one. In Group C, two students collected four, one collected six, and two collected one. In Group D, four students collected one, and one collected two. In Group E, one student collected four, three collected three, and one student collected two.

Which group collected the most baseballs? _____

How many baseballs did each group collect?

Group A _____   Group D _____

Group B _____   Group E _____

Group C _____

The Complete Book of Challenge Math

Name _____

Running a Truck Farm

Mark and his family live on a farm. They raise fruits and vegetables and ship them to market by truck. Read about the farm and answer the questions. Show your work.

1. They planted 98 rows of corn with 125 plants in each row. How many corn plants did they plant?

_____

2. While picking peaches, they filled 742 bushel baskets. Each basket held 45 peaches. How many peaches did they pick?

_____

3. 41 plums were packed in 1-peck cartons. If there were 237 cartons, how many plums were packed?

_____

4. The truck made deliveries in a 191-kilometer route each day for 23 days of the busiest month. How many total kilometers did the truck travel in that one month?

_____

5. The family picked 15 cartons of green beans. If each carton held 300 green beans, how many green beans did they pick?

_____

6. When the cantaloupes were ripe, they shipped 430 cases each day. If a case held 12 cantaloupes, how many cantaloupes were shipped each day?

_____

7. Mark's father works an average of 48 hours a week. If he works 45 weeks a year, about how many hours does he work in a year?

_____

Dividing Whole Numbers

Name _____

$= \pi \ \frac{4}{5} \ 2 \div {}^3 A - r^2 + 8 \ 1 \times 6^{mm} \ 7 \ 32°F \ 10 \ 63\% \ 8 \ cm \ \frac{7}{8}$

Gobble These Facts

These wild turkeys are displaying division facts. Solve each division problem and find the quotient that does not match the others. Shade this feather. Unscramble the letters from the shaded feathers to write a Thanksgiving word.

___ ___ ___ ___ ___ ___ ___ !

Name _____

= π $\frac{4}{5}$ 2 ÷ ^{3}A − r^2 + 8 1 × 6^{mm} 7 32°F 10 63% 8cm $\frac{7}{8}$

Domino Dots

Write multiplication and division facts for each domino. The first one has been done for you.

1.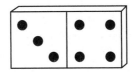

$3 \times 4 = 12$

$4 \times 3 = 12$

$12 \div 3 = 4$

$12 \div 4 = 3$

2.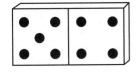

3.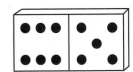

4.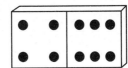

5.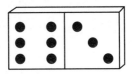

6.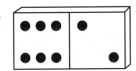

7.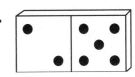

8.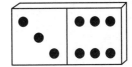

Place a handful of dominoes upside down on a table. Turn over four dominoes. Draw the dots on the dominoes below. Write multiplication and division facts for each domino.

1.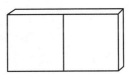

2.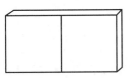

3.

4.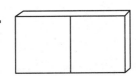

49

The Complete Book of Challenge Math

Name _____

$= \pi \ \frac{4}{5} \ 2 \div \ ^5A - r^2 + 8 \ 1 \times 6^{mm} \ 7 \ 32°F \ 10 \ 63\% \ 8_{cm} \ \frac{7}{8}$

Domino Trivia

Divide and show your work. Then, cross out the matching answers in the letter grid below. The remaining letters will answer the trivia question.

1. $3\overline{)49}$

2. $6\overline{)85}$

3. $5\overline{)93}$

4. $3\overline{)71}$

5. $7\overline{)97}$

6. $3\overline{)88}$

7. $4\overline{)91}$

8. $3\overline{)74}$

DOMINOES ARE BELIEVED TO HAVE ORIGINATED IN CHINA!

What name is given to one of the little dots on a domino?

___ ___ ___

B	A	P	R	E	I	S	G	O	P	L
16 r1	13 r6	17 r1	29 r1	18 r3	21 r2	14 r1	23 r2	24 r2	24 r4	22 r3

The Complete Book of Challenge Math

Name _____

Sick Bunny

Divide and show your work. Then, cross out the boxes with the matching answers in the letter grid below. The remaining letters will answer the riddle.

I. 3)86

2. 4)67

3. 9)97

4. 4)93

5. 4)69

6. 3)79

7. 2)37

8. 7)92

9. 7)186

10. 3)193

11. 7)296

12. 9)471

I DON'T FEEL SO HOT....

What do you give sick rabbits?

___ ___ ___ ___ ___   ___ ___ ___ ___ ___

R	U	H	T	A	B	A	R	Y	C	E
28 r2	26 r4	21 r3	17 r1	17 r2	23 r1	64 r1	54 r3	42 r2	52 r3	45 r2
B	**X**	**D**	**O**	**T**	**O**	**N**	**A**	**I**	**C**	**!**
18 r1	13 r1	26 r1	16 r3	16 r2	12 r1	81 r6	10 r7	71 r4	16 r6	15 r3

The Complete Book of Challenge Math

Name _____

$= \pi \frac{4}{5}\ 2 \div\ ^3 A - r^2 + 8\ 1 \times 6^{mm}\ 7\ 32°F\ 10\ 63\%\ 8\,cm\ \frac{7}{8}$

Mary's Thanksgiving

Thanksgiving Day wasn't always celebrated in the U.S. In 1863, Sarah Josepha Hale, a well-known writer and editor, convinced President Abraham Lincoln to declare the last Thursday in November a National Day of Thanksgiving. Since then, the U.S. celebrates a National Thanksgiving Day each November.

Sarah Josepha Hale is also famous for writing a well-known children's poem. What is it?

Divide and show your work. Then, write each letter in the blank above the matching answer to name the poem.

1. $6\overline{)216}$ **R**   2. $7\overline{)336}$ **A**   3. $5\overline{)185}$ **D**   4. $9\overline{)378}$ **B**

5. $4\overline{)332}$ **I**   6. $8\overline{)536}$ **E**   7. $7\overline{)546}$ **H**   8. $6\overline{)444}$ **T**

9. $6\overline{)210}$ **L**   10. $8\overline{)608}$ **M**   11. $4\overline{)308}$ **Y**

___ ___ ___ ___   ___ ___ ___   ___
76   48   36   77   78   48   37   48

___ ___ ___ ___ ___ ___   ___ ___ ___ ___
35   83   74   74   35   67   35   48   76   42

The Complete Book of Challenge Math

Teatime

Is there a friend that you haven't talked to in a while? Today is the day to invite that friend over to enjoy a cup of tea together!

Divide and show your work. Then, cross out the boxes with the matching answers in the letter grid below. The remaining letters will answer the riddle.

$5\overline{)93}$ $4\overline{)73}$ $3\overline{)88}$ $6\overline{)86}$

$7\overline{)175}$ $3\overline{)143}$ $8\overline{)174}$ $6\overline{)264}$

$8\overline{)265}$ $6\overline{)188}$

Y	T	U	E	R	A	Y	M
31 r2	44 r1	47 r2	16 r2	18 r1	45 r2	21 r6	29 r1
R	P	O	R	M	G	T	W
44	13 r2	15 r3	33 r1	25	18 r3	22 r4	14 r2

What starts with *T*, ends with *T*, and is filled with *T*?

_____

The Complete Book of Challenge Math

Name _____

$= \pi \ \frac{4}{5} \ 2 \div {}^3 A - r^2 + 8 \ 1 \times 6^{mm} \ 7 \ 32°F \ 10 \ 63\% \ 8 \ cm \ \frac{7}{8}$

Salute to Soldiers

Find each quotient. Then, write each letter in the blank above the matching answer to solve the riddle.

1. $27\overline{)135}$ **T**

2. $16\overline{)544}$ **R**

3. $24\overline{)360}$ **Y**

4. $14\overline{)378}$ **I**

5. $31\overline{)354}$ **H**

6. $22\overline{)423}$ **T**

7. $57\overline{)295}$ **N**

8. $46\overline{)334}$ **E**

9. $26\overline{)244}$ **N**

10. $61\overline{)732}$ **A**

11. $19\overline{)536}$ **F**

12. $16\overline{)306}$ **!**

ANSWER THIS RIDDLE CORRECTLY AND YOU'RE A FULL-FLEDGED MEMBER OF THE DIAPER DIVISION!

To what regiment in the army do baby soldiers belong?

____ ____ ____   ____ ____ ____   ____   ____   ____   ____   ____   ____
19 r5   11 r13   7 r12   27   5 r10   28 r4   12   9 r10   5   34   15   19 r2

Name _____

= π 4/5 2 ÷ 3A − r² + 8 1 × 6 mm 7 32°F 10 63% 8 cm 7/8

Every"body" Dance!

Divide and show your work. Then, write each letter in the box above the matching answer to solve the riddle.

1. 12)265 **H**

2. 21)467 **W**

3. 25)529 **E**

4. 32)996 **I**

5. 11)480 **N**

6. 15)365 **A**

7. 12)263 **D**

8. 10)186 **O**

9. 14)304 **Y**

10. 51)591 **B**

11. 23)492 **T**

12. 11)471 **G**

HA! THIS RIDDLE IS PRETTY HUMERUS!

Why didn't the skeleton go to the school dance?

___ ___   ___ ___ ___
22 r1 21 r4   22 r1 24 r5 21 r11

___ ___   ___ ___ ___ ___
43 r7 18 r6   11 r30 18 r6 21 r11 21 r10

___ ___   ___ ___
21 r9 18 r6   42 r9 18 r6

___ ___ ___ ___ .
22 r5 31 r4 21 r9 22 r1

The Complete Book of Challenge Math

Dividing Whole Numbers

Name _____

Leaping Leroy

Leap Day occurs only once every four years. During leap year, February 29 is added to the calendar year to make it almost equal to the solar year. Leap year is a year that can be divided evenly by 4.

Shade in the lilypads that lead Leaping Leroy to the party. You may move vertically, horizontally, or diagonally.

The Complete Book of Challenge Math   © 2006 American Education Publishing

$$= \pi \ \frac{4}{5} \ 2 \div {}^{5}A - r^{2} + 8 \ 1 \times 6^{mm} \ 7 \ 32^{\circ}F \ 10 \ 63\% \ 8 \, cm \ \frac{7}{8}$$

Check Your Division

Find the quotient.

Tyrell's Answer:

$$
\begin{array}{r}
108 \text{ r} 17 \\
37\overline{)683} \\
-37 \\
\hline
31 \\
-0 \\
\hline
313 \\
-296 \\
\hline
17
\end{array}
$$

I. Look at Tyrell's answer to the problem. Where did he place the first digit of his answer—above the ones, tens, or hundreds? _____

2. Paul thinks Tyrell should have placed the first digit in a different place. Here is Paul's thought process:

"Does 37 go into 6?   No. 37 > 6
Does 37 go into 68?   Yes. 37 < 68
The first digit should be placed above the 8, which is the tens place."

Do you agree with Paul? _____

3. Place the first digit of the answer in the correct place. Then, solve the division problem. Show your work.

$$37\overline{)683}$$

4. How does Tyrell's answer compare to yours? Explain to Tyrell why it is important to place the first digit in the correct place.

Name _____

Check Your Division

Check each of Camilla's answers by working the problems backwards. Make any necessary corrections.

Example:

Larry checked Camilla's answer to problem **1** by working the problem backwards. Finish Larry's work.

$$24 \times 22 = 528 \longrightarrow 528 + 15 = 543 \qquad \text{correct}$$

Camilla's Answers:

1. $24\overline{)543}$ 22 r15

4. $39\overline{)3,276}$ 84

2. $34\overline{)891}$ 26 r7

5. $21\overline{)918}$ 48 r10

3. $52\overline{)3,172}$ 62 r48

6. $56\overline{)3,652}$ 74 r12

The Complete Book of Challenge Math

$= \pi \ \frac{4}{5} \ 2 \div \ ^3A - r^2 + 8 \ 1 \times 6^{mm} \ 7 \ 32°F \ 10 \ 63\% \ 8_{cm} \ \frac{7}{8}$

Check Your Division

Find the quotient. Show your work.

Sydney's Answer:

$$\begin{array}{r} 17\ r13 \\ 42\overline{)4,507} \\ -42\downarrow\downarrow \\ \hline 307 \\ -\ 294 \\ \hline 13 \end{array}$$

Look carefully at each step of Sydney's work.

1. Did she place the first digit of the answer in the correct place? _____

2. Did she multiply correctly? _____ $42 \times 1 =$ ____

3. Did she subtract correctly? _____ $45 - 42 =$ ____

4. Did she bring down the tens? _____

   Is the difference less than 42? _____

$$\begin{array}{r} 1 \\ 42\overline{)4,507} \\ -42\downarrow \\ \hline 30 \end{array}$$

5. How many times does 42 go into 30? _____

   Did she put this answer in the right place? _____

$$\begin{array}{r} 1? \\ 42\overline{)4,507} \\ -42 \\ \hline 30 \end{array}$$

6. What did Sydney forget? Finish the problem correctly.

Make sure you include 0 in your quotient if you can't divide that place value.
For any wrong answers, look carefully at your work and make corrections.

The Complete Book of Challenge Math

Name _____

Check Your Division

Find the quotients. Show your work. Check each answer by working the problem backwards.

1. $17 \overline{)145}$

4. $44 \overline{)2{,}746}$

2. $54 \overline{)573}$

5. $29 \overline{)3{,}782}$

3. $62 \overline{)7{,}239}$

6. $38 \overline{)6{,}177}$

Make sure you place the first digit above the correct place value. Don't forget to include 0 in your quotient if you can't divide that place value.

The Complete Book of Challenge Math

Name _____

$= \pi \frac{4}{5} \ 2 \div \ ^3A - r^2 + 8 \ 1 \times \ 6^{mm} \ 7 \ 32°F \ 10 \ 63\% \ 8 \ cm \ \frac{7}{8}$

Division Practice (One-Digit Divisors)

Find each quotient. Show your work.

1. $8)\overline{3,216}$ **2.** $4)\overline{1,272}$ **3.** $7)\overline{1,502}$ **4.** $3)\overline{296}$ **5.** $6)\overline{4,811}$

6. $9)\overline{788}$ **7.** $5)\overline{554}$ **8.** $8)\overline{1,143}$ **9.** $4)\overline{362}$ **10.** $3)\overline{1,553}$

11. $6)\overline{5,554}$ **12.** $7)\overline{487}$ **13.** $2)\overline{1,694}$ **14.** $4)\overline{1,550}$ **15.** $9)\overline{7,155}$

With practice, you can do it!

16. $5)\overline{2,093}$ **17.** $7)\overline{4,778}$ **18.** $3)\overline{316}$

The Complete Book of Challenge Math

Name _____

Division Practice (Two-Digit Divisors)

Find each quotient. Show your work.

1. 27)216   **2.** 48)432   **3.** 35)245   **4.** 81)729   **5.** 32)192

6. 21)168   **7.** 84)588   **8.** 74)444   **9.** 65)520   **10.** 25)225

11. 92)644   **12.** 75)450   **13.** 24)192   **14.** 58)464   **15.** 42)252

Practice makes perfect!

16. 65)455   **17.** 25)250   **18.** 42)504

= π $\frac{4}{5}$ 2 ÷ ^3A − r^2 + 8 1 × 6ᵐᵐ 7 32°F 10 63% 8 cm $\frac{7}{8}$

Division Practice (Two-Digit Divisors)

Find each quotient. Show your work.

1. $14\overline{)326}$ **2.** $34\overline{)888}$ **3.** $21\overline{)298}$ **4.** $46\overline{)690}$ **5.** $31\overline{)843}$

6. $17\overline{)578}$ **7.** $54\overline{)918}$ **8.** $62\overline{)1,143}$ **9.** $20\overline{)706}$ **10.** $42\overline{)675}$

11. $23\overline{)653}$ **12.** $81\overline{)2,195}$ **13.** $71\overline{)3,550}$ **14.** $24\overline{)872}$ **15.** $19\overline{)825}$

16. $32\overline{)1,997}$ **17.** $44\overline{)1,678}$ **18.** $38\overline{)2,482}$ **Practice = Success!**

    The Complete Book of Challenge Math

Name _____

Division Practice (Two-Digit Divisors)

Find each quotient. Show your work.

1. $14\overline{)7,415}$ **2.** $22\overline{)6,750}$ **3.** $16\overline{)7,672}$ **4.** $19\overline{)5,640}$ **5.** $51\overline{)7,749}$

6. $32\overline{)8,558}$ **7.** $12\overline{)7,543}$ **8.** $15\overline{)5,856}$ **9.** $24\overline{)8,757}$ **10.** $31\overline{)7,991}$

11. $23\overline{)8,314}$ **12.** $13\overline{)4,536}$ **13.** $17\overline{)4,872}$ **14.** $25\overline{)9,240}$ **15.** $33\overline{)7,085}$

16. $20\overline{)9,657}$ **17.** $14\overline{)7,244}$ **18.** $48\overline{)6,960}$

With practice, you can do it!

Division Practice (Three-Digit Divisors)

Find each quotient. Show your work.

1. $143\overline{)1,287}$ **2.** $623\overline{)12,460}$ **3.** $431\overline{)3,448}$ **4.** $264\overline{)2,376}$

5. $172\overline{)2,064}$ **6.** $532\overline{)3,747}$ **7.** $803\overline{)12,090}$ **8.** $515\overline{)3,138}$

9. $634\overline{)17,443}$ **10.** $572\overline{)8,033}$ **11.** $145\overline{)5,539}$ **12.** $924\overline{)7,448}$

13. $232\overline{)4,908}$ **14.** $297\overline{)3,888}$ **15.** $128\overline{)2,304}$ **Practice brings success!**

The Complete Book of Challenge Math

Name _____

Ghosts and Bats

Solve each problem. Then, find the matching answers in the tic-tac-toe games. Draw a ghost over the answers for the odd-numbered problems and a bat over the answers for the even-numbered problems.

1. $56\overline{)27,384}$ **2.** $36\overline{)23,472}$ **3.** $15\overline{)9,450}$

4. $33\overline{)14,619}$ **5.** $57\overline{)10,203}$ **6.** $23\overline{)12,489}$

7. $47\overline{)12,549}$ **8.** $61\overline{)16,043}$ **9.** $82\overline{)12,218}$

10. $76\overline{)25,156}$ **11.** $42\overline{)33,264}$ **12.** $59\overline{)37,937}$

13. $27\overline{)16,146}$ **14.** $80\overline{)34,240}$

 THAT ABOUT WRAPS IT UP!

winner

179	543	489
267	443	180
630	642	652

winner

643	331	428
640	263	149
546	792	598

Name _____

$$= \pi \ \tfrac{4}{5} \ 2 \div {}^{3}A - r^2 + 8 \ 1 \times 6^{mm} \ 7 \ 32°F \ 10 \ 63\% \ 8\,cm \ \tfrac{7}{8}$$

Name That Inventor

Solve each problem. Find the matching answer in the letter grid. Then, write the letters on the blanks above the matching numbers to name the inventor.

3,741	197	243	518	268	669	864	635	5,410	725	299	411
A	D	E	H	I	L	M	N	O	S	T	V

1. $66\overline{)246{,}906}$

2. $42\overline{)11{,}256}$

3. $97\overline{)524{,}770}$

4. $55\overline{)34{,}925}$

5. $38\overline{)15{,}618}$

6. $61\overline{)31{,}598}$

7. $13\overline{)8{,}697}$

8. $94\overline{)18{,}518}$

9. $71\overline{)21{,}229}$

10. $76\overline{)18{,}468}$

11. $18\overline{)15{,}552}$

12. $25\overline{)18{,}125}$

This person, born on February 11, 1847, invented the carbon telephone transmitter, the phonograph, and the incandescent lamp. Who is this famous inventor?

___ ___ ___ ___ ___ ___   ___ ___ ___ ___   ___ ___ ___ ___ ___ ___
9   6   3   11 1   12   1   7   5   1   10 8   2   12 3   4

The Complete Book of Challenge Math

Dividing Whole Numbers

Name _____

$= \pi \frac{4}{5} \ 2 \div \frac{5}{A} - r^2 + 8 \ 1 \times 6^{mm} \ 7 \ 32°F \ 10 \ 63\% \ 8cm \frac{7}{8}$

Bert's Job

Samantha's big brother, Bert, works at a service station. Read about Bert's job and answer the questions. Show your work.

1. The service station has a supply of 95 tires. How many sets of 4 tires can be sold from this supply?

_____

2. If 4 tires cost $259, how much does one tire cost?

_____

3. The service station made $207.00 changing oil in one day. If they changed the oil for 9 cars, how much did each oil change cost?

_____

4. Samantha's father filled up his car with $9.81 of gasoline. If he got 9 gallons of gasoline, how much did gas cost per gallon?

_____

5. Bert counted the service station's supply of spark plugs. Each car takes 4 spark plugs, and he counted 84 spark plugs. How many cars can they service with spark plugs before they need to reorder?

_____

6. The service station made $315 in one week on car washes. If each car wash cost $7, how many cars were washed that week?

_____

7. Bert makes $35 per day for working at the service station. If he gets paid $5 per hour, how many hours does he work in a day?

_____

8. During the summer, when Bert isn't in school, he makes $700 a month. If he is paid $35 per day, how many days per month does he work in the summer?

_____

68

The Complete Book of Challenge Math

$= \pi \; \frac{4}{5} \; 2 \div \; {}^{3}A - r^2 + 8 \; 1 \times 6^{mm} \; 7 \; 32°F \; 10 \; 63\% \; 8\,cm \; \frac{7}{8}$

Preparing for the Prom

Wayne helped his sister who was on the prom preparation committee. Read about the preparations and answer the questions. Show your work.

1. The committee hired a band for the dance for $500. If the dance lasts from 8 P.M. until 12 A.M., how much will the band be paid per hour?

_____

2. The dance band has 5 members. How much does each band member get paid per hour?

_____

3. The committee rented 4 special-effects lights for $100. How much would it cost to rent one light?

_____

4. The committee will rent 256 chairs for the dance. If 4 chairs fit around one table, how many tables will they need to rent?

_____

5. There is a fountain in the middle of the dance floor that holds 150 gallons of water. The committee has a 5-gallon bucket. How many buckets of water will it take to fill the fountain?

_____

6. The committee has ordered 192 flowers to be put in vases on the tables. If 3 flowers go in each vase, how many vases will they need?

_____

7. Wayne helped his sister put crepe paper around the walls of the room. Each wall was 20 yards long. They used 40 yards of crepe paper per wall. Will 160 yards of crepe paper be enough to decorate the square room?

_____

8. After the prom was over, a cleanup crew of 7 people worked a total of 21 hours to get the room back to order. How many hours did they each work?

_____

The Complete Book of Challenge Math

Dividing Whole Numbers

Name _____

The Young Eagle's Club

The Young Eagle's Club made an informational book about airplanes to show what they were learning. Complete each problem they proposed.

1. Ray read about the first airplane made by the Wright brothers. It reached 30 miles per hour on its first flight. If a small, propeller-driven, single-engine plane flies about 5 times this fast, at what speed can it fly?

_____

2. Amy's father is a pilot on a jet airliner. He flies from Chicago to Los Angeles, a distance of 2,000 miles. If the jet flew at 500 miles per hour, how long would it take him to fly from Chicago to Los Angeles?

_____

3. Last summer, Barbara's family flew in a four-engine propeller plane from Chicago to Glacier National Park. It took them 3 hours. If the plane flew 400 miles per hour, how many miles was it from Chicago to Glacier National Park?

_____

4. The supersonic transport travels 1,500 miles per hour. If it takes 2 hours to fly from New York to London, how many miles is the flight between these cities?

_____

5. If a twin-engine jet flies about 500 miles an hour, which plane described above travels about 3 times as fast?

_____

6. Most people choose to fly on the jumbo jet. If it travels at 600 miles per hour, how long would it take to travel the 3,000 miles from New York to London?

_____

7. How long would it take to fly the 3,000 miles from New York to London in a twin-engine jet if it flies 500 miles per hour?

_____

Adding and Subtracting Fractions

$= \pi \frac{4}{5} \ 2 \div \frac{3}{4} - r^2 + 8 \ 1 \times 6mm \ 7 \ 32°F \ 10 \ 63\% \ 8cm \ \frac{7}{8}$

Common Factors Through Time

Let's consider the history of numbers. Eratosthenes, an ancient Greek mathematician, developed a method to determine prime numbers. His method for finding the 25 prime numbers between 1 and 100 is explained below. A prime number is a number with only two factors, itself and 1. Circle all of the prime numbers. Then, cross out all of the composite numbers (those with more than two factors).

1	2	3	4	5	6	7	8	9	10
11	12	13	14	15	16	17	18	19	20
21	22	23	24	25	26	27	28	29	30
31	32	33	34	35	36	37	38	39	40
41	42	43	44	45	46	47	48	49	50
51	52	53	54	55	56	57	58	59	60
61	62	63	64	65	66	67	68	69	70
71	72	73	74	75	76	77	78	79	80
81	82	83	84	85	86	87	88	89	90
91	92	93	94	95	96	97	98	99	100

1. Cross out 1.

2. Circle the smallest prime number. What is it? _____

3. Cross out all multiples of this number.

4. Circle the next prime number. What is it? _____

5. Cross out all multiples of this number.

6. Circle the next prime number. What is it? _____

7. Cross out all multiples of this number.

8. Circle the next prime number. What is it? _____

9. Cross out all multiples of this number.

10. Circle the prime numbers.

THIS METHOD OF FINDING PRIME NUMBERS IS CALLED THE SIEVE OF ERATOSTHENES!

72

Greatest Common Factors

Factors are numbers that, when multiplied together, yield a given product.

   3 and 8 are factors of 24 because 3 × 8 = 24.
   12 and 3 are factors of 36 because 12 × 3 = 36.

Both 24 and 36 have 3 as a factor, so it is a common factor. But, it is not their greatest common factor (GCF) because 12 is also a factor of both and is larger than 3. 12 is their greatest common factor and can be found by using factor trees.

Example A

24
12   **2**
6   **2**
3   2

common factors:
2 × 2 × 3 = 12

36
6   6
2   3   **2**   **3**

Example B

Find the GCF of 18 and 54.

18
9   **2**
3   **3**

common factors:
3 × 3 × 2 = 18

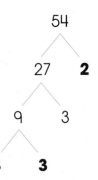

54
27   **2**
9   3
3   **3**

Find the GCF of the following numbers. Use a separate sheet of paper, if necessary.

1. 45 and 20

2. 16 and 30

3. 15 and 60

_____

_____

_____

4. 22 and 4

5. 6 and 33

6. 21 and 28

_____

_____

_____

The Complete Book of Challenge Math

Name _____

Winter Fences

Write the factors of each composite number below it on the fence post. Write the greatest common factors (GCF) in the rungs between the posts. The first one is done for you.

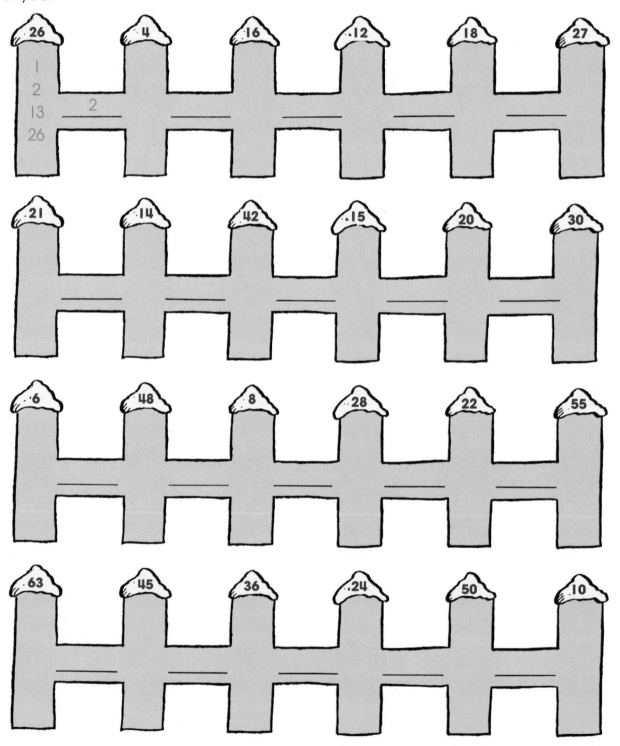

The Complete Book of Challenge Math

$= \pi \ \frac{4}{5} \ 2 \div 3 \ A - r^2 + 8 \ 1 \times 6 mm \ 7 \ 32°F \ 10 \ 63\% \ 8 cm \ \frac{7}{8}$

Reducing Fractions

A fraction is in lowest terms when 1 is the only common factor of the numerator and the denominator.

To reduce a fraction to lowest terms, divide the numerator and the denominator by their greatest common factor (GCF).

Example A	$\frac{6}{8}$ 2 is the largest number (GCF) that goes into both 6 and 8.

$$\frac{6 \ (\div 2)}{8 \ (\div 2)} = \frac{3}{4}$$

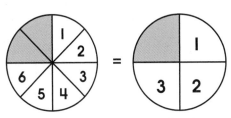

Example B	$\frac{12}{15}$ 3 is their GCF.

$$\frac{12 \ (\div 3)}{15 \ (\div 3)} = \frac{4}{5}$$

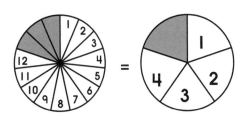

Example C	$\frac{11}{12}$ 1 is their GCF so this cannot be reduced.

Reducing to lowest terms.

1. $\frac{20}{25}$

2. $\frac{12}{18}$

3. $\frac{2}{11}$

4. $\frac{16}{20}$

5. $\frac{7}{21}$

6. $\frac{6}{9}$

7. $\frac{14}{49}$

8. $\frac{30}{50}$

9. $\frac{27}{63}$

10. $\frac{40}{64}$

11. $\frac{5}{13}$

12. $\frac{36}{96}$

    The Complete Book of Challenge Math

Name _____

That's Entertaining

Cross out each box that contains a fraction in its lowest terms. Then, write the remaining letters in order on the blanks to answer the riddle.

K	T	E	O	N	T	D	R
$\frac{2}{5}$	$\frac{3}{6}$	$\frac{3}{5}$	$\frac{2}{8}$	$\frac{2}{3}$	$\frac{4}{12}$	$\frac{3}{4}$	$\frac{1}{8}$
H	A	E	M	M	A	O	O
$\frac{6}{12}$	$\frac{2}{7}$	$\frac{3}{9}$	$\frac{1}{4}$	$\frac{4}{12}$	$\frac{3}{8}$	$\frac{4}{8}$	$\frac{6}{9}$
T	V	T	H	I	E	W	S
$\frac{9}{10}$	$\frac{3}{15}$	$\frac{5}{8}$	$\frac{11}{12}$	$\frac{4}{20}$	$\frac{2}{10}$	$\frac{7}{8}$	$\frac{3}{12}$

Where do cows like to go on Saturday night?

____ ____   ____ ____ ____

" ____ ____ ____ ____ ____ ____ ____ "

Write each fraction in lowest terms.

1. $\frac{8}{12}$

2. $\frac{4}{6}$

3. $\frac{6}{9}$

4. $\frac{9}{12}$

5. $\frac{5}{15}$

6. $\frac{8}{16}$

$= \pi \frac{4}{5} 2 \div \frac{3}{4} A - \frac{1}{2} + 8 \ 1 \times 6mm \ 7 \ 32°F \ 10 \ 63\% \ 8cm \ \frac{7}{8}$

Reduce It

Reduce each fraction in the sentences below to its lowest terms. Rewrite the sentence correctly on the line.

1. Daniel slept $\frac{8}{24}$ of a day.

_____

2. Emilia rides the bus to school $\frac{6}{8}$ of the time.

_____

3. Jim spent $\frac{5}{25}$ of his dollar at the candy store.

_____

4. Josie completed $\frac{80}{100}$ of her math problems correctly.

_____

5. Amy scored $\frac{4}{8}$ of the points in the soccer game.

_____

6. The sun was hidden by clouds $\frac{20}{30}$ of the days in January.

_____

7. The cars raced $\frac{20}{60}$ of the hour.

_____

8. The baby cried for $\frac{10}{60}$ of an hour.

_____

9. Of the students in Maureen's room, $\frac{8}{24}$ have pets.

_____

10. Ethan drank $\frac{6}{12}$ of the sodas in one day.

_____

The Complete Book of Challenge Math

Name _____

Finding Least Common Multiples (LCM)

Multiples are numbers that can be divided by a number without a remainder.

> The first six multiples of 7 are: 7, 14, 21, 28, 35, 42
>
> The first ten multiples of 4 are: 4, 8, 12, 16, 20, 24, 28, 32, 36, 40
>
> The first ten multiples of 5 are: 5, 10, 15, 20, 25, 30, 35, 40, 45, 50

When comparing multiples of 4 and 5, notice that they have 20 and 40 in common. Therefore, 20 is the least common multiple (LCM) of 4 and 5.

Write the next 11 multiples of 6 and 9.

6, ___ , ___ , ___ , ___ , ___ , ___ , ___ , ___ , ___ , ___ , ___

9, ___ , ___ , ___ , ___ , ___ , ___ , ___ , ___ , ___ , ___ , ___

What are their common multiples? _____

What is their LCM? _____

Find the LCM of the following numbers.

1. 3, 4 _____   **2.** 5, 6 _____   **3.** 8, 6 _____

4. 15, 3 _____   **5.** 6, 15 _____   **6.** 16, 24 _____

7. 5, 9 _____   **8.** 15, 75 _____   **9.** 8, 14 _____

10. 3, 5, 9 _____   **11.** 4, 7, 2 _____   **12.** 3, 20, 15 _____

$$= \pi \; \frac{4}{5} \; 2 \div {}^{3}A - r^{2} + 8 \; 1 \times 6\,mm \; 7 \; 32°F \; 10 \; 63\% \; 8\,cm \; \frac{7}{8}$$

Practice With Least Common Multiples

> The least common multiple (LCM) is the smallest number that both values go into evenly.

Find the LCM for each pair of numbers. Check your answers and correct any mistakes.

1. 16 and 24

5. 6 and 27

_____

_____

2. 14 and 21

6. 8 and 14

_____

_____

3. 24 and 30

7. 12 and 40

_____

_____

4. 8 and 12

8. 7 and 15

_____

_____

The Complete Book of Challenge Math

Name _____

In the Table

Write the multiples for each number in the table.

1												
2												
3												
4												
5												
6												
7												
8												
9												

Use the table to write common multiples for the following number pairs. Circle the least common multiple (LCM) for each pair.

1. 8 and 6 _____

2. 5 and 3 _____

3. 2 and 3 _____

4. 7 and 2 _____

5. 4 and 6 _____

6. 9 and 6 _____

$= \pi \quad \frac{4}{5} \quad 2 \div {}^{3} A - r^2 + 8 \ 1 \times 6mm \ 7 \ 32°F \ 10 \ 63\% \ 8cm \ \frac{7}{8}$

Mountain-Climbing Madge

Help Madge the Mountain Climber find the easiest path to the top of the mountain. Find the LCM of the numbers in the trees and connect them in order. Write the sum of the LCMs and put it on the line at the top of the mountain.

Sum of LCMs

3, 10

7, 5

5, 8

3, 5

8, 3

7, 3

8, 16

6, 4

9, 6

4, 5

10, 2

3, 2

4, 8

3, 9

The Complete Book of Challenge Math

Name _____

Equivalent Fractions

Equivalent fractions are fractions that name the same amount. To find equivalent fractions, multiply or divide the numerator and denominator by the same non-zero number.

$$\frac{18}{24} = \frac{18 \, (\times 2)}{24 \, (\times 2)} = \frac{36}{48}$$

So, $\frac{3}{4}$, $\frac{18}{24}$, and $\frac{36}{48}$ are equivalent.

$$\frac{18}{24} = \frac{18 \, (\div 6)}{24 \, (\div 6)} = \frac{3}{4}$$

Cross-multiplication can also be used to determine if fractions are equivalent. If the cross products are the same, the fractions are equivalent.

$$\frac{24}{36} \bowtie \frac{2}{3} \qquad \begin{array}{l} 24 \times 3 = 72 \\ 36 \times 2 = 72 \end{array} \qquad \text{Since } 72 = 72, \frac{24}{36} = \frac{2}{3}$$

$$\frac{4}{5} \bowtie \frac{17}{20} \qquad \begin{array}{l} 4 \times 20 = 80 \\ 5 \times 17 = 85 \end{array} \qquad \text{Since } 80 \neq 85, \frac{4}{5} \neq \frac{17}{20}$$

Find equivalent fractions.

1. $\dfrac{3}{7} = \dfrac{3 \, (\times 3)}{7 \, (\times 3)} = $ ___

2. $\dfrac{3}{4} = \dfrac{3 \, (\times 8)}{4 \, (\times 8)} = $ ___

3. $\dfrac{45}{55} = \dfrac{45 \, (\div 5)}{55 \, (\div 5)} = $ ___

4. $\dfrac{18}{22} = \dfrac{18 \, (\div 2)}{22 \, (\div 2)} = $ ___

Find the missing number.

5. $\dfrac{3}{7} = \dfrac{15}{}$

6. $\dfrac{}{18} = \dfrac{7}{9}$

7. $\dfrac{}{8} = \dfrac{24}{64}$

8. $\dfrac{6}{30} = \dfrac{1}{}$

The Complete Book of Challenge Math

"Tri" These

Two of the three fractions in each shamrock are equivalent fractions. Put an **X** on the fraction that is not equal to the other two. Circle the fraction that is simplified to lowest terms.

The Complete Book of Challenge Math

Name _____

Outrageous Outfits

Flaky Frannie the Fashion Consultant has a unique sense of style. Draw lines connecting the equivalent fractions to see the outfits Frannie has coordinated.

 $= \dfrac{3}{7}$

 $= \dfrac{15}{18}$

 $= \dfrac{3}{10}$

 $= \dfrac{35}{42}$

 $= \dfrac{3}{8}$

 $= \dfrac{10}{40}$

 $= \dfrac{1}{4}$

 $= \dfrac{17}{68}$

 $= \dfrac{12}{32}$

 $= \dfrac{21}{70}$

 $= \dfrac{12}{28}$

 $= \dfrac{35}{45}$

 $= \dfrac{28}{36}$

 $= \dfrac{7}{9}$

 $= \dfrac{18}{42}$

 $= \dfrac{18}{48}$

 $= \dfrac{9}{30}$

 $= \dfrac{5}{6}$

The Complete Book of Challenge Math

$= \pi \ \frac{4}{3} \ 2 \div 3 \ A - r^2 + 8 \ 1 \times 6mm \ 7 \ 32°F \ 10 \ 63\% \ 8cm \ \frac{7}{3}$

Ha-Ha-Ha

April is National Humor Month. Cheer up a friend's day with a good, healthy chuckle!

Find the missing numerators and denominators. Use the answers and the code to solve the riddle. Follow the example.

1	2	3	4	5	6	7	8	9	10	11
O	K	E	A	C	P	Y	L	R	I	T

1. $\dfrac{2}{3} = \dfrac{\boxed{4}}{6}$

2. $\dfrac{3}{4} = \dfrac{\boxed{}}{8}$

3. $\dfrac{3}{7} = \dfrac{\boxed{}}{21}$

4. $\dfrac{1}{\boxed{}} = \dfrac{2}{8}$

5. $\dfrac{1}{\boxed{}} = \dfrac{3}{15}$

6. $\dfrac{1}{\boxed{}} = \dfrac{3}{33}$

7. $\dfrac{\boxed{}}{12} = \dfrac{5}{6}$

8. $\dfrac{2}{\boxed{}} = \dfrac{4}{10}$

9. $\dfrac{15}{20} = \dfrac{3}{\boxed{}}$

10. $\dfrac{3}{\boxed{}} = \dfrac{6}{16}$

11. $\dfrac{3}{21} = \dfrac{1}{\boxed{}}$

12. $\dfrac{4}{16} = \dfrac{\boxed{}}{4}$

13. $\dfrac{1}{4} = \dfrac{2}{\boxed{}}$

14. $\dfrac{6}{12} = \dfrac{1}{\boxed{}}$

15. $\dfrac{3}{9} = \dfrac{1}{\boxed{}}$

16. $\dfrac{6}{\boxed{}} = \dfrac{12}{18}$

THIS JOKE REALLY CRACKS ME UP!

What do you call an egg who loves April Fool's Day?

$\underset{1}{\overline{\text{A}}}$ $\underset{2}{\overline{}}$ $\underset{3}{\overline{}}$ $\underset{4}{\overline{}}$ $\underset{5}{\overline{}}$ $\underset{6}{\overline{}}$ $\underset{7}{\overline{}}$ $\underset{8}{\overline{}}$ $\underset{9}{\overline{}}$ $\underset{10}{\overline{}}$ $\quad$ $\underset{11}{\overline{}}$ $\underset{12}{\overline{}}$ $\underset{13}{\overline{}}$ $\underset{14}{\overline{}}$ $\underset{15}{\overline{}}$ $\underset{16}{\overline{}}$

The Complete Book of Challenge Math

Name _____

Comparing Fractions

It is easier to compare fraction sizes if they both have the same denominator. Find a common denominator. For each fraction, create an equivalent fraction by multiplying the numerator and denominator by the same number.

Example:

Which is larger, $\dfrac{2}{8}$ or $\dfrac{6}{12}$?

The LCM of 8 and 12 is 24.

$$\frac{2}{8} = \frac{}{24} \qquad\qquad\qquad \frac{6}{12} = \frac{}{24}$$

$$\frac{2}{8} \times \frac{3}{3} = \frac{6}{24} \qquad\qquad \frac{6}{12} \times \frac{2}{2} = \frac{12}{24}$$

$$\frac{6}{24} \; ? \; \frac{12}{24}$$

$$\frac{6}{24} < \frac{12}{24}$$

$$\text{So } \frac{2}{8} < \frac{6}{12}$$

Which fraction is larger? Place the greater than sign (>) or less than sign (<) between each pair of fractions. Show your work.

1. $\dfrac{2}{3} \;\square\; \dfrac{1}{4}$

2. $\dfrac{3}{4} \;\square\; \dfrac{2}{6}$

3. $\dfrac{4}{7} \;\square\; \dfrac{2}{3}$

4. $\dfrac{4}{6} \;\square\; \dfrac{2}{8}$

5. $\dfrac{1}{12} \;\square\; \dfrac{3}{8}$

6. $\dfrac{2}{8} \;\square\; \dfrac{3}{14}$

The Complete Book of Challenge Math

© 2006 American Education Publishing

$= \pi \; \frac{4}{5} \; 2 \div \; {}^3A - P^2 + 8 \; 1 \times 6mm \; 7 \; 32°F \; 10 \; 63\% \; 8cm \; \frac{7}{8}$

Pick a Pie

Change the unlike fractions in each pie to like (equivalent) fractions. Then, number them from least to greatest.

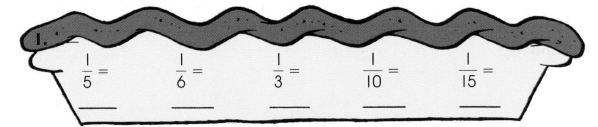

1. $\frac{1}{5} =$ $\frac{1}{6} =$ $\frac{1}{3} =$ $\frac{1}{10} =$ $\frac{1}{15} =$

    _____   _____   _____   _____   _____

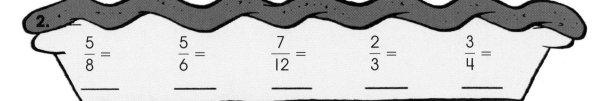

2. $\frac{5}{8} =$ $\frac{5}{6} =$ $\frac{7}{12} =$ $\frac{2}{3} =$ $\frac{3}{4} =$

    _____   _____   _____   _____   _____

3. $\frac{4}{5} =$ $\frac{3}{4} =$ $\frac{3}{10} =$ $\frac{1}{2} =$ $\frac{11}{20} =$

    _____   _____   _____   _____   _____

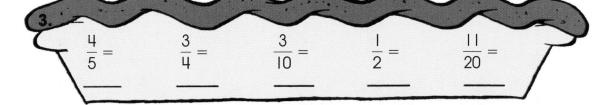

4. $\frac{3}{4} =$ $\frac{1}{2} =$ $\frac{5}{6} =$ $\frac{2}{3} =$ $\frac{1}{4} =$

    _____   _____   _____   _____   _____

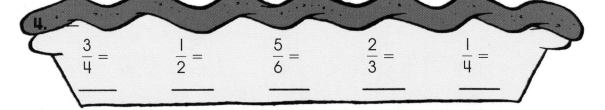

5. $\frac{2}{3} =$ $\frac{1}{4} =$ $\frac{7}{9} =$ $\frac{5}{6} =$ $\frac{11}{18} =$

    _____   _____   _____   _____   _____

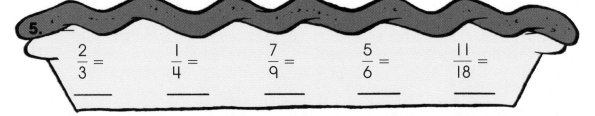

6. $\frac{1}{2} =$ $\frac{5}{8} =$ $\frac{3}{4} =$ $\frac{3}{8} =$ $\frac{11}{16} =$

    _____   _____   _____   _____   _____

The Complete Book of Challenge Math

Improper Fractions and Mixed Numbers

Renaming Improper Fractions

In an improper fraction, the numerator is greater than the denominator. To write as a mixed number, divide.

$$\frac{17}{5} = 17 \div 5 = 5\overline{)17}$$

$$2 \leftarrow \text{remainder}$$
$$3\frac{2}{5} \leftarrow \text{divisor}$$
$$-15$$
$$\overline{2}$$

Renaming Mixed Numbers

A mixed number has a whole number part and a fraction part. These can be written as improper fractions by multiplying and adding.

$$4\frac{2}{3}$$

$3 \times 4 = 12$

$12 + 2 = 14$

$$4\frac{2}{3} = \frac{14}{3}$$

1. Multiply denominator by whole number.

2. Add the numerator to the product.

3. Write this sum over the denominator.

Write as mixed numbers. Show your work.

1. $\frac{19}{6} = 6\overline{)19} = $ $\begin{array}{r}3\\-18\\\hline 1\end{array}$

2. $\frac{21}{4}$

3. $\frac{33}{10}$

4. $\frac{49}{5}$

5. $\frac{38}{4}$

6. $\frac{85}{9}$

Write as improper fractions.

7. $5\frac{1}{8} = \frac{8 \times 5 + 1}{8} = \frac{41}{8}$

8. $6\frac{1}{6}$

9. $10\frac{4}{7}$

10. $11\frac{3}{5}$

11. $8\frac{2}{3}$

12. $7\frac{5}{11}$

Improper Fractions and Mixed Numbers

Write each improper fraction as a mixed number in lowest terms.

1. $\dfrac{12}{5}$

2. $\dfrac{9}{2}$

3. $\dfrac{14}{9}$

4. $\dfrac{13}{3}$

5. $\dfrac{10}{8}$

6. $\dfrac{11}{4}$

7. $\dfrac{5}{2}$

8. $\dfrac{10}{3}$

9. $\dfrac{32}{12}$

10. $\dfrac{40}{3}$

11. $\dfrac{7}{5}$

12. $\dfrac{39}{8}$

13. $\dfrac{26}{5}$

14. $\dfrac{9}{4}$

15. $\dfrac{34}{6}$

16. $\dfrac{52}{10}$

The Complete Book of Challenge Math

Name _____

Cactus Fractions

Draw lines from the mixed numbers to the correct improper fractions.

The Complete Book of Challenge Math

Name _____

$= \pi \ \frac{4}{5} \ 2 \div \ ^3\sqrt{A} - r^3 + 8 \ 1 \times 6mm \ 7 \ 32°F \ 10 \ 63\% \ 8cm \ \frac{7}{8}$

Toad-ally Mixed-Up Numbers

Match each improper fraction to the equivalent mixed number. Then, write the letter in the matching number blank to solve the riddle.

____ 1. $\frac{5}{3}$

____ 2. $\frac{7}{4}$

____ 3. $\frac{9}{4}$

____ 4. $\frac{5}{2}$

____ 5. $\frac{6}{5}$

____ 6. $\frac{11}{4}$

____ 7. $\frac{13}{2}$

____ 8. $\frac{8}{5}$

____ 9. $\frac{11}{3}$

____ 10. $\frac{21}{10}$

____ 11. $\frac{7}{6}$

____ 12. $\frac{9}{8}$

$2\frac{1}{4}$ **O**

$2\frac{1}{2}$ **D**

$2\frac{3}{4}$ **T**

$1\frac{2}{3}$ **A**

$1\frac{3}{4}$ **O**

$6\frac{1}{2}$ **O**

$2\frac{1}{10}$ **T**

$1\frac{1}{5}$ **S**

$1\frac{3}{5}$ **A**

$3\frac{2}{3}$ **L**

$1\frac{1}{6}$ **O**

$1\frac{1}{8}$ **N**

AAAHH...

Where do amphibians rest their weary feet?

____ ____   ____   ____ ____ ____ ____   ____ ____ ____ ____ ____
11   12   1   6   2   8   4   5   10   7   3   9

     The Complete Book of Challenge Math

Name _____

Teacher Tool

Draw a line with a ruler from each improper fraction to the equivalent mixed number. Then, to solve the riddle, write each letter in the correctly numbered blank.

1. $\frac{4}{3}$ •

2. $\frac{6}{5}$ •

3. $\frac{9}{4}$ •

4. $\frac{7}{3}$ •

5. $\frac{5}{3}$ •

6. $\frac{7}{4}$ •

7. $\frac{10}{4}$ •

8. $\frac{7}{2}$ •

9. $\frac{10}{3}$ •

10. $\frac{11}{4}$ •

• $2\frac{3}{4}$ D

• $1\frac{2}{3}$ K

• $1\frac{3}{4}$ B

• $1\frac{1}{5}$ H

• $2\frac{1}{2}$ O

• $2\frac{1}{3}$ L

• $1\frac{1}{3}$ C

• $2\frac{1}{4}$ A

• $3\frac{1}{3}$ R

• $3\frac{1}{2}$ A

What is white when it is dirty?

A ___ ___ ___ ___ ___ ___ ___ ___ ___
   1   2   3   4   5   6   7   8   9   10

$= \pi \ \frac{4}{5} \ 2 \div {}^{3}\!A - r^2 + 8 \ 1 \times 6mm \ 7 \ 32°F \ 10 \ 63\% \ 8cm \ \frac{7}{8}$

Mixed Numbers

Change these mixed numbers to improper fractions. Show your work.

1. $3\frac{2}{5}$

2. $6\frac{2}{5}$

3. $2\frac{1}{4}$

4. $7\frac{3}{8}$

5. $4\frac{2}{7}$

6. $12\frac{3}{4}$

7. $8\frac{2}{3}$

8. $4\frac{1}{8}$

9. $3\frac{2}{4}$

10. $5\frac{2}{7}$

11. $8\frac{2}{5}$

12. $4\frac{3}{7}$

13. $2\frac{3}{8}$

14. $9\frac{2}{3}$

15. $4\frac{3}{9}$

Practice hard. You'll win!

16. $8\frac{3}{5}$

17. $15\frac{1}{3}$

The Complete Book of Challenge Math

Name _____

$= \pi \ \frac{4}{5} \ 2 \div \ {}^5A - {}^P + 8 \ 1 \times 6mm \ 7 \ 32°F \ 10 \ 63\% \ 8cm \ \frac{7}{8}$

Fractions

Change these improper fractions to mixed numbers. Show your work.

1. $\dfrac{36}{6}$

2. $\dfrac{14}{6}$

3. $\dfrac{28}{9}$

4. $\dfrac{13}{5}$

5. $\dfrac{17}{8}$

6. $\dfrac{51}{10}$

7. $\dfrac{13}{6}$

8. $\dfrac{43}{8}$

9. $\dfrac{24}{5}$

10. $\dfrac{34}{6}$

11. $\dfrac{29}{4}$

12. $\dfrac{91}{10}$

13. $\dfrac{37}{7}$

14. $\dfrac{21}{4}$

15. $\dfrac{83}{9}$

16. $\dfrac{15}{6}$

17. $\dfrac{37}{5}$

Anything's possible with practice!

The Complete Book of Challenge Math

$= \pi \ \frac{4}{5} \ 2 \div \frac{5}{7} - r^2 + 8 \ 1 \times 6mm \ 7 \ 32°F \ 10 \ 63\% \ 8cm \ \frac{7}{8}$

Adding Like Denominators

Example A $\frac{1}{8} + \frac{5}{8}$

add

$\frac{1}{8} + \frac{5}{8} = \frac{6}{8} \frac{(\div 2)}{(\div 2)} = \frac{3}{4}$

same

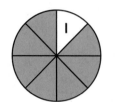 + 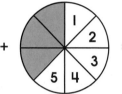 = 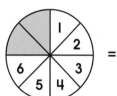 =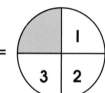

Example B $\frac{9}{10} + \frac{7}{10}$

add

$\frac{9}{10} + \frac{7}{10} = \frac{16}{10} = 1\frac{16}{10} \frac{(\div 2)}{(\div 2)} = 1\frac{3}{5}$

same

1. Add numerators.

2. Denominators stay the same.

3. Write improper fractions as mixed numbers.

4. Reduce.

Add.

add

1. $\frac{5}{12} + \frac{11}{12} = \frac{16}{12} = 1\frac{1}{3}$

same

2. $\frac{4}{5} + \frac{3}{5}$

3. $\frac{4}{9} + \frac{8}{9}$

4. $\frac{11}{15} + \frac{7}{15}$

5. $\frac{3}{10} + \frac{1}{10}$

6. $\frac{19}{25} + \frac{11}{25}$

7. $\frac{7}{9} + \frac{5}{9}$

8. $\frac{31}{35} + \frac{19}{35}$

The Complete Book of Challenge Math

Name _____

$= \pi \frac{4}{5} 2 \div 5 \sqrt{} - r^2 + 8 \ 1 \times 6mm \ 7 \ 32°F \ 10 \ 63\% \ 8cm \ \frac{7}{8}$

Adding Like Denominators

Add the fractions. Complete the answers. Then, fill in the crossword puzzle.

Across

1. $\frac{7}{10} + \frac{9}{10}$ = one and three-_____

2. $\frac{5}{6} + \frac{5}{6}$ = one and _____-thirds

6. $\frac{1}{8} + \frac{5}{8}$ = three-_____

9. $\frac{7}{15} + \frac{4}{15}$ = _____-fifteenths

10. $\frac{2}{9} + \frac{5}{9}$ = _____-ninths

11. $\frac{11}{16} + \frac{7}{16}$ = one and one-_____

13. $\frac{3}{11} + \frac{7}{11}$ = _____-elevenths

16. $\frac{4}{9} + \frac{2}{9}$ = two-_____

18. $\frac{14}{15} + \frac{4}{15}$ = one and one-_____

21. $\frac{1}{18} + \frac{5}{18}$ = one-_____

22. $\frac{5}{7} + \frac{6}{7}$ = one and _____-sevenths

Down

1. $\frac{1}{15} + \frac{13}{15}$ = fourteen-_____

3. $\frac{7}{12} + \frac{7}{12}$ = one and _____-sixth

4. $\frac{7}{10} + \frac{2}{10}$ = _____-tenths

5. $\frac{13}{20} + \frac{13}{20}$ = one and three-_____

7. $\frac{15}{16} + \frac{13}{16}$ = one and _____-fourths

8. $\frac{4}{7} + \frac{2}{7}$ = _____-sevenths

9. $\frac{7}{9} + \frac{1}{9}$ = _____-ninths

12. $\frac{1}{12} + \frac{5}{12}$ = one-_____

14. $\frac{8}{9} + \frac{2}{9}$ = one and one-_____

15. $\frac{4}{18} + \frac{17}{18}$ = one and one-_____

17. $\frac{3}{11} + \frac{2}{11}$ = _____-elevenths

19. $\frac{1}{10} + \frac{7}{10}$ = _____-fifths

20. $\frac{3}{4} + \frac{3}{4}$ = one and one-_____

Adding Unlike Denominators

Denominators must be the same to add, so multiply each fraction by a number to make their least common multiple (LCM).

Example A

$$\frac{2}{5} + \frac{1}{3}$$

add

$$\frac{2 \,(\times 3)}{5 \,(\times 3)} + \frac{1 \,(\times 5)}{3 \,(\times 5)} = \frac{6}{15} + \frac{5}{15} = \frac{11}{15}$$

15 is LCM   same

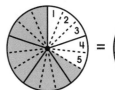

$$\frac{2}{5} = \frac{6}{15} \qquad \frac{1}{3} = \frac{5}{15} \qquad \frac{11}{15}$$

Remember: Since you multiply both numerator and denominator by the same number, you are really just multiplying the fraction by 1.

$$\left(\frac{3}{3} = 1, \frac{5}{5} = 1\right)$$

1. Find LCM of denominators.
2. Multiply numerator and denominator of each fraction by a number to make LCM.
3. Add numerators.
4. Denominators stay the same (LCM).
5. Write improper fractions as mixed numbers.
6. Reduce.

Example B

$$\frac{9}{10} + \frac{1}{2}$$

add

$$\frac{9}{10} + \frac{1 \,(\times 5)}{2 \,(\times 5)} = \frac{9}{10} + \frac{5}{10} = \frac{14}{10} = 1\frac{4}{10}\frac{(\div 2)}{(\div 2)} = 1\frac{2}{5}$$

10 is LCM   same

Add.

1. $\dfrac{5}{6} + \dfrac{2}{9} = \dfrac{5 \,(\times 3)}{6 \,(\times 3)} + \dfrac{2 \,(\times 2)}{9 \,(\times 2)} = 1\dfrac{1}{18}$

18 is LCM

2. $\dfrac{1}{4} + \dfrac{1}{2}$

3. $\dfrac{2}{3} + \dfrac{5}{12}$

4. $\dfrac{1}{7} + \dfrac{3}{14}$

5. $\dfrac{1}{8} + \dfrac{1}{6}$

6. $\dfrac{3}{4} + \dfrac{2}{3}$

The Complete Book of Challenge Math

Name _____

$= \pi \ \frac{4}{5} \ 2 \div \frac{3}{4} - r^2 + 8 \ 1 \times 6mm \ 7 \ 32°F \ 10 \ 63\% \ 8 \, cm \ \frac{7}{8}$

Adding Like Fractions and Mixed Numbers

Fractions	$\frac{5}{8} + \frac{7}{8}$

add

$$\frac{5}{8} + \frac{7}{8} = \frac{12}{8} = 1\frac{4}{8} = 1\frac{1}{2}$$

same

Steps:
1. Add numerators.
2. Denominators stay the same.
3. Write improper fractions as mixed numbers.
4. Reduce to lowest terms.

Mixed Numbers	$8\frac{4}{5} + 3\frac{2}{5}$

add

$$8\frac{4}{5} + 3\frac{2}{5} = 11\frac{6}{5} = 12\frac{1}{5}$$

same

Steps:
1. Add whole numbers.
2. Add numerators.
3. Denominators stay the same.
4. Write improper fractions as mixed numbers and add to whole numbers.
5. Reduce to lowest terms.

Add.

1. $\frac{2}{9} + \frac{4}{9}$

2. $\frac{5}{6} + \frac{5}{6}$

3. $\frac{9}{10} + \frac{7}{10}$

4. $4\frac{1}{7} + 5\frac{4}{7}$

5. $3\frac{7}{8} + 8\frac{7}{8}$

6. $6\frac{13}{15} + 2\frac{7}{15}$

Name _____

Gotta Have the Beat

Wolfgang Amadeus Mozart, one of the world's greatest composers, was born on January 27, 1756. Mozart learned to play the harpsichord at the age of 4, was writing music at the age of 5, and played for the Austrian empress at the age of 6.

Even though Mozart never went to school, he probably understood fractions. Refer to the Note Chart and add the notes. Reduce to the lowest terms. The first one has been done for you.

Note Chart

$\bigcirc$ = 1   Whole note

$\textEighth$ = $\frac{1}{2}$ Half note

= $\frac{1}{4}$ Quarter note

= $\frac{1}{8}$ Eighth note

= $\frac{1}{16}$ Sixteenth note

$= 1 + \dfrac{1}{16} + \dfrac{1}{16} = 1\dfrac{2}{16} = 1\dfrac{1}{8}$

   The Complete Book of Challenge Math

Name _____

Race to the Finish

Find the sums. Then, cross out the answers in the box at the bottom of the page to help the race car reach the finish line.

1. $1\dfrac{3}{4}$

$+ \ 2\dfrac{2}{4}$

_____

2. $3\dfrac{4}{8}$

$+ \ 2\dfrac{5}{8}$

_____

3. $1\dfrac{4}{5}$

$+ \ 3\dfrac{4}{5}$

_____

4. $2\dfrac{1}{4}$

$+ \ 3\dfrac{2}{4}$

_____

5. $1\dfrac{4}{5}$

$+ \ 3\dfrac{3}{5}$

_____

6. $3\dfrac{3}{6}$

$+ \ 1\dfrac{4}{6}$

_____

7. $2\dfrac{3}{8}$

$+ \ 4\dfrac{6}{8}$

_____

8. $5\dfrac{5}{6}$

$+ \ 3\dfrac{2}{6}$

_____

9. $3\dfrac{3}{9}$

$+ \ 2\dfrac{8}{9}$

_____

10. $5\dfrac{2}{3}$

$+ \ 1\dfrac{2}{3}$

_____

11. $5\dfrac{7}{8}$

$+ \ 1\dfrac{6}{8}$

_____

$4\dfrac{1}{4}$	$6\dfrac{1}{8}$	$5\dfrac{4}{5}$	$7\dfrac{1}{3}$	$7\dfrac{5}{8}$
$6\dfrac{3}{8}$	$5\dfrac{3}{5}$	$5\dfrac{1}{8}$	$6\dfrac{2}{9}$	$6\dfrac{2}{5}$
$5\dfrac{1}{6}$	$5\dfrac{3}{4}$	$5\dfrac{3}{7}$	$9\dfrac{1}{6}$	$7\dfrac{4}{8}$
$4\dfrac{2}{8}$	$5\dfrac{2}{5}$	$5\dfrac{1}{6}$	$7\dfrac{1}{8}$	$7\dfrac{3}{8}$

$= \pi \frac{4}{5} 2 \div 3 - t^2 + 8 \ 1 \times 6mm \ 7 \ 32°F \ 10 \ 63\% \ 8cm \frac{7}{8}$

Adding Unlike Mixed Numbers

| Example | $52\frac{7}{10} + 18\frac{3}{4}$ |

$$52\frac{7}{10} + 18\frac{3}{4} = 52\frac{7\,(\times 2)}{10\,(\times 2)} + 18\frac{3\,(\times 5)}{4\,(\times 5)} = 52\frac{14}{20} + 18\frac{15}{20} = 70\frac{29}{20} = 71\frac{9}{20}$$

add

same

$\downarrow$

10, (20)

4, 8, 12, 16, (20)

Steps:

1. Find LCM of denominators (20).

2. Multiply numerator and denominator of each fraction by a number to make LCM.

3. Add whole numbers.

4. Add numerators.

5. Denominators stay the same.

6. Write improper fractions as mixed numbers.

7. Reduce to lowest terms.

Add.

1. $13\frac{7}{10} + 22\frac{7}{15}$

2. $2\frac{1}{2} + 2\frac{4}{5}$

3. $14\frac{7}{8} + 8\frac{11}{16}$

4. $9\frac{3}{4} + 11\frac{2}{5}$

5. $30\frac{2}{7} + 15\frac{2}{3}$

6. $6\frac{1}{6} + 18\frac{8}{9}$

7. $8\frac{5}{6} + 2\frac{5}{12}$

8. $6\frac{3}{5} + 4\frac{7}{10}$

9. $15\frac{3}{7} + 21\frac{11}{21}$

The Complete Book of Challenge Math

Name _____

Electrifying Mr. Franklin

"An ounce of prevention is worth a pound of cure." These electrifying words of wisdom are credited to one of America's famous scientists, Benjamin Franklin.

Solve the problems and reduce the answers to the lowest terms. Then, connect the answers in order. You'll discover one of Mr. Franklin's most electrifying experiments.

1. $\dfrac{3}{4} + \dfrac{1}{8}$

2. $\dfrac{4}{14} + \dfrac{2}{7}$

3. $\dfrac{3}{10} + \dfrac{5}{20}$

4. $\dfrac{1}{3} + \dfrac{3}{6}$

5. $\dfrac{1}{3} + \dfrac{1}{4}$

6. $\dfrac{3}{5} + \dfrac{2}{15}$

7. $\dfrac{4}{8} + \dfrac{3}{16}$

8. $\dfrac{3}{8} + \dfrac{3}{16}$

9. $\dfrac{3}{12} + \dfrac{4}{12}$

10. $\dfrac{4}{9} + \dfrac{1}{3}$

11. $\dfrac{1}{16} + \dfrac{3}{8}$

12. $\dfrac{1}{2} + \dfrac{1}{5}$

13. $\dfrac{3}{4} + \dfrac{3}{16}$

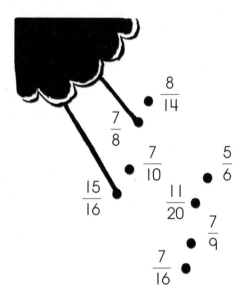

YOWSA!

The Complete Book of Challenge Math

© 2006 American Education Publishing

$= \pi \ \frac{4}{5} \ 2 \div 3 \ \sqrt{\ } \ r^2 + 8 \ 1 \times 6\,mm \ 7 \ 32°F \ 10 \ 63\% \ 8\,cm \ \frac{7}{8}$

Climbing to New Heights

Fill in the missing fractions or mixed numbers.

$\frac{2}{3}$	+	$\frac{4}{5}$	=	
+				
$\frac{1}{10}$	+	$\frac{1}{20}$	=	
=		+		
		$\frac{2}{5}$		
		=		
$\frac{3}{4}$	+		=	
+				
$\frac{7}{16}$	+	$\frac{3}{8}$	=	
=		+		+
		$\frac{5}{6}$		$\frac{1}{2}$
		=		=

The Complete Book of Challenge Math

Name _____

$= \pi \ \frac{4}{5} \ 2 \div \ ^3A - r^2 + 8 \ 1 \times 6mm \ 7 \ 32°F \ 10 \ 63\% \ 8cm \ \frac{7}{8}$

A New Planet

In 1996, scientists discovered a new planet that was 17 times larger than Earth. It was discovered 600 trillion miles away from Earth, outside of our solar system in the constellation Cygnus. Something is very unusual about this planet. Solve each problem and use the Letter Bank and code to determine what is so unusual about this planet.

Letter Bank

A	$1\frac{1}{2}$	**H**	$1\frac{9}{14}$	**N**	$1\frac{11}{18}$	**S**	$1\frac{11}{24}$
B	$1\frac{5}{8}$	**I**	$1\frac{7}{15}$	**O**	$1\frac{7}{20}$	**T**	2
G	$1\frac{11}{12}$	**L**	$1\frac{13}{16}$	**R**	$1\frac{11}{21}$		

1. $\frac{1}{3} + \frac{3}{4} + \frac{5}{6}$

2. $\frac{1}{2} + \frac{6}{7} + \frac{2}{7}$

3. $\frac{5}{8} + \frac{3}{4} + \frac{1}{8}$

4. $\frac{3}{8} + \frac{1}{4} + \frac{5}{6}$

5. $\frac{5}{7} + \frac{2}{3} + \frac{1}{7}$

6. $\frac{2}{3} + \frac{1}{2} + \frac{5}{6}$

7. $\frac{4}{9} + \frac{5}{6} + \frac{1}{3}$

8. $\frac{3}{5} + \frac{1}{3} + \frac{8}{15}$

9. $\frac{5}{8} + \frac{1}{4} + \frac{15}{16}$

10. $\frac{3}{4} + \frac{3}{8} + \frac{1}{2}$

11. $\frac{1}{4} + \frac{1}{2} + \frac{3}{5}$

___ ___   ___ ___ ___   ___ ___
 8 6   2 3 4   3 7

___ ___ ___ ___ ___ ___   ___ ___ ___ ___ ___
11 10 9 11 7 1   11 5 10 8 6

Mixed-Up Mummy!

Help the mummy complete the pyramid using this rule:

$a + b = c$

Bottom row values:
$3\frac{1}{2}$ $5\frac{1}{4}$ $1\frac{1}{3}$ $6\frac{1}{2}$ $10\frac{1}{5}$

The Complete Book of Challenge Math

Name _____

Extra Credit

The students in Mrs. Keepbusy's class could choose from several different extra credit projects. Find out how long it took each of the following students to complete his/her projects.

1. Juanita chose a different extra credit project to work on each day. On Monday she read for $\frac{8}{16}$ of an hour. She spent $\frac{4}{8}$ of an hour Tuesday working on an art project. Juanita wrote a poem in $\frac{1}{4}$ of an hour on Wednesday. On Thursday she spent $\frac{3}{4}$ of an hour planning a report. On Friday she worked $\frac{6}{8}$ of an hour finishing earlier projects. How much time did Juanita spend on extra credit projects that week?

_____

2. Frank decided to work on an extra credit project on the Komodo dragon over the weekend. First he spent $1\frac{5}{12}$ hours in the library looking for books with information. That evening at home he read through the books, taking notes for $1\frac{3}{4}$ hours. The next day Frank spent $\frac{2}{3}$ of an hour organizing his notes, and later he spent another $2\frac{1}{6}$ hours writing his first draft. After receiving his first draft back from Mrs. Keepbusy, Frank spent another hour writing the final draft. How long did it take Frank to complete the report?

_____

3. Juan worked on his extra credit project for $\frac{6}{8}$ of an hour, then $\frac{4}{5}$ of an hour, $\frac{3}{4}$, $\frac{6}{10}$, and finally $1\frac{2}{4}$ hours. How long did he work all together?

_____

The Complete Book of Challenge Math

$$= \pi \ \tfrac{4}{5} \ 2 \div {}^{3}A - r^{2} + 8 \ 1 \times 6\,mm \ 7 \ 32°F \ 10 \ 63\% \ 8\,cm \ \tfrac{7}{8}$$

Subtracting Like Fractions and Mixed Numbers

Fractions $\qquad \dfrac{7}{8} - \dfrac{1}{8}$

subtract

$$\dfrac{7}{8} - \dfrac{1}{8} = \dfrac{6}{8} = \dfrac{3}{4}$$

same

Steps:

1. Subtract numerators.
2. Denominators stay the same.
3. Reduce to lowest terms.

Mixed Numbers $\qquad 11\dfrac{1}{6} - 3\dfrac{5}{6}$

subtract

$$11\dfrac{1}{6} - 3\dfrac{5}{6} = 10\dfrac{7}{6} - 3\dfrac{5}{6} = 7\dfrac{2}{6} = 7\dfrac{1}{3}$$

same

$$1 = \dfrac{6}{6}, \text{ so } 11\dfrac{1}{6} = 10\dfrac{7}{6}$$

Steps:

1. When regrouping, borrow a whole number and write fraction as an improper fraction.
2. Subtract whole numbers.
3. Subtract numerators.
4. Denominators stay the same.
5. Reduce to lowest terms.

Subtract

1. $\dfrac{8}{9} - \dfrac{2}{9}$

2. $\dfrac{3}{4} - \dfrac{1}{4}$

3. $8\dfrac{4}{5} - 1\dfrac{3}{5}$

4. $100\dfrac{7}{8} - 18\dfrac{3}{8}$

5. $10\dfrac{3}{10} - 4\dfrac{7}{10}$

6. $28\dfrac{5}{12} - 13\dfrac{7}{12}$

7. $8\dfrac{3}{8} - 2\dfrac{5}{8}$

8. $101\dfrac{1}{3} - 17\dfrac{2}{3}$

9. $6\dfrac{3}{10} - 2\dfrac{9}{10}$

The Complete Book of Challenge Math

Name _____

$$= \pi \ \tfrac{4}{3} \ 2 \div \ ^3A - r^2 + 8 \ 1 \times 6mm \ 7 \ 32°F \ 10 \ 63\% \ 8cm \ \tfrac{7}{8}$$

Can Captain Kook Subtract?

Help Captain Kook find his hidden treasure by shading in the path of the incorrect subtraction problems.

$\frac{8}{9} - \frac{2}{9} = \frac{2}{5}$	$\frac{4}{15} - \frac{1}{15} = \frac{1}{5}$	$\frac{8}{9} - \frac{1}{9} = \frac{2}{3}$	$\frac{71}{100} - \frac{27}{100} = \frac{1}{2}$	$\frac{4}{5} - \frac{1}{5} = \frac{7}{10}$	$\frac{13}{14} - \frac{1}{14} = \frac{6}{7}$
$\frac{5}{6} - \frac{1}{6} = \frac{1}{3}$	$\frac{3}{7} - \frac{1}{7} = \frac{2}{7}$	$\frac{11}{15} - \frac{1}{15} = \frac{3}{4}$	$\frac{11}{25} - \frac{6}{25} = \frac{1}{5}$	$\frac{11}{12} - \frac{5}{12} = \frac{2}{5}$	$\frac{7}{15} - \frac{2}{15} = \frac{1}{3}$
$\frac{4}{7} - \frac{2}{7} = \frac{1}{3}$	$\frac{5}{18} - \frac{1}{18} = \frac{2}{9}$	$\frac{9}{10} - \frac{7}{10} = \frac{2}{5}$	$\frac{4}{5} - \frac{3}{5} = \frac{1}{5}$	$\frac{3}{25} - \frac{2}{25} = \frac{1}{50}$	$\frac{7}{10} - \frac{5}{10} = \frac{1}{5}$
$\frac{7}{10} - \frac{3}{10} = \frac{3}{5}$	$\frac{3}{8} - \frac{1}{8} = \frac{1}{4}$	$\frac{5}{12} - \frac{1}{12} = \frac{1}{4}$	$\frac{7}{20} - \frac{1}{20} = \frac{3}{10}$	$\frac{9}{14} - \frac{1}{14} = \frac{5}{7}$	$\frac{11}{19} - \frac{3}{19} = \frac{8}{19}$
$\frac{7}{12} - \frac{5}{12} = \frac{3}{12}$	$\frac{4}{9} - \frac{2}{9} = \frac{2}{9}$	$\frac{10}{11} - \frac{5}{11} = \frac{1}{2}$	$\frac{2}{7} - \frac{1}{7} = \frac{1}{7}$	$\frac{5}{11} - \frac{2}{11} = \frac{1}{4}$	$\frac{7}{8} - \frac{1}{8} = \frac{3}{4}$
$\frac{3}{5} - \frac{1}{5} = \frac{3}{5}$	$\frac{11}{15} - \frac{7}{15} = \frac{4}{15}$	$\frac{9}{20} - \frac{3}{20} = \frac{1}{5}$	$\frac{9}{10} - \frac{3}{10} = \frac{3}{5}$	$\frac{5}{8} - \frac{1}{8} = \frac{5}{16}$	$\frac{9}{22} - \frac{5}{22} = \frac{2}{11}$
$\frac{7}{8} - \frac{1}{8} = \frac{1}{4}$	$\frac{17}{20} - \frac{3}{20} = \frac{7}{10}$	$\frac{23}{25} - \frac{11}{25} = \frac{1}{2}$	$\frac{8}{9} - \frac{1}{9} = \frac{7}{9}$	$\frac{13}{16} - \frac{3}{16} = \frac{1}{2}$	$\frac{18}{25} - \frac{3}{25} = \frac{3}{5}$
$\frac{8}{9} - \frac{4}{9} = \frac{2}{3}$	$\frac{11}{12} - \frac{5}{12} = \frac{5}{12}$	$\frac{31}{40} - \frac{10}{40} = \frac{1}{2}$	$\frac{6}{7} - \frac{2}{7} = \frac{4}{7}$	$\frac{11}{18} - \frac{5}{18} = \frac{1}{4}$	$\frac{11}{12} - \frac{5}{12} = \frac{1}{2}$
$\frac{2}{3} - \frac{1}{3} = \frac{1}{3}$	$\frac{11}{14} - \frac{9}{14} = \frac{1}{7}$	$\frac{5}{8} - \frac{1}{8} = \frac{1}{2}$	$\frac{13}{18} - \frac{5}{18} = \frac{4}{9}$	$\frac{7}{15} - \frac{1}{15} = \frac{3}{5}$	$\frac{3}{5} - \frac{1}{5} = \frac{2}{5}$
$\frac{19}{20} - \frac{1}{20} = \frac{9}{10}$	$\frac{7}{9} - \frac{4}{9} = \frac{1}{3}$	$\frac{5}{6} - \frac{1}{6} = \frac{2}{3}$	$\frac{3}{4} - \frac{1}{4} = \frac{1}{2}$	$\frac{9}{10} - \frac{3}{10} = \frac{2}{5}$	$\frac{5}{6} - \frac{1}{6} = \frac{5}{12}$

Subtracting Unlike Fractions

| **Example** | $\dfrac{8}{9} - \dfrac{1}{6}$ |

Steps:

1. Find LCM of denominators (18).

$$\dfrac{8}{9} - \dfrac{1}{6} = \dfrac{8\,(\times 2)}{9\,(\times 2)} - \dfrac{1\,(\times 3)}{6\,(\times 3)} = \dfrac{16}{18} - \dfrac{3}{18} = \dfrac{13}{18}$$

subtract

same

2. Multiply numerator and denominator of each fraction by a number to make LCM.

3. Subtract numerators.

4. Denominators stay the same.

5. Reduce to lowest terms.

9, (18)
6, 12, (18)

Remember: Since you are multiplying both numerator and denominator by the same number, you are just multiplying the fraction by 1.

$$\left(\dfrac{2}{2} = 1, \dfrac{3}{3} = 1\right)$$

Subtract

1. $\dfrac{9}{10} - \dfrac{1}{4}$

2. $\dfrac{7}{12} - \dfrac{1}{3}$

3. $\dfrac{5}{8} - \dfrac{1}{2}$

4. $\dfrac{8}{9} - \dfrac{5}{6}$

5. $\dfrac{6}{7} - \dfrac{2}{3}$

6. $\dfrac{4}{5} - \dfrac{1}{4}$

7. $\dfrac{4}{5} - \dfrac{2}{3}$

8. $\dfrac{3}{4} - \dfrac{2}{3}$

9. $\dfrac{5}{8} - \dfrac{3}{6}$

Name _____

Sick Sentences

Examine these number sentences. Fill in the missing fractions.

$\frac{9}{10}$	$-$	$\frac{2}{5}$	$=$			
$-$						
$\frac{1}{4}$	$-$	$\frac{3}{16}$	$=$			
$=$		$-$				
	$-$	$\frac{1}{8}$	$=$			
		$=$			$-$	
$\frac{1}{2}$	$-$	$\frac{7}{16}$	$=$		$\frac{3}{8}$
$-$					$=$
$\frac{1}{6}$		$\frac{9}{10}$	$-$	$\frac{3}{4}$	$=$	
$=$		$-$		$-$	
		$\frac{2}{3}$	$-$	$\frac{5}{12}$	$=$	
		$=$		$=$	

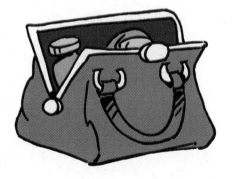

$= \pi \ \frac{4}{5} \ 2 \div \ ^3\sqrt{\ } \ - r^2 + 8 \ 1 \times 6mm \ 7 \ 32°F \ 10 \ 63\% \ 8cm \ \frac{7}{8}$

Tic-Tac-Toe Is Cool

Solve each problem. Then, find the matching answers in the tic-tac-toe games. Draw a snowman over the answer for the even-numbered problems and a mitten over the answers for the odd-numbered problems.

1. $\dfrac{1}{3} - \dfrac{1}{12}$

2. $\dfrac{5}{8} - \dfrac{1}{4}$

3. $\dfrac{9}{10} - \dfrac{3}{4}$

$\dfrac{3}{8}$	$\dfrac{1}{5}$	$\dfrac{3}{20}$
$\dfrac{7}{18}$	$\dfrac{7}{12}$	$\dfrac{1}{4}$
$\dfrac{1}{6}$	$\dfrac{4}{7}$	$\dfrac{1}{8}$

4. $\dfrac{5}{8} - \dfrac{1}{2}$

5. $\dfrac{3}{4} - \dfrac{1}{6}$

6. $\dfrac{2}{3} - \dfrac{1}{2}$

7. $\dfrac{5}{9} - \dfrac{1}{6}$

8. $\dfrac{4}{5} - \dfrac{1}{2}$

9. $\dfrac{13}{14} - \dfrac{6}{7}$

$\dfrac{3}{10}$	$\dfrac{1}{14}$	$\dfrac{2}{3}$
$\dfrac{2}{15}$	$\dfrac{4}{15}$	$\dfrac{2}{5}$
$\dfrac{5}{12}$	$\dfrac{1}{18}$	$\dfrac{7}{12}$

10. $\dfrac{2}{3} - \dfrac{1}{4}$

11. $\dfrac{4}{5} - \dfrac{2}{3}$

12. $\dfrac{5}{6} - \dfrac{1}{4}$

13. $\dfrac{1}{3} - \dfrac{5}{18}$

14. $\dfrac{13}{15} - \dfrac{3}{5}$

15. $\dfrac{2}{3} - \dfrac{4}{7}$

16. $\dfrac{12}{15} - \dfrac{1}{5}$

17. $\dfrac{3}{4} - \dfrac{2}{7}$

18. $\dfrac{5}{6} - \dfrac{1}{2}$

$\dfrac{13}{28}$	$\dfrac{2}{7}$	$\dfrac{3}{5}$
$\dfrac{1}{16}$	$\dfrac{1}{3}$	$\dfrac{3}{4}$
$\dfrac{1}{2}$	$\dfrac{1}{9}$	$\dfrac{2}{21}$

19. $\dfrac{2}{3} - \dfrac{1}{6}$

20. $\dfrac{7}{9} - \dfrac{2}{3}$

21. $\dfrac{5}{8} - \dfrac{9}{16}$

The Complete Book of Challenge Math

Name _____

Subtracting Unlike Mixed Numbers

Example $41\frac{2}{8} - 20\frac{2}{3}$

subtract

$$41\frac{2}{8} - 20\frac{2}{3} = 41\frac{2(\times 3)}{8(\times 3)} - 20\frac{2(\times 8)}{3(\times 8)} = 41\frac{6}{24} - 20\frac{16}{24} = 40\frac{30}{24} - 20\frac{16}{24} =$$

same

↓

8, 16, ⃝24

3, 6, 9, 12, 15,
18, 21, ⃝24

$$20\frac{14}{24} = 20\frac{7}{12}$$

Steps:

1. Find LCM of denominators (24).

2. Multiply numerator and denominator of each fraction by a number to make LCM.

3. When regrouping, borrow a whole number and write

fraction as an improper fraction.

4. Subtract whole numbers.

5. Subtract numerators.

6. Denominators stay the same.

7. Reduce to lowest terms.

Subtract.

1. $24\frac{2}{9} - 11\frac{2}{3}$

2. $86\frac{1}{5} - 72\frac{7}{10}$

3. $44\frac{3}{8} - 26\frac{5}{6}$

4. $19\frac{1}{4} - 12\frac{2}{3}$

5. $17\frac{4}{5} - 8\frac{1}{4}$

6. $50\frac{2}{9} - 26\frac{1}{2}$

7. $10\frac{1}{2} - 3\frac{2}{3}$

8. $12\frac{1}{5} - 7\frac{2}{3}$

9. $28\frac{5}{12} - 11\frac{2}{3}$

Name _____

$= \pi \; \frac{4}{5} \; 2 \div \frac{3}{A} - r^2 + 8 \; 1 \times 6mm \; 7 \; 32°F \; 10 \; 63\% \; 8\,cm \; \frac{7}{8}$

Nine Planets?

Subtract the mixed numbers. Find the matching answers in the letter grid. Then, write the letters on the blanks above the matching numbers to name eight of the nine planets in our solar system.

1. $5\frac{1}{3}$
$-1\frac{2}{3}$

2. $7\frac{1}{5}$
$-4\frac{4}{5}$

3. $11\frac{2}{7}$
$-8\frac{5}{7}$

4. $6\frac{4}{9}$
$-5\frac{5}{9}$

5. $15\frac{5}{8}$
$-10\frac{7}{8}$

6. $9\frac{1}{4}$
$-2\frac{3}{4}$

7. $12\frac{7}{12}$
$-6\frac{9}{12}$

8. $14\frac{1}{2}$
$-11\frac{5}{6}$

9. $3\frac{2}{5}$
$-1\frac{3}{5}$

10. $2\frac{1}{3}$
$-1\frac{7}{12}$

11. $9\frac{3}{5}$
$-4\frac{7}{10}$

12. $8\frac{1}{3}$
$-5\frac{5}{6}$

13. $16\frac{5}{7}$
$-13\frac{18}{21}$

14. $11\frac{2}{3}$
$-7\frac{7}{9}$

15. $6\frac{1}{8}$
$-1\frac{3}{4}$

___ ___ ___ ___ ___
4   9   10   5   1

___ ___ ___ ___ ___ ___ ___
12   7   2   6   5   4   10

___ ___ ___ ___ ___ ___ ___ ___ ___ ___ ___
14   9   10   15   8   4   2   5   7   8   4

___ ___ ___ ___ ___ ___ ___ ___ ___ ___ ___
2   3   7   5   13   15   9   5   7   10   8

___ ___ ___ ___ ___ ___ ___ ___ ___ ___ ___
7   10   9   8   7   15   11   4   8   7   15

Which planet is missing? _____

Letter Box			
$1\frac{4}{5}$	$\frac{8}{9}$	$3\frac{2}{3}$	$6\frac{1}{2}$
A	**E**	**H**	**I**
$2\frac{1}{2}$	$2\frac{4}{7}$	$3\frac{8}{9}$	$2\frac{2}{3}$
J	**L**	**M**	**N**
$2\frac{6}{7}$	$2\frac{2}{5}$	$\frac{3}{4}$	$4\frac{3}{8}$
O	**P**	**R**	**S**
$4\frac{3}{4}$	$5\frac{5}{6}$	$4\frac{9}{10}$	
T	**U**	**V**	

The Complete Book of Challenge Math

Name _____

Subtracting Mixed Numbers and Whole Numbers

Subtract and complete the answers. Then, fill in the crossword puzzle.

Across

1. $9 - 8\frac{1}{11} =$ ten-_____

3. $3\frac{3}{4} - 1\frac{1}{5} =$ two and eleven-_____

5. $14\frac{3}{10} - 2\frac{1}{2} =$ eleven and four-_____

8. $5\frac{1}{2} - \frac{4}{5} =$ four and seven-_____

10. $15 - 11\frac{17}{20} =$ three and _____-twentieths

11. $15\frac{1}{3} - 2\frac{1}{2} =$ twelve and _____-sixths

12. $7\frac{7}{9} - 3\frac{1}{9} =$ four and _____-thirds

13. $12\frac{3}{5} - 2\frac{1}{10} =$ _____ and one-half

14. $8 - 2\frac{1}{8} =$ five and _____-eighths

16. $10\frac{3}{8} - 1\frac{5}{8} =$ eight and three-_____

17. $17\frac{1}{5} - 7\frac{7}{10} =$ nine and one-_____

18. $18 - 11\frac{1}{6} =$ six and five-_____

Down

2. $6\frac{3}{4} - 3\frac{1}{3} =$ three and five-_____

3. $10\frac{1}{5} - 2\frac{1}{3} =$ seven and _____-fifteenths

4. $8\frac{2}{9} - 2\frac{1}{3} =$ five and _____-ninths

6. $4 - 1\frac{1}{3} =$ two and two-_____

7. $9\frac{17}{18} - 3\frac{7}{9} =$ _____ and one-sixth

9. $6\frac{7}{9} - 1\frac{2}{3} =$ five and one-_____

11. $7\frac{1}{20} - 3\frac{1}{4} =$ three and _____-fifths

13. $10\frac{1}{12} - 6\frac{3}{4} =$ three and one-_____

15. $9\frac{1}{2} - 4\frac{1}{8} =$ five and three-_____

The Complete Book of Challenge Math

Water the Flowers

Solve each problem. Then, find the matching answers in the tic-tac-toe boards at the bottom of the page. Draw a raindrop on the answers for the odd-numbered problems and a flower on the answers for the even-numbered problems.

1. $2\dfrac{1}{3}$
$+\ 7\dfrac{1}{6}$

2. $8\dfrac{4}{5}$
$+\ 1\dfrac{4}{15}$

3. $7\dfrac{3}{4}$
$-\ 2\dfrac{1}{6}$

4. $1\dfrac{6}{7}$
$+\ 5\dfrac{1}{2}$

5. $8\dfrac{3}{8}$
$-\ 5\dfrac{3}{4}$

6. $4\dfrac{1}{4}$
$-\ 1\dfrac{2}{3}$

7. $1\dfrac{5}{6}$
$+\ 1\dfrac{8}{9}$

8. $10\dfrac{1}{2}$
$-\ 6\dfrac{2}{3}$

9. $2\dfrac{5}{6}$
$+\ 4\dfrac{1}{3}$

10. $1\dfrac{3}{8}$
$+\ 1\dfrac{3}{4}$

11. $5\dfrac{1}{8}$
$-\ 3\dfrac{3}{4}$

12. $3\dfrac{5}{16}$
$+\ 2\dfrac{5}{8}$

13. $2\dfrac{3}{5}$
$+\ 3\dfrac{2}{3}$

14. $6\dfrac{1}{4}$
$-\ 1\dfrac{4}{5}$

15. $11\dfrac{13}{15}$
$-\ 9\dfrac{1}{5}$

$5\dfrac{7}{12}$	$9\dfrac{1}{2}$	$7\dfrac{5}{14}$
$4\dfrac{1}{2}$	$3\dfrac{13}{18}$	$2\dfrac{5}{8}$
$2\dfrac{7}{12}$	$3\dfrac{5}{6}$	$10\dfrac{1}{15}$

$7\dfrac{1}{6}$	$5\dfrac{15}{16}$	$1\dfrac{3}{8}$
$2\dfrac{2}{3}$	$4\dfrac{9}{20}$	$1\dfrac{5}{7}$
$6\dfrac{4}{15}$	$3\dfrac{5}{9}$	$3\dfrac{1}{8}$

The Complete Book of Challenge Math

Name _____

A Trip to the Ocean

Maria's club earned enough money from their cookie sale to have a camp out at the ocean. Read about their trip and answer the questions. Show your work.

1. The bus started with $6\frac{1}{2}$ gallons of gasoline. When the driver added $9\frac{1}{2}$ more gallons of gasoline, how much gasoline did the bus have in it?

_____

2. The girls and their leaders stopped for a picnic after driving $58\frac{1}{5}$ miles. After the picnic, they drove $43\frac{4}{5}$ miles before reaching the ocean. How far were they from home?

_____

3. Before leaving home, they had made sandwiches for their lunch. They had $7\frac{1}{2}$ tuna sandwiches, $4\frac{1}{4}$ cheese sandwiches, $2\frac{3}{4}$ peanut butter sandwiches, and $5\frac{1}{2}$ beef sandwiches. How many total sandwiches did they bring?

_____

4. The leader cut their watermelon into 16 slices for lunch. They ate 8 of the slices. What fraction of the watermelon did they eat?

_____

5. If they saved the rest of the watermelon for dinner, how much was left for their dinner?

_____

6. When they arrived, they took $1\frac{1}{3}$ hours to set up the tents. They spent another $\frac{2}{3}$ hour getting their bedrolls ready. How long did they work before they could play in the ocean?

_____

Multiplying and Dividing Fractions

$= \pi \frac{4}{5} \ 2 \div {}^{3}A - r^{2} + 8 \ 1 \times 6\text{mm} \ 7 \ 32°F \ 10 \ 63\% \ 8\text{cm} \frac{7}{8}$

Multiplying Fractions

Example A	multiply $\frac{3}{5} \times \frac{1}{4} = \frac{3}{5} \times \frac{1}{4} = \frac{3}{20}$ multiply
Example B	multiply $\frac{20}{21} \times \frac{7}{10} = \frac{\overset{2}{20}}{\underset{3}{21}} \times \frac{\overset{1}{7}}{\underset{1}{10}} = \frac{2}{3}$ multiply
Example C	multiply $\frac{5}{16} \times \frac{4}{9} = \frac{5}{\underset{4}{16}} \times \frac{\overset{1}{4}}{9} = \frac{5}{36}$ multiply

Steps:

1. Cancel if possible by dividing numerators and denominators by their greatest common factor (GCF).

2. Multiply numerators.

3. Multiply denominators.

Multiply.

1. multiply $\frac{1}{15} \times \frac{2}{3} = \frac{2}{45}$ multiply

2. $\frac{7}{18} \times \frac{6}{7}$

3. $\frac{5}{14} \times \frac{7}{10}$

4. $\frac{1}{4} \times \frac{2}{3}$

5. $\frac{3}{8} \times \frac{4}{9}$

6. $\frac{4}{25} \times \frac{5}{6}$

The Complete Book of Challenge Math   © 2006 American Education Publishing

$= \pi \ \frac{4}{5} \ 2 \div {}^{3}A - r^{2} + 8 \ 1 \times 6^{mm} \ 7 \ 32°F \ 10 \ 63\% \ 8_{cm} \ \frac{7}{8}$

Can Crushers

Crush these number sentences. Fill in the missing fractions.

$\frac{5}{8}$	×	$\frac{4}{15}$	=	
×		×		
$\frac{12}{25}$	×	$\frac{5}{6}$	=	
=		=		
	×		=	
				×
$\frac{7}{12}$	×	$\frac{9}{14}$	=	
×		×		=
$\frac{6}{35}$		$\frac{21}{36}$		
=		=		
	×		=	

The Complete Book of Challenge Math

$$= \pi \tfrac{4}{5}\ 2 \div \ ^3A - r^2 + 8\ 1 \times 6^{mm}\ 7\ 32°F\ 10\ 63\%\ 8\,cm\ \tfrac{7}{8}$$

Practice Multiplying Fractions

> Remember the steps for multiplying fractions. Multiply the numerators together. Then, multiply the denominators together. Don't forget to reduce the fraction to lowest terms.

Find the products. Write each answer as a fraction in lowest terms.

1. $\dfrac{1}{2} \times \dfrac{4}{5}$ **2.** $\dfrac{1}{4} \times \dfrac{4}{5}$ **3.** $\dfrac{1}{3} \times \dfrac{3}{4}$

4. $\dfrac{1}{5} \times \dfrac{5}{6}$ **5.** $\dfrac{3}{5} \times \dfrac{1}{3}$ **6.** $\dfrac{2}{3} \times \dfrac{6}{8}$

7. $\dfrac{1}{6} \times \dfrac{3}{5}$ **8.** $\dfrac{1}{8} \times \dfrac{4}{5}$ **9.** $\dfrac{4}{7} \times \dfrac{1}{2}$

10. $\dfrac{3}{4} \times \dfrac{2}{12}$ **11.** $\dfrac{3}{7} \times \dfrac{1}{4}$ **12.** $\dfrac{7}{8} \times \dfrac{3}{4}$

Compare answers with a friend. If you have different answers, decide on a right answer. Be prepared to explain how you know the answer is correct.

The Complete Book of Challenge Math

$$= \pi \quad \frac{4}{5} \quad 2 \div \quad ^3 A \quad - r^2 + 8 \quad 1 \times 6mm \quad 7 \quad 32°F \quad 10 \quad 63\% \quad 8cm \quad \frac{7}{8}$$

Problems With the Pyramid

Help the camel complete the pyramid using this rule:

$$a \times b = c$$

The Complete Book of Challenge Math

$= \pi \ \frac{4}{5} \ 2 \div {}^{3}A - r^2 + 8 \ 1 \times 6^{mm} \ 7 \ 32°F \ 10 \ 63\% \ 8^{cm} \ \frac{7}{8}$

Leprechaun's Gold

Find the products. Show your work. Shade the corresponding pieces of gold to find out which leprechaun has the most gold.

1. $\frac{2}{5} \times \frac{3}{8}$ **2.** $\frac{3}{8} \times \frac{4}{9}$ **3.** $\frac{3}{5} \times \frac{5}{6}$

4. $\frac{8}{9} \times \frac{3}{10}$ **5.** $\frac{2}{9} \times \frac{6}{7}$ **6.** $\frac{1}{5} \times \frac{10}{11}$

7. $\frac{4}{13} \times \frac{1}{8}$ **8.** $\frac{14}{15} \times \frac{5}{6}$ **9.** $\frac{4}{9} \times \frac{3}{4}$

10. $\frac{2}{3} \times \frac{9}{10}$ **11.** $\frac{4}{5} \times \frac{1}{4}$ **12.** $\frac{15}{16} \times \frac{2}{5}$

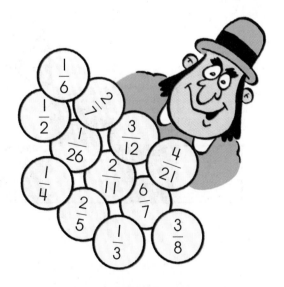

More Fraction Practice

Find each product. Show your work. Reduce your answers to lowest terms.

1. $\dfrac{1}{3} \times \dfrac{2}{4}$

2. $\dfrac{1}{4} \times \dfrac{3}{6}$

3. $\dfrac{1}{2} \times \dfrac{3}{4}$

4. $\dfrac{1}{3} \times \dfrac{1}{5}$

5. $\dfrac{1}{6} \times \dfrac{3}{7}$

6. $\dfrac{2}{6} \times \dfrac{1}{8}$

7. $\dfrac{3}{5} \times \dfrac{2}{4}$

8. $\dfrac{2}{3} \times \dfrac{1}{5}$

9. $\dfrac{3}{8} \times \dfrac{1}{6}$

10. $\dfrac{1}{2} \times \dfrac{2}{3}$

11. $\dfrac{1}{4} \times \dfrac{2}{5}$

12. $\dfrac{4}{6} \times \dfrac{1}{7}$

13. $\dfrac{1}{3} \times \dfrac{4}{5}$

14. $\dfrac{1}{5} \times \dfrac{3}{6}$

15. $\dfrac{1}{4} \times \dfrac{5}{6}$

16. $\dfrac{2}{6} \times \dfrac{3}{5}$

17. $\dfrac{1}{3} \times \dfrac{1}{4}$

18. $\dfrac{3}{5} \times \dfrac{6}{7}$

The Complete Book of Challenge Math

$$= \pi \ \frac{4}{5} \ 2 \div \ ^5A = r^2 + 8 \ 1 \times 6mm \ 7 \ 32°F \ 10 \ 63\% \ 8\,cm \ \frac{7}{8}$$

Improper Fractions and Mixed Numbers

Improper Fraction to Mixed Number

In an improper fraction, the numerator is larger than the denominator. To write an improper fraction as a mixed number, divide.

$$\frac{31}{6} = 31 \div 6 = \begin{array}{r} 5\ \frac{1}{6} \\ 6\overline{)31} \\ -30 \\ \hline 1 \end{array}$$ ←remainder
←divisor

Mixed Number to Improper Fraction

A mixed number has a whole number part and a fraction part. It can be written as an improper fraction by multiplying and adding.

$7\frac{3}{4}$

$4 \times 7 = 28$ Multiply denominator by whole number.

$28 + 3 = 31$ Add the numerator to this product.

$\frac{31}{4}$ Write this sum over the denominator.

Write as mixed numbers.

1. $\dfrac{42}{5}$

2. $\dfrac{83}{4}$

3. $\dfrac{46}{7}$

4. $\dfrac{57}{8}$

5. $\dfrac{63}{10}$

6. $\dfrac{29}{12}$

Write as improper fractions.

7. $5\dfrac{2}{7}$

8. $4\dfrac{11}{12}$

9. $6\dfrac{3}{8}$

10. $1\dfrac{1}{2}$

11. $30\dfrac{4}{5}$

12. $15\dfrac{2}{3}$

$$= \pi \; \tfrac{4}{5} \; 2 \div {}^{3}A - r^2 + 8 \; 1 \times 6^{mm} \; 7 \; 32°F \; 10 \; 63\% \; 8\,cm \; \tfrac{7}{8}$$

Multiplying Fractions and Whole Numbers

Example A (no canceling)	multiply $$10 \times \frac{2}{3} = \frac{10}{1} \times \frac{2}{3} = \frac{20}{3} = 6\frac{2}{3}$$ multiply
Example B (canceling)	multiply $$\frac{3}{5} \times 15 = \frac{3}{\cancel{5}_1} \times \frac{\cancel{15}^3}{1} = \frac{9}{1} = 9$$ multiply
Example C (canceling)	multiply $$12 \times \frac{5}{8} = \frac{\cancel{12}^3}{1} \times \frac{5}{\cancel{8}_2} = \frac{15}{2} = 7\frac{1}{2}$$ multiply

Steps:

1. Write whole number as a fraction.

2. Cancel by dividing numerators and denominators by their GCFs.

3. Multiply numerators.

4. Multiply denominators.

5. Write improper fractions as mixed numbers.

Multiply.

1. $\dfrac{2}{3} \times 9$

2. $\dfrac{11}{12} \times 8$

3. $6 \times \dfrac{8}{9}$

4. $\dfrac{7}{13} \times 11$

5. $15 \times \dfrac{12}{25}$

6. $18 \times \dfrac{5}{9}$

The Complete Book of Challenge Math

$= \pi \frac{4}{5} \ 2 \div \ ^3 4 - r^2 + 8 \ 1 \times 6^{mm} \ 7 \ 32°F \ 10 \ 63\% \ 8 cm \frac{7}{8}$

Multiplying Fractions by Mixed Numbers

multiply

Example A $\frac{3}{4} \times 1\frac{1}{2} = \frac{3}{4} \times \frac{3}{2} = \frac{9}{8} = 1\frac{1}{8}$

multiply

multiply

Example B $2\frac{4}{7} \times \frac{5}{9} = \frac{18}{7} \times \frac{5}{9} = \frac{\overset{2}{18}}{7} \times \frac{5}{\underset{1}{9}} = \frac{10}{7} = 1\frac{3}{7}$

multiply

Steps:

1. Change mixed numbers to improper fractions.
2. Cancel if possible.
3. Multiply numerators.
4. Multiply denominators.
5. Write improper fractions as mixed numbers.

Multiply.

1. $\frac{1}{2} \times 8\frac{3}{4} = \frac{1}{2} \times \frac{35}{4} = 4\frac{3}{8}$

2. $7\frac{1}{2} \times \frac{8}{9}$

3. $5\frac{1}{3} \times \frac{6}{7}$

4. $\frac{2}{5} \times 2\frac{1}{12}$

5. $\frac{11}{12} \times 11\frac{1}{3}$

6. $8\frac{2}{3} \times \frac{1}{4}$

The Complete Book of Challenge Math   © 2006 American Education Publishing

$= \pi \ \frac{4}{5} \ 2 \div {}^3 A - r^2 + 8 \ 1 \times 6 \text{mm} \ 7 \ 32°F \ 10 \ 63\% \ 8 \text{cm} \ \frac{7}{8}$

Daredevil Danny

Daredevil Danny has many dangerous pastimes. Solve the problems. Find the matching answers in Danny's wheels. Then, write the letters on the blanks above the matching numbers to find out Danny's favorite pastime.

1. $3\frac{1}{2} \times \frac{4}{6}$

2. $\frac{3}{19} \times 4\frac{2}{9}$

3. $\frac{3}{4} \times 5\frac{1}{7}$

4. $4\frac{1}{5} \times \frac{3}{4}$

5. $\frac{7}{10} \times 3\frac{3}{4}$

6. $\frac{4}{15} \times 6\frac{7}{8}$

7. $\frac{10}{11} \times 1\frac{1}{2}$

8. $3\frac{1}{3} \times \frac{3}{5}$

9. $8\frac{3}{8} \times \frac{4}{5}$

10. $2\frac{2}{7} \times \frac{7}{10}$

11. $5\frac{1}{3} \times \frac{1}{4}$

12. $\frac{2}{3} \times 5\frac{1}{4}$

O = $1\frac{4}{11}$ O = $\frac{2}{3}$ O = $3\frac{3}{20}$ R = $1\frac{5}{6}$

C = $2\frac{5}{8}$ I = $1\frac{3}{5}$ G = $3\frac{1}{2}$ T = $3\frac{6}{7}$

S = $6\frac{7}{10}$ S = 2   M = $2\frac{1}{3}$ N = $1\frac{1}{3}$

___ ___ ___ ___ ___ ___ ___ ___ ___ ___ ___ ___
1   2   3   4   5   6   7   8   9   10 11 12

The Complete Book of Challenge Math

Name _____

$= \pi \frac{4}{5} \; 2 \div \frac{3}{A} - r^2 + 8 \; 1 \times 6^{mm} \; 7 \; 32°F \; 10 \; 63\% \; 8 \, cm \frac{7}{8}$

Multiplying Mixed Numbers

Example A

multiply

$4\frac{1}{3} \times 2\frac{1}{2} = \frac{13}{3} \times \frac{5}{2} = \frac{65}{6} = 10\frac{5}{6}$

multiply

Steps:

1. Change mixed numbers to improper fractions.

2. Cancel if possible.

Example B

multiply

$1\frac{3}{5} \times 4\frac{1}{6} = \frac{8}{5} \times \frac{25}{6} = \frac{\overset{4}{\cancel{8}}}{\underset{1}{\cancel{5}}} \times \frac{\overset{5}{\cancel{25}}}{\underset{3}{\cancel{6}}} = \frac{20}{3} = 6\frac{2}{3}$

multiply

3. Multiply numerators.

4. Multiply denominators.

Example C

multiply

$8\frac{1}{4} \times 3\frac{7}{11} = \frac{33}{4} \times \frac{40}{11} = \frac{\overset{3}{\cancel{33}}}{\underset{1}{\cancel{4}}} \times \frac{\overset{10}{\cancel{40}}}{\underset{1}{\cancel{11}}} = \frac{30}{1} = 30$

multiply

5. Write improper fractions as mixed numbers.

Multiply.

1. $5\frac{1}{3} \times 4\frac{1}{2} = \frac{16}{3} \times \frac{9}{2} = 24$

2. $1\frac{2}{3} \times 1\frac{3}{4}$

3. $1\frac{3}{10} \times 3\frac{3}{4}$

4. $1\frac{7}{8} \times 2\frac{2}{5}$

5. $2\frac{6}{7} \times 2\frac{4}{5}$

6. $4\frac{3}{8} \times 1\frac{1}{15}$

$= \pi \; \frac{4}{5} \; 2 \div \; ^3\!A - r^2 + 8 \; 1 \times 6^{mm} \; 7 \; 32°F \; 10 \; 63\% \; 8\,cm \; \frac{7}{8}$

Sarah's Sweet Solution

Sweet-tooth Sarah altered the recipe for banana splits. Make the changes to the recipe. Then, write the letters of the problems in the blanks above the matching answers to find out what Sarah gets from eating too many sweets.

Banana Split

$1\frac{2}{5}$ bananas

$1\frac{1}{8}$ scoops vanilla ice cream

$2\frac{2}{3}$ scoops chocolate ice cream

$1\frac{1}{6}$ scoops strawberry ice cream

$1\frac{1}{4}$ cups hot fudge

$3\frac{3}{4}$ tablespoons marshmallow sauce

$2\frac{2}{3}$ teaspoons sprinkles

$1\frac{1}{2}$ teaspoons chopped nuts

Sarah likes:

A. $6\frac{2}{3}$ times the marshmallow sauce

E. $1\frac{5}{9}$ times the chopped nuts

I. $7\frac{1}{2}$ times the chocolate ice cream

T. $3\frac{3}{4}$ times the bananas

I. $1\frac{4}{5}$ times the strawberry ice cream

S. $2\frac{7}{10}$ times the sprinkles

C. $2\frac{2}{7}$ times the hot fudge

V. $1\frac{1}{3}$ times the vanilla ice cream

_____ _____ _____ _____ _____ _____ _____ _____
$2\frac{6}{7}$ 25 $1\frac{1}{2}$ 20 $5\frac{1}{4}$ $2\frac{1}{10}$ $2\frac{1}{3}$ $7\frac{1}{5}$

The Complete Book of Challenge Math

$= \pi \ \frac{4}{5} \ 2 \div \ ^3A - r^2 + 8 \ 1 \times 6mm \ 7 \ 32°F \ 10 \ 63\% \ 8 cm \ \frac{7}{8}$

Cooking Conversions

Beth and her mother were serving dinner for ten people. The recipe served only four people. They multiplied each ingredient by $2\frac{1}{2}$ to get the correct amount. Read each recipe ingredient and write the amount they will use on the line.

1. $\frac{1}{4}$ pound of butter _____

2. $\frac{1}{3}$ cup of flour _____

3. $2\frac{1}{2}$ cups chicken stock _____

4. $\frac{3}{4}$ cup cream _____

5. $\frac{1}{4}$ cup wine _____

6. 2 teaspoons salt _____

7. $\frac{1}{4}$ teaspoon pepper _____

8. 1 cup sliced mushrooms _____

9. 6 mushroom caps _____

10. 1 cup cooked ham _____

11. $\frac{1}{2}$ pound pasta dough _____

12. 2 cups cooked chicken _____

13. $\frac{1}{3}$ cup grated cheese _____

The Complete Book of Challenge Math

$= \pi \; \frac{4}{5} \; 2 \div \; {}^{3}A - r^{2} + 8 \; 1 \times 6^{mm} \; 7 \; 32°F \; 10 \; 63\% \; 8 \, cm \; \frac{7}{8}$

Willie the Worm

Help Willie the Worm reach the apple by solving the multiplication problems. Find the path by following the answers from least to greatest.

The Complete Book of Challenge Math

Name _____

$= \pi \frac{4}{5} 2 \div {}^3 A - r^2 + 8 1 \times 6 \text{mm} 7 \ 32°F \ 10 \ 63\% \ 8 \text{cm} \frac{7}{8}$

Playing Soccer

Soccer was a popular sport last year at Forestview Middle School. Using what you've learned about multiplying fractions, solve the problems below.

1. 30 students were in one seventh-grade classroom. If one-third of them played soccer, how many played soccer?   _____

2. One-sixth of 24 soccer players were girls. How many boys were on the team?   _____

3. The coach ordered 48 uniforms for the seventh-grade team. The sizes varied. Two-thirds of the uniforms were large. How many were large?   _____

4. 84 people came to watch one game. Six-eighths of the spectators were parents. How many were parents?   _____

5. 32 candy bars were sold at the first game. Two-eighths of them had peanuts. How many bars with peanuts were sold?   _____

6. One sixth-grade team played 10 games. Three-fifths of the games were played at home. How many were away games?   _____

7. The eighth graders won eight of their games. One-fourth of the games were won by only two points. How many were won by two points?   _____

8. Out of the 486 students at Forestview Middle School, one-third of them played soccer. How many of the students did not play soccer?   _____

$= \pi \ \frac{4}{5} \ 2 \div \ ^{5}A - r^{2} + 8 \ 1 \times 6^{mm} \ 7 \ 32°F \ 10 \ 63\% \ 8 \, cm \ \frac{7}{8}$

McCauley Middle School

A businesswoman from the community visited McCauley Middle School to observe students' understanding of word problems. Use what you've learned about multiplying fractions to solve the problems the students prepared for her.

1. It took Carla $2\frac{3}{4}$ hours to find the different leaves she needed for her leaf collection for science. It took Emily $\frac{3}{4}$ as long. How long did it take Emily?   _____

2. The play lasted $3\frac{1}{3}$ hours. Last year's play was $\frac{3}{4}$ as long. How long was last year's play?   _____

3. Antonio's report was $6\frac{3}{4}$ pages long. It only needed to be $\frac{1}{9}$ as long. How long did it need to be?   _____

4. On Arbor Day, Mr. Conservation's class planted one tree $20\frac{2}{3}$ yards from the building. They planted a second tree $\frac{3}{5}$ as far from the building. How far from the building did they plant the second tree?   _____

5. Deyana's speech took $12\frac{3}{4}$ minutes. Tara's speech lasted $\frac{8}{12}$ as long. How long was Tara's speech?   _____

6. During gym class, Jason kicked a ball $15\frac{2}{6}$ yards. Darnell kicked it only $\frac{1}{3}$ as far. How far did Darnell kick the ball?   _____

7. It took $6\frac{2}{7}$ yards of material to make four replacement flags for the flag team. Last year they used $\frac{3}{4}$ as much material. How much did they use the previous year?   _____

The Complete Book of Challenge Math

Name _____

$= \pi \; \frac{4}{5} \; 2 \div \frac{3}{4} A - r^2 + 8 \; 1 \times 6^{mm} \; 7 \; 32°F \; 10 \; 63\% \; 8\,cm \; \frac{7}{8}$

Dividing Fractions

Example A	$\frac{2}{3} \div \frac{7}{9}$	multiply

$$\frac{2}{3} \div \frac{7}{9} = \frac{2}{3} \times \frac{9}{7} = \frac{2}{3} \times \frac{\overset{3}{\cancel{9}}}{7} = \frac{6}{7}$$

multiply

Example B	$\frac{7}{9} \div \frac{2}{3}$	multiply

$$\frac{7}{9} \div \frac{2}{3} = \frac{7}{9} \times \frac{3}{2} = \frac{7}{\underset{3}{\cancel{9}}} \times \frac{\overset{1}{\cancel{3}}}{2} = \frac{7}{6} = 1\frac{1}{6}$$

multiply

Steps:

1. Change the problem to multiplication.
2. Invert the divisor (called the reciprocal).
3. Cancel if possible.

4. Multiply numerators.
5. Multiply denominators.
6. Write improper fractions as mixed numbers.

Divide.

1. $\frac{3}{10} \div \frac{4}{5}$

2. $\frac{5}{6} \div \frac{3}{8}$

3. $\frac{2}{9} \div \frac{1}{3}$

4. $\frac{5}{12} \div \frac{3}{4}$

5. $\frac{7}{9} \div \frac{7}{18}$

6. $\frac{2}{7} \div \frac{1}{2}$

7. $\frac{2}{5} \div \frac{4}{5}$

8. $\frac{3}{4} \div \frac{9}{14}$

9. $\frac{8}{9} \div \frac{2}{3}$

The Complete Book of Challenge Math

$= \pi \ \frac{4}{5} \ 2 \div \ ^{3}A - r^2 + 8 \ 1 \times 6^{mm} \ 7 \ 32°F \ 10 \ 63\% \ 8\,cm \ \frac{7}{8}$

Practice Dividing Fractions

	multiply
Example A	$\dfrac{3}{10} \div \dfrac{4}{5} = \dfrac{3}{10} \times \dfrac{5}{4} = \dfrac{3}{\overset{}{10}} \times \dfrac{\overset{1}{5}}{4} = \dfrac{3}{8}$
	multiply

Steps:

1. Change problem to multiplication.
2. Invert the divisor.
3. Cancel if possible.
4. Multiply numerators.
5. Multiply denominators.
6. Write improper fractions as mixed numbers.

multiply

Example B $\dfrac{3}{8} \div \dfrac{5}{12} = \dfrac{3}{8} \times \dfrac{12}{5} = \dfrac{3}{\overset{}{8}} \times \dfrac{\overset{3}{12}}{5} = \dfrac{9}{10}$

multiply

multiply

Example C $\dfrac{4}{5} \div \dfrac{3}{10} = \dfrac{4}{5} \times \dfrac{10}{3} = \dfrac{4}{\overset{}{5}} \times \dfrac{\overset{2}{10}}{3} = \dfrac{8}{3} = 2\dfrac{2}{3}$

multiply

multiply

Example D $\dfrac{5}{12} \div \dfrac{3}{8} = \dfrac{5}{12} \times \dfrac{8}{3} = \dfrac{5}{\overset{}{12}} \times \dfrac{\overset{2}{8}}{3} = \dfrac{10}{9} = 1\dfrac{1}{9}$

multiply

Divide.

1. $\dfrac{1}{2} \div \dfrac{3}{10} = \dfrac{1}{2} \times \dfrac{10}{3} = \dfrac{5}{3} = 1\dfrac{2}{3}$

2. $\dfrac{1}{10} \div \dfrac{2}{5}$

3. $\dfrac{3}{8} \div \dfrac{1}{4}$

4. $\dfrac{5}{6} \div \dfrac{11}{12}$

5. $\dfrac{4}{9} \div \dfrac{2}{3}$

6. $\dfrac{14}{15} \div \dfrac{2}{3}$

The Complete Book of Challenge Math

Multiplying and Dividing Fractions

Name _____

"Corny" Number Sentences

Fill in the missing fractions or mixed numbers.

The Complete Book of Challenge Math

© 2006 American Education Publishing

$= \pi \frac{4}{5} 2 \div {}^3 A - r^2 + 8 1 \times 6^{mm} 7\ 32°F\ 10\ 63\%\ 8\,cm\ \frac{7}{8}$

Double-Crossing Fractions

Solve each problem. Find the matching answers and write the letters to the problems on the lines to answer the question.

A. $\frac{2}{5} \div \frac{3}{10}$

B. $\frac{7}{12} \div \frac{3}{4}$

C. $\frac{9}{16} \div \frac{3}{4}$

D. $\frac{2}{7} \div \frac{4}{5}$

D. $\frac{3}{4} \div \frac{3}{8}$

E. $\frac{8}{9} \div \frac{4}{7}$

I. $\frac{5}{6} \div \frac{2}{3}$

L. $\frac{3}{20} \div \frac{9}{10}$

N. $\frac{8}{9} \div \frac{1}{4}$

O. $\frac{3}{8} \div \frac{3}{4}$

R. $\frac{8}{11} \div \frac{2}{5}$

E. $\frac{5}{6} \div \frac{1}{5}$

T. $\frac{5}{6} \div \frac{5}{18}$

N. $\frac{14}{15} \div \frac{4}{5}$

My name has become a synonym for the word traitor. Who am I?

$$\overline{\ \ }\ \overline{\ \ }\ \overline{\ \ }\ \overline{\ \ }\ \overline{\ \ }\ \overline{\ \ }\ \overline{\ \ }\ \overline{\ \ }\qquad \overline{\ \ }\ \overline{\ \ }\ \overline{\ \ }\ \overline{\ \ }\ \overline{\ \ }\ \overline{\ \ }$$

$\frac{7}{9}\quad 4\frac{1}{6}\quad 3\frac{5}{9}\quad 1\frac{5}{9}\quad 2\quad 1\frac{1}{4}\quad \frac{3}{4}\quad 3\qquad 1\frac{1}{3}\quad 1\frac{9}{11}\quad 1\frac{1}{6}\quad \frac{1}{2}\quad \frac{1}{6}\quad \frac{5}{14}$

The Complete Book of Challenge Math

Name _____

$= \pi \quad \frac{4}{5} \quad 2 \div \quad {}^3A - r^2 + 8 \quad 1 \times 6^{mm} \quad 7 \quad 32°F \quad 10 \quad 63\% \quad 8\,cm \quad \frac{7}{8}$

Dividing Mixed Numbers

| **Example** | $8\frac{3}{4} \div 5\frac{5}{8}$ |

multiply

$$8\frac{3}{4} \div 5\frac{5}{8} = \frac{35}{4} \div \frac{45}{8} = \frac{35}{4} \times \frac{8}{45} = \frac{35}{4} \times \frac{\overset{2}{\cancel{8}}}{\cancel{45}} = \frac{14}{9} = 1\frac{5}{9}$$

multiply

Steps:

1. Write mixed numbers as improper fractions.
2. Change the problem to multiplication.
3. Invert the divisor.
4. Cancel if possible.
5. Multiply numerators.
6. Multiply denominators.
7. Write improper fractions as mixed numbers.

Divide.

1. $6\frac{1}{2} \div 3\frac{9}{10}$

2. $5\frac{5}{6} \div 5\frac{1}{4}$

3. $3\frac{1}{3} \div 2\frac{4}{9}$

4. $5\frac{5}{8} \div 3\frac{3}{5}$

5. $4\frac{1}{8} \div 4\frac{7}{12}$

6. $4\frac{7}{12} \div 4\frac{1}{8}$

7. $3\frac{3}{4} \div 2\frac{11}{12}$

8. $4\frac{6}{7} \div 5\frac{8}{14}$

$= \pi \frac{4}{5} 2 \div {}^{3}A - r^{2} + 8 \ 1 \times 6^{mm} \ 7 \ 32°F \ 10 \ 63\% \ 8 \ cm \ \frac{7}{8}$

More Mixed Number Division

Solve each problem. Find the matching answers in the Code box. Then, write the letters on the blanks above the matching numbers to complete the secret message.

1. $4\frac{1}{3} \div 2\frac{8}{9}$

2. $2\frac{1}{5} \div 1\frac{1}{10}$

3. $5\frac{1}{4} \div 2\frac{1}{3}$

4. $4\frac{1}{6} \div 1\frac{2}{3}$

5. $2\frac{1}{7} \div 1\frac{2}{9}$

6. $3\frac{8}{9} \div 8\frac{1}{3}$

7. $4\frac{1}{2} \div 2\frac{8}{9}$

8. $2\frac{2}{3} \div 4\frac{2}{3}$

9. $2\frac{3}{4} \div 4\frac{1}{8}$

10. $9\frac{3}{7} \div 5\frac{1}{2}$

11. $3\frac{3}{4} \div 2\frac{1}{2}$

12. $5\frac{1}{3} \div 2\frac{2}{15}$

Code

E $1\frac{1}{2}$	**S** $1\frac{5}{7}$
I $\frac{4}{7}$	**T** $2\frac{1}{2}$
N $2\frac{1}{4}$	**V** $1\frac{58}{77}$
O 2	**W** $\frac{2}{3}$
R $1\frac{1}{3}$	**Y** $\frac{7}{15}$

___ ___ ___ , ___
 8 10 3   4

___ ___ ___ ___ ___ ___
 9 8 3 12 11 7

___ ___ ___ ___   ___ ___ ___?
 2 5 1 7   6 11 4

The Complete Book of Challenge Math

Name _____

$$= \pi \; \frac{4}{5} \; 2 \div {}^{3}A - r^2 + 8 \; 1 \times 6^{mm} \; 7 \; 32°F \; 10 \; 63\% \; 8^{cm} \; \frac{7}{8}$$

Fruity Fractions

Divide the mixed numbers. Complete the answers. Then, fill in the crossword puzzle.

Across

2. $2\frac{1}{10} \div 8\frac{2}{5} =$ one-_____

3. $5\frac{2}{5} \div 2\frac{17}{20} =$ one and _____-nineteenths

5. $1\frac{11}{15} \div 1\frac{19}{20} =$ _____-ninths

7. $7\frac{1}{2} \div 5\frac{5}{8} =$ one and one-_____

10. $8\frac{3}{4} \div 5\frac{3}{5} =$ one and nine-_____

Down

1. $6\frac{2}{3} \div 2\frac{1}{12} =$ _____ and one-fifth

2. $2\frac{5}{8} \div 4\frac{9}{10} =$ _____-twenty-eighths

3. $5\frac{5}{6} \div 4\frac{4}{9} =$ one and five-_____

4. $15\frac{3}{4} \div 10\frac{1}{8} =$ one and five-_____

6. $5\frac{2}{3} \div 25\frac{1}{2} =$ _____-ninths

8. $16\frac{1}{2} \div 6\frac{7}{8} =$ two and two-_____

9. $4\frac{5}{6} \div 5\frac{4}{5} =$ five-_____

$$= \pi \frac{4}{5} \ 2 \div \ ^3\!A - l^2 + 8 \ 1 \times 6^{mm} \ 7 \ 32°F \ 10 \ 63\% \ 8^{cm} \frac{7}{8}$$

Art Show

Ms. Creative had her students busy preparing for the year-end art show. Using what you've learned about dividing fractions, solve the problems below.

1. Kelly needed to finish seven paintings for the show. If he painted $\frac{1}{3}$ of a painting each session, how many sessions would it take him to finish all seven? _____

2. Morgan's responsibility was to glaze six pieces of pottery. She was able to complete $\frac{1}{4}$ of a pot's glaze in one class. How many classes will it take her to glaze all six pieces? _____

3. The art department had 102 pounds of paper. Each student uses approximately $\frac{3}{4}$ of a pound in one semester. Is there enough paper for 125 students this semester? _____

4. Karen needed to have nine black-and-white sketches finished for the show. If she finished about $\frac{2}{4}$ of one each class, how many classes would it take Karen to finish all nine? _____

5. Two sculptures were needed to highlight the entrance of the exhibit. One-sixteenth of each sculpture was completed in each art class. How many classes will it take to complete both sculptures? _____

6. The students took a piece of art paper that was $\frac{8}{9}$ of a yard long to make a mural. Once the mural was complete it needed to be cut into sections, each $\frac{2}{18}$ of a yard long. How many pieces will there be? _____

7. A painted carousel horse was the hit of the show. Three-tenths was painted each day. How many days did it take to finish? _____

The Complete Book of Challenge Math

$= \pi \ \frac{4}{5} \ 2 \div \ ^{3}\!A - r^2 + 8 \ 1 \times 6^{mm} \ 7 \ 32°F \ 10 \ 63\% \ 8_{cm} \ \frac{7}{8}$

Getting Ready for the Auction

Worthington Middle School was having a school auction. The students were learning about finance and organization while planning the auction. Solve the problems below.

1. Brad was making model airplane kits to sell at the auction. It took him $2\frac{1}{3}$ hours to make one kit. If he works for $9\frac{1}{3}$ total hours, how many airplane kits can he make?   _____

2. Suki was making origami kits. Each one took her $1\frac{2}{3}$ hours to make. If she worked for $11\frac{2}{3}$ hours, how many kits could she complete?   _____

3. Patrick's contribution was making the signs to advertise the auction. He could make four in $1\frac{1}{4}$ hours. If he worked $6\frac{2}{8}$ hours, how many signs could he make?   _____

4. Melissa, Sabrina, and Alyson worked together making boxed lunches. It took them an hour and a half to put five together. They worked for $7\frac{1}{2}$ hours. How many boxed lunches did they make?   _____

5. Kimberly was making bracelets. It took her $2\frac{3}{4}$ hours to make each one. If she worked $16\frac{1}{2}$ hours all together, how many could she make?   _____

Help was sought in making the bracelets because 30 were needed for the auction. How many additional hours of work would it take to complete that many?   _____

6. Pedro, Tanya, and Corey were making cupcakes. Working as a team, it took them $1\frac{1}{6}$ hours to make two dozen. If they worked $8\frac{1}{6}$ hours, how many cupcakes could they make?   _____

Adding and Subtracting Decimals

Name _____

Decimal Place Value

1 2 3 . 4 5 6 7 8

↑ hundreds
↑ tens
↑ ones
↑ tenths
↑ hundredths
↑ thousandths
↑ ten-thousandths
↑ hundred-thousandths

.0498 has 8 ten-thousandths
2.1376 has 3 hundredths
.458 has 4 tenths
.192 has 9 hundredths
4.60125 has 5 hundred-thousandths

1. The number 24.56137 has:

6 _____

3 _____

7 _____

5 _____

1 _____

2. What number has:

4 hundredths
0 tenths
3 ten-thousandths
5 hundred-thousandths
8 thousandths

_____

Profound Pork

Write the word name for each underlined number. Then, read the circled letters from top to bottom to answer the question.

67.071<u>4</u> = f o u r -

t (e) n - t h o u s a n d t h s

14.56<u>9</u> = __ (__) __ __-

__ __ __ __ __ (__) __ __ __ __

.<u>3</u>47 = __ __ __ __ - __ __ __ (__)

3.511<u>2</u> = __ (__) __-

__ __ __ - __ __ __ __ __ __ __ __ __ __

63.<u>8</u>5 = __ (__) __ __ - __ __ (__) __ __ __

8.1<u>7</u>04 = __ __ __ __ -

__ __ __ __ __ (__) __ __ __

What do you call a smart pig?

__ __ __ __ __ __ __ __

Name _____

Goofy Giggles

Draw a line from each dot to the letter to match each number word to its decimal. Then, write each letter in the correctly numbered blank to solve the riddle.

1. five-hundredths	●	L	0.05
2. two-tenths	●	T	0.9
3. five-thousandths	●	N	0.42
4. nine-hundredths	●	K	1.1
5. five-tenths	●	A	0.2
6. two-hundredths	●	O	42.2
7. forty-two hundredths	●	G	100.1
8. one hundred and one-tenth	●	H	0.5
9. forty and two-hundredths	●	U	0.005
10. nine-tenths	●	C	900.9
11. forty-two and two-tenths	●	G	0.09
12. nine hundred and nine-tenths	●	I	0.02
13. one and one-tenth	●	S	40.02

What do you call cows with a sense of humor?

___ ___ ___ ___ ___ ___ ___ ___
1   2   3   4   5   6   7   8

___ ___ ___ ___ ___
9 10 11 12 13

$= \pi \quad \frac{4}{5} \quad 2 \div \quad ^{3}A - r^{2} + 8 \quad 1 \times 6^{mm} \quad 7 \quad 32°F \quad 10 \quad 63\% \quad 8_{cm} \quad \frac{7}{8}$

Comparing and Ordering Decimals

Compare: 14.0397, 14.0386

To compare decimals, line up decimal points and compare each place value starting from the left until they differ.

same →
14 . 03	97
14 . 03	86
← different

Since 9 is greater than 8, 14.0397 > 14.0386.

Put in increasing order: 5.144, 5.141, 5.1441

To put decimals in order, compare the decimals.

same →
5 . 14	4
5 . 14	1
5 . 14	41
← different

Since 1 < 4 < 41, increasing order is:
5.141, 5.144, 5.1441

Compare.

1. .683, .681

2. 40.056, 40.065

3. 5.5515, 5.5155

4. .8031, .8013

5. .1167, .1617

6. .203, .23

Put in increasing order.

7. 3.224, 3.223, 3.225

8. 5.0041, 5.0039, 5.005

9. .6238, .6233, .6328

Put in decreasing order.

10. 20.080, 20.07, 20.074

11. 3.154, 3.1541, 3.155

12. 7.793, 7.739, 7.794

The Complete Book of Challenge Math

Name _____

$= \pi \ \frac{4}{5} \ 2 \div \ \overset{3}{A} - r^2 + 8 \ 1 \times 6 \text{mm} \ 7 \ 32°F \ 10 \ 63\% \ 8 \text{cm} \ \frac{7}{8}$

Marvelous Mentor!

What is another word for teacher? To find out, solve problems 1–9. Then, find the answers in the box and put the corresponding letter beside the answers.

O = .0111	**U** = 17.666	**G** = 8.04	**B** = 31.039
U = 6.499	**P** = .1368	**A** = 5.614	**I** = 5.6
T = 26.892	**E** = 26.98	**G** = 12.82	**E** = 17.675
M = .1376	**L** = 8.043	**U** = .0049	**D** = 31.0299

Which decimal is largest?

1. 5.614, 5.6114, 5.6

2. 26.892, 26.98

3. .0049, .0005, .0111

4. 17.675, 17.666

Which decimal is smallest?

5. 8.043, 8.04

6. 31.0349, 31.0299, 31.0329

7. 6.5, 6.499, 6.511

8. .1376, .1369, .1368

9. 12.82, 12.821, 12.9

___ ___ ___ ___ ___ ___ ___ ___ ___
8   4   6   1   9   3   5   7   2

Put in increasing order.

10. 16.198, 16.199, 16.189

11. 102.09, 102.101, 102.011

12. 8.0321, 8.0322, 8.03121

13. .6032, .6132, .6022

Put in decreasing order.

14. .301, .311, .302

15. 12.1212, 12.1221, 12.1222

16. 4.404, 4.414, 4.441

17. .7811, .7812, .7821

The Complete Book of Challenge Math

$= \pi\ \frac{4}{5}\ 2 \div {}^{3}A - r^{2} + 8\ 1 \times 6\text{mm}\ 7\ 32°\text{F}\ 10\ 63\%\ 8\text{cm}\ \frac{7}{8}$

Rounding Decimals

1. Locate the number immediately to the right of the place value you are rounding to.

2. If that number is less than 5, stay the same. If that number is greater than or equal to 5, round up.

3. All numbers before the place value being rounded stay the same. All numbers after are dropped.

Example: 254.17389

rounded to the nearest hundred: 2<u>5</u>4.17389 = 300
rounded to the nearest ten: 25<u>4</u>.17389 = 250
rounded to the nearest one: 254.<u>1</u>7389 = 254
rounded to the nearest tenth: 254.1<u>7</u>389 = 254.2
rounded to the nearest hundredth: 254.17<u>3</u>89 =254.17
rounded to the nearest thousandth: 254.173<u>8</u>9 = 254.174
rounded to the nearest ten-thousandth: 254.1738<u>9</u> = 254.1739

Round: 1,482.155634

1. to the nearest tenth _____

2. to the nearest hundred _____

3. to the nearest ten-thousandth _____

4. to the nearest hundredth _____

5. to the nearest one _____

6. to the nearest thousandth _____

7. to the nearest ten _____

8. to the nearest hundred-thousandth _____

9. to the nearest thousand _____

Name _____

$= \pi \quad \frac{4}{5} \quad 2 \quad \div \quad {}^{3}A \quad - \quad r^{2} \quad + \quad 8 \quad 1 \quad \times \quad 6mm \quad 7 \quad 32°F \quad 10 \quad 63\% \quad 8cm \quad \frac{7}{8}$

"Egg-sact" Numbers

International Egg Day is an "egg-citing" day. Maybe you'll want to go "eggs-ploring," or just hang around and share some good "yokes" with friends. Just make it an "egg-citing" day!

Complete the number puzzle. Round off the "egg-sact" decimal number. An entire box should be used for a decimal point. The first one is an "egg-sample."

Across

Round off . . .

1. 36.19 to the nearest tenth.

3. 23.634 to the nearest hundredth.

5. 1.536 to the nearest hundredth.

7. 1.78 to the nearest tenth.

Down

Round off . . .

1. 3,454.8 to the nearest whole number.

2. 2.342 to the nearest hundredth.

4. 650.61 to the nearest whole number.

6. 4.08 to the nearest tenth.

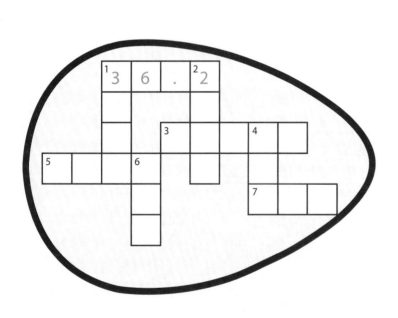

YOU MIGHT SCRAMBLE YOUR BRAIN ON THIS ONE!

$= \pi \quad \frac{4}{5} \quad 2 \div {}^{5}A - r^{2} + 8 \quad 1 \times 6\text{mm} \quad 7 \quad 32°F \quad 10 \quad 63\% \quad 8\text{cm} \quad \frac{7}{8}$

Soar into Summer

Complete the number puzzle. An entire box should be used for a decimal point.

Across

Round . . .

2. 346.28 to the nearest tenth.

4. 1,672.56 to the nearest whole number.

7. 5.163 to the nearest tenth.

8. 39.22 to the nearest tenth.

9. 54.899 to the nearest hundredth.

Down

Round . . .

1. 24.263 to the nearest tenth.

3. 341.276 to the nearest hundredth.

5. 299.61 to the nearest whole number.

6. 4,123.499 to the nearest whole number.

7. 5.246 to the nearest hundredth.

The Complete Book of Challenge Math

= π $\frac{4}{5}$ 2 ÷ ³ A − r² + 8 1 × 6 mm 7 32°F 10 63% 8 cm $\frac{7}{8}$

Itchy Insects

Only some mosquitoes bite. To find out which ones, follow the directions below.

1. Put an E above number 2 if 3.596 rounded to the nearest one is 4.
2. Put an A above number 1 if 23.4512 rounded to the nearest ten is 23.
3. Put an O above number 5 if 649.3 rounded to the nearest hundred is 650.
4. Put an E above number 6 if 2.19 rounded to the nearest tenth is 2.2.
5. Put an M above number 1 if .0388 rounded to the nearest hundredth is .039.

6. Put a C above number 5 if 57.86 rounded to the nearest ten is 58.9.
7. Put a D above number 3 if 4.355 rounded to the nearest hundredth is 4.35.
8. Put an A above number 4 if 14.86 rounded to the nearest one is 15.
9. Put an L above number 5 if .2315 rounded to the nearest thousandth is .232.
10. Put a B above number 2 if 717.1717 rounded to the nearest tenth is 717.17.
11. Put an M above number 3 if 5.066 rounded to the nearest one is 5.
12. Put a D above number 6 if 44.689 rounded to the nearest ten is 44.7.
13. Put an F above number 1 if .86424 rounded to the nearest ten-thousandth is .8642

____ ____ ____ ____ ____ ____
  1   2   3   4   5   6

$= \pi \; \frac{4}{5} \; 2 \div {}^3 A - r^2 + 8 \; 1 \times 6^{mm} \; 7 \; 32°F \; 10 \; 63\% \; 8^{cm} \; \frac{7}{8}$

Fractions to Decimals

Example A

$$\frac{13}{20} = 20\overline{)13.00} \;\; .65$$
$$-120$$
$$100$$
$$-100$$
$$0$$

To change a fraction to a decimal, divide the numerator by the denominator.

1. Put numbers in position to divide.
2. Add decimal point after numerator.
3. Bring decimal point up.
4. Divide, adding zeros at the end of the numerator.

Example B

$$\frac{7}{25} = 25\overline{)7.00} \;\; .28$$
$$-50$$
$$200$$
$$-200$$
$$0$$

Write as a decimal.

1. $\frac{5}{8} = 8\overline{)5.00} = .625$

2. $\frac{3}{10}$

3. $\frac{3}{8}$

4. $\frac{7}{20}$

5. $\frac{4}{25}$

6. $\frac{3}{4}$

7. $\frac{1}{8}$

8. $\frac{4}{5}$

9. $\frac{7}{8}$

The Complete Book of Challenge Math

Name _____

Decimal Delight

Kooky Claude Clod, the cafeteria cook, has some strange ideas about cooking. He does not understand fractions—only decimals. Help Claude convert these measurements to decimals so he can get cooking!

Fractions	**Decimals**
Mix together and sauté:	Mix together and sauté:
$\frac{9}{20}$ cup minced cat whiskers	_____ cup minced cat whiskers
$\frac{7}{8}$ cup crushed snails	_____ cup crushed snails
$\frac{3}{5}$ cup toothpaste	_____ cup toothpaste
$\frac{3}{4}$ tablespoon vinegar	_____ tablespoon vinegar
$\frac{11}{25}$ cup pig slop	_____ cup pig slop
Simmer $93\frac{1}{2}$ days.	Simmer _____ days.
Gradually fold in:	Gradually fold in:
$\frac{1}{5}$ teaspoon soot	_____ teaspoon soot
$\frac{3}{8}$ cup car oil	_____ cup car oil
$\frac{9}{10}$ tablespoon lemon juice	_____ tablespoon lemon juice
$\frac{11}{20}$ cup chopped poison ivy	_____ cup chopped poison ivy
$6\frac{1}{4}$ rotten eggs	_____ rotten eggs

Brew for $1,500\frac{24}{25}$ years. Enjoy!   Brew for _____ years. Enjoy!

The Complete Book of Challenge Math   © 2006 American Education Publishing

$$= \pi \ \tfrac{4}{5} \ 2 \div \ ^3A - r^2 + 8 \ 1 \times 6mm \ 7 \ 32°F \ 10 \ 63\% \ 8cm \ \tfrac{7}{8}$$

Decimals to Fractions

Problem	.24

1. Read the decimal mentally.   24 hundredths

2. Write the number you read.

3. Reduce this fraction to lowest terms by dividing both numerator and denominator by their greatest common factor (GCF).

$$\frac{24}{100}$$

$$\frac{24 \ (\div 4)}{100 \ (\div 4)} = \frac{6}{25}$$

Example A	.4

4 tenths

$$\frac{4}{10}$$

$$\frac{4 \ (\div 2)}{10 \ (\div 2)} = \frac{2}{5}$$

Example B	.875

875 thousandths

$$\frac{875}{1000}$$

$$\frac{875 \ (\div 125)}{1000 \ (\div 125)} = \frac{7}{8}$$

Write as a fraction in reduced form. The first one has been started for you.

1. .7
= 7 tenths =

2. .35

3. .75

4. .51

5. .64

6. .18

7. .25

8. .625

9. .125

The Complete Book of Challenge Math

Name _____

$$= \pi \quad \frac{4}{5} \quad 2 \div \quad ^3 A - r^2 + 8 \quad 1 \times 6^{mm} \quad 7 \quad 32°F \quad 10 \quad 63\% \quad 8\,cm \quad \frac{7}{8}$$

Peggy's Problem!

Help poor Peggy the bald porcupine find her quills by shading in the boxes of the correct equations. Remember to reduce the fractions to lowest terms.

$.41 = \frac{41}{100}$	$.26 = \frac{13}{50}$	$.55 = \frac{11}{20}$	$.15 = \frac{3}{20}$	$.68 = \frac{27}{25}$	$.48 = \frac{13}{25}$	$.34 = \frac{17}{25}$	$.82 = \frac{43}{50}$
$.635 = \frac{129}{500}$	$.4 = \frac{4}{5}$	$.38 = \frac{19}{25}$	$.9 = \frac{9}{10}$	$.27 = \frac{13}{50}$	$.65 = \frac{17}{20}$	$.56 = \frac{13}{25}$	$.74 = \frac{39}{50}$
$.95 = \frac{19}{25}$	$.6 = \frac{6}{100}$	$.11 = \frac{1}{10}$	$.234 = \frac{117}{500}$	$.8 = \frac{8}{100}$	$.72 = \frac{17}{20}$	$.29 = \frac{13}{50}$	$.62 = \frac{13}{20}$
$.385 = \frac{77}{100}$	$.502 = \frac{253}{500}$	$.81 = \frac{41}{50}$	$.18 = \frac{9}{50}$	$.45 = \frac{9}{25}$	$.28 = \frac{7}{25}$	$.82 = \frac{41}{50}$	$.36 = \frac{9}{25}$
$.76 = \frac{18}{25}$	$.7 = \frac{7}{100}$	$.24 = \frac{3}{20}$	$.52 = \frac{13}{25}$	$.69 = \frac{34}{50}$	$.93 = \frac{93}{100}$	$.95 = \frac{17}{20}$	$.61 = \frac{61}{100}$
$.3 = \frac{3}{5}$	$.19 = \frac{7}{20}$	$.73 = \frac{14}{20}$	$.38 = \frac{19}{50}$	$.73 = \frac{18}{25}$	$.12 = \frac{3}{25}$	$.36 = \frac{9}{20}$	$.59 = \frac{59}{100}$
$.48 = \frac{13}{25}$	$.63 = \frac{31}{50}$	$.444 = \frac{111}{200}$	$.92 = \frac{23}{25}$	$.66 = \frac{13}{20}$	$.65 = \frac{13}{20}$	$.52 = \frac{27}{50}$	$.46 = \frac{23}{50}$
$.99 = \frac{49}{50}$	$.47 = \frac{47}{50}$	$.58 = \frac{27}{50}$	$.88 = \frac{22}{25}$	$.74 = \frac{37}{50}$	$.2 = \frac{1}{5}$	$.91 = \frac{9}{10}$	$.14 = \frac{7}{50}$
$.93 = \frac{23}{50}$	$.84 = \frac{19}{25}$	$.77 = \frac{33}{50}$	$.42 = \frac{11}{25}$	$.5 = \frac{1}{5}$	$.89 = \frac{88}{100}$	$.49 = \frac{98}{100}$	$.32 = \frac{8}{25}$
$.27 = \frac{27}{50}$	$.1 = \frac{1}{100}$	$.14 = \frac{7}{10}$	$.89 = \frac{21}{25}$	$.22 = \frac{11}{20}$	$.38 = \frac{9}{25}$	$.18 = \frac{4}{25}$	$.24 = \frac{6}{25}$

$= \pi \ \frac{4}{5} \ 2 \div \ ^3\!A - r^2 + 8 \ 1 \times 6mm \ 7 \ 32°F \ 10 \ 63\% \ 8cm \ \frac{7}{8}$

Baby Faces

Draw the correct hair on the babies by finding the decimal for each fraction. Then, draw the correct mouths on the babies by finding the fraction for each decimal.

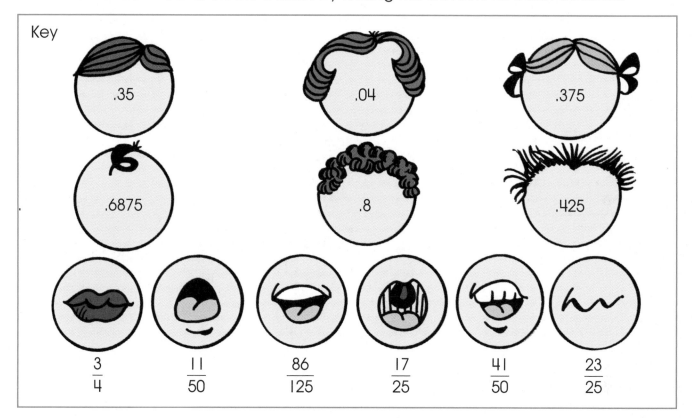

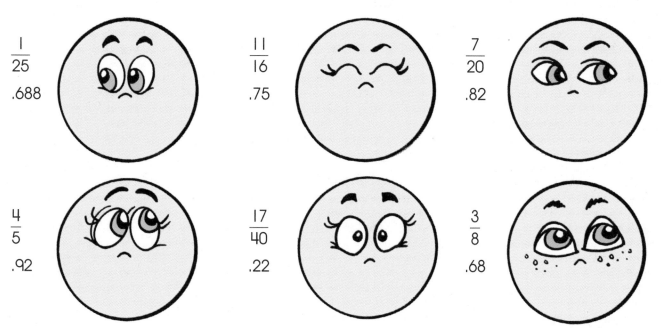

The Complete Book of Challenge Math

Name _____

$$= \pi \ \tfrac{4}{5} \ 2 \div \ ^3 A \ - \ r^0 \ + \ 8 \ 1 \times 6^{mm} \ 7 \ 32°F \ 10 \ 63\% \ 8_{cm} \ \tfrac{7}{8}$$

Adding Decimals

Example A (no regrouping)	63.248 + 5,741 ↓ 68.989	**1.** Line up decimals. **2.** Bring decimal point down. **3.** Add, carrying when needed.

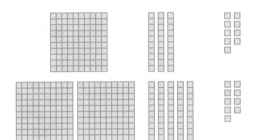

Example B (regrouping)	.139 +.259 ↓ .398

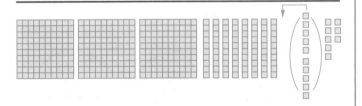

Add.

1.   62.059
    + 14.027

2.   .3586
    + .2795

3.   8.42
    + 1.37

4. 28.211 + .082

5. .976 + .834

6. 3.22 + .406

7. 21.09 + 16.8

8. 33.73 + 105.59

9. 8.937 + 16.99

$= \pi \; \frac{4}{5} \; 2 \div \; ^3A - r^2 + 8 \; 1 \times 6mm \; 7 \; 32°F \; 10 \; 63\% \; 8 \, cm \; \frac{7}{8}$

More Decimal Addition

Example A 3.498 + 2.056	$\begin{array}{r} 3.498 \\ + \; 2.056 \\ \hline 5.554 \end{array}$	**1.** Line up decimal points.

2. Add zeros to keep position if necessary.

3. Bring decimal point down.

4. Add, carrying when needed.

Example B 1.18 + .5782	$\begin{array}{r} 1.1800 \\ + \; .5782 \\ \hline 1.7582 \end{array}$

Add.

1. 4.98 + .0052

$\begin{array}{r} 4.9800 \\ + \quad .0052 \end{array}$

2. .9704 + .332

3. 18.8853 + .658

4. 3.4052 + 3.669

5. .0103 + .8888

6. 5.6674 + 8.3326

7. 6.801 + 16.59

8. 212.98 + 16.813

9. 17.414 + 211.99

© 2006 American Education Publishing   The Complete Book of Challenge Math

Name _____

Blast Off!

Have a blast with this number puzzle! An entire box should be used for a decimal point.

Across

3. $1.068 + 5.086$

4. $.444 + .53$

5. $521.8 + 312.4$

6. $7.32 + .99$

8. $.502 + .191$

12. $40.389 + 38.076$

14. $270.85 + 90.57$

15. $.033 + .066$

16. $8.749 + 3.388$

Down

1. $33.333 + .896$

2. $2.587 + 3.191$

3. $5.78 + 1.09$

7. $22.05 + 15.91$

9. $2.057 + .008$

10. $.531 + .19$

11. $7.852 + 1.489$

13. $3.012 + 1.025$

Swiss Sentences

Fill in the missing numbers.

1.862	+	.9854	=	
+		+		
.53	+	6.72	=	
=		=		
	+		=	

				+
.9076	+	.995	=	
+		+		=
6.53	+	5.47	=	
=		=		
	+		=	

The Complete Book of Challenge Math

Name _____

$= \pi \ \frac{4}{5} \ 2 \div \ ^3A - r^2 + 8 \ 1 \times 6^{mm} \ 7 \ 32°F \ 10 \ 63\% \ 8 \ cm \ \frac{7}{8}$

Practice With Decimal Addition

Find the sums. Show your work.

1.
```
  32.50
   0.89
+ 46.27
```

2.
```
  842.9
   56.32
+ 912.8
```

3.
```
  362.54
    3.85
+  46.39
```

4.
```
  200.69
  463.2
+   8.56
```

5.
```
   0.87
   6.42
+ 8.965
```

6.
```
  642.36
   58.29
+   0.37
```

7.
```
  845.236
   32.873
+    0.46
```

8.
```
  27.5
  34.62
+  5.38
```

9.
```
   7.64
  37.46
+ 29.583
```

10.
```
  526.9
   38.62
+ 300.18
```

11.
```
  9,642.31
    821.24
+      9.56
```

12.
```
  47.312
  314.25
+  82.74
```

13.
```
  602.45
   86.37
+   2.48
```

14.
```
  68.75
  214.23
+   9.462
```

15.
```
  312.46
   46.231
+   0.59
```

16.
```
  84.06
  246.23
+  38.4
```

17.
```
  918.06
   54.08
+ 312.04
```

18.
```
   0.75
  28.14
+  7.32
```

**Success ahoy!
Just practice!**

Build a Snowman

Solve each addition problem.

1.
```
    4.571
   24.85
  360.521
 +   .0391
```

2.
```
   981.1
    89.344
     2.013
 + 10.906
```

3.
```
   108.61
     3.386
    51.105
 +    .009
```

4.
```
    31.61
   111.364
     8.008
 + 942.1
```

5.
```
     .4632
   50.11
    9.0501
 +  8.76
```

6.
```
   833.3
    68.89
   361.275
 +   5.687
```

7.
```
    69.125
   152.96
     3.892
 +2,115.6
```

8.
```
     .785
   432.1
    41.52
 + 962.38
```

9.
```
    36.54
   147.02
  6,205.6
 +    8.699
```

10.
```
    85.36
   397.6
  5,900.369
 +   77.1205
```

Look at each sum. Follow the directions.

1. Circle all 8s in the hundredths place. Draw one piece of coal on the snowman for the mouth for each.

2. Underline all 1s in the tenths place. Draw one eye for each.

3. Put a triangle around each 5 in the ten-thousandths place. Draw one carrot nose for each.

4. Draw an arrow beneath each 3 in the thousandths place. Draw one stick arm for each.

5. Put a box around each 6 in the tens place. Draw one charcoal button for each.

6. Underline each 3 in the ten-thousandths place. Draw one hat for each.

The Complete Book of Challenge Math

$= \pi \; \frac{4}{5} \; 2 \div \; ^3A - r^2 + 8 \; 1 \times 6mm \; 7 \; 32°F \; 10 \; 63\% \; 8\,cm \; \frac{7}{8}$

Estimating Decimal Sums

When estimating decimal sums, round to whole numbers to make the addition easy. If you were at the market and had a $10 bill and wanted to buy items that cost $2.27, $4.83, and $1.95, you could estimate their sum to know if you had enough money with you.

Nearest One

```
   2.27    →      2
   4.83    →      5
+  1.95    →    + 2
 _____         ____
   9.05          9
```

Actual = 9.05
Estimated = 9
Difference = .05

Nearest Ten

```
   48.99    →      50
 + 22.25    →    + 20
 _____          ____
   71.24           70
```

Actual = 71.24
Estimated = 70
Difference = 1.24

Remember, look at the number to the right of the place value you are rounding to. If that number is < 5, the number you are rounding stays the same. If that number is ≥ 5, the number you are rounding goes up by 1.

Estimate.

1.
```
   3.864   →   4
   5.27    →   5
 + 6.911   →  +7
 _____       ___
```

2.
```
   33.96
 + 48.13
 _____
```

3.
```
   28.034
 + 74.105
 _____
```

4. 3.4 + 7.2 + 8.8

5. 81.6 + 52.7 + 49.8

6. 1.2 + 1.9 + 3.5

7. 79.8 + 63.9 + 82.4

8. 5.68 + 4.39 + 5.42

9. 77.41 + 63.92 + 18.88

Name _____

Scoops and Cones

Each cone contains an estimated sum. Write each estimated sum in a matching scoop. Then, draw a line to the correct cone.

The Complete Book of Challenge Math

Name _____

$= \pi \ \frac{4}{5} \ 2 \div \ ^3A - r^2 + 8 \ 1 \times 6^{mm} \ 7 \ 32°F \ 10 \ 63\% \ 8^{cm} \ \frac{7}{8}$

Time for Science

The Science Fair exhibitors from Scioto Middle School were being timed during practice sessions to see how long it would take each exhibitor to present his or her project. Use what you've learned about adding decimals to solve the problems below.

1. Brian prepared a complicated electrical circuit exhibit. The first time he tried his demonstration, he had trouble with a couple of connections and it took 10.52 minutes. His second try went much better and it took only 8.76 minutes. Finally, on the third try he was down to 4.65 minutes. What was his total practice time?

_____

2. Karen's buoyancy project took 13.28 minutes the first time. It went much smoother the second time and took only 10.24 minutes. She was finally successful on her third try. It took 4.46 minutes. What was Karen's total practice time?

_____

3. Bill's project dealt with circulation. It took him four minutes to set it up, .628 minutes to complete the circulation, and 1.245 minutes to finalize. Did he perform his demonstration in under six minutes?   _____

What was his time?   _____

4. Sheryl entered her photography project. It took .46 minutes to set her project up, 1.72 minutes to photograph her first subject, 3.84 minutes to photograph her second subject, and 3.46 minutes to complete the processing. How long did the project take?   _____

5. Tom's project focused on aerodynamics. He used different types of materials, various designs, and the addition of different types of weights to make his point. His first plane flew 20.676 feet, the second one flew 32.4689 feet, the third flew 18.62 feet, and the fourth flew 28.431 feet. What is the total distance all four planes flew?

$$= \pi \; \tfrac{4}{5} \; 2 \div {}^3 A - r^2 + 8 \; 1 \times 6 \, mm \; 7 \; 32°F \; 10 \; 63\% \; 8 \, cm \; \tfrac{7}{8}$$

Keeping Track of Time

Each student was given a stopwatch to time themselves for a whole week doing chores, homework, watching TV, or reading. Solve each of the following problems using decimal addition.

1. Carlos was amazed at the time he spent watching television in a week. On Monday he spent 1.45 hours in front of the television. Tuesday was better with only .54 hours. He watched 1.24 hours on Wednesday. On Thursday, he spent .28 hours. Friday, he watched for 1.07 hours. Saturday was a record with 3.49 hours. On Sunday, he watched only .18 hours. What was Carlos' total TV-watching time?

_____

2. Kim timed her homework sessions. Sunday she spent 48.05 minutes on homework, Monday 28.8 minutes, Tuesday 31.25 minutes, Wednesday 49.8 minutes, Thursday 57.85 minutes, and no time on Friday or Saturday. What was the total time Kim spent on homework?

_____

3. David did quite a few chores around the house because he was saving money for a new bike. On Monday, he worked .36 of an hour cleaning the garage. On Tuesday, he spent 1.19 hours cleaning his room. On Wednesday and Thursday together, he spent 1.44 hours vacuuming and dusting the house. On Friday he took a break. On Saturday, he spent 2.4 hours raking leaves. On Sunday, he helped his dad clean the workshop for 1.08 hours. How many total hours did David spend doing chores that week?

_____

4. Mandy decided to keep track of the amount of time she spent reading. On Monday she read after dinner for 1.45 hours. Tuesday, she was only able to read for .32 of an hour. Wednesday was rainy and cold, a great day for Mandy to spend 2.25 hours reading. On Thursday, she spent .50 of an hour. On Friday, she read for 1.36 of an hour. On Saturday, she had two reading sessions which totaled 3.55 hours. On Sunday, she squeezed in .25 hours. How many total hours did Mandy read in a week?

_____

The Complete Book of Challenge Math

Name _____

$= \pi \; \frac{4}{5} \; 2 \div \; ^3A - r^2 + 8 \; 1 \times 6^{mm} \; 7 \; 32°F \; 10 \; 63\% \; 8_{cm} \; \frac{7}{8}$

Subtracting Decimals

Example A 35.0469 − 14.0378	35.0469 − 14.0378 21.0091	
		1. Line up decimal points. With whole numbers, add a decimal point at the end.
Example B 8.5 − 6.345	8.500 − 6.345 2.155	**2.** Add zeros to keep position if necessary.
		3. Bring decimal point down.
		4. Subtract, borrowing when needed.
Example C 13 − .54	13.00 − .54 12.46	

Subtract.

1. 3 − 2.598

$$\begin{array}{r} 3.000 \\ -\; 2.598 \\ \hline \end{array}$$

2. .8175 − .623

3. 9.86 − .0426

4. 29.586 − 14.4211

5. .8747 − .0996

6. 17 − 5.8032

7. 42.816 − 9.9123

8. 212 − 11.916

9. 21.3 − 11.815

$$= \pi \ \tfrac{4}{5} \ 2 \div {}^{3}A - r^{2} + 8 \ 1 \times 6mm \ 7 \ 32°F \ 10 \ 63\% \ 8cm \ \tfrac{7}{8}$$

Subtracting Decimals from Whole Numbers

Example A $3 - .26$	$\overset{9}{\underset{}{\overset{2\ \ 11}{3.\cancel{0}0}}}$ $\underline{- \ \ .26}$ 2.74

1. Put decimal point after whole number.

2. Line up decimals.

3. Add zero(s) after decimal.

4. Bring decimal point down.

5. Subtract, borrowing when needed.

Example B $58 - 12.09$	$\overset{9}{\underset{}{\overset{7\ \ 11}{5\cancel{8}.\cancel{0}0}}}$ $\underline{- \ 12.09}$ 45.91

Subtract.

1. $\begin{array}{r} 79.00 \\ - \ \ \ .84 \\ \hline \end{array}$

2. $\begin{array}{r} 25.0 \\ - \ 24.3 \\ \hline \end{array}$

3. $\begin{array}{r} 16.00 \\ - \ 11.04 \\ \hline \end{array}$

4. $5 - .112$

5. $57 - 1.08$

6. $98 - 58.36$

7. $123 - 12.91$

8. $85 - 6.07$

9. $29 - 19.456$

The Complete Book of Challenge Math

Name _____

$= \pi \frac{4}{5} 2 \div \sqrt[3]{A} - r^2 + 8\ 1 \times 6mm\ 7\ 32°F\ 10\ 63\%\ 8cm\ \frac{7}{8}$

Subtracting Decimals from Whole Numbers

Solve each problem. Find the matching answer in the cannon. Then, write the letters on the blanks above the matching numbers to answer the trivia question.

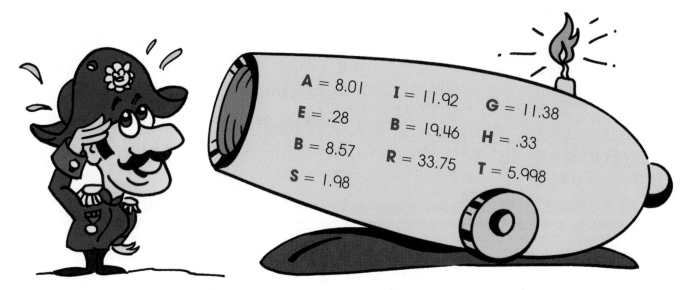

A = 8.01   I = 11.92   G = 11.38
E = .28   B = 19.46   H = .33
B = 8.57   R = 33.75   T = 5.998
S = 1.98

1. 9 − .43

2. 12 − .08

3. 15 − 3.62

4. 20 − .54

5. 1 − .72

6. 46 − 12.25

7. 6 − .002

8. 21 − 20.67

9. 9 − .99

10. 4 − 2.02

What were the large cannons used by Germany in World War I called?

___ ___ ___   ___ ___ ___ ___ ___ ___ ___
 1   2   3   4   5   6   7   8   9   10

Name _____

= π $\frac{4}{5}$ 2 ÷ 3_A − r^2 + 8 1 × 6mm 7 32°F 10 63% 8cm $\frac{7}{8}$

Who Planted More?

On Arbor Day, two classes planted trees. Solve each problem. Then, circle the answers on the trees and total the amounts to find out which class planted the most.

Mr. Larson's Homeroom

954.228
.579
5.628
6.2197
474.64
58.559
6.512
644.74
32.571
226.839

Ms. Young's Homeroom

709.69
290.479
4.9032
17.445
1.1148
329.059
755.87
350.738
302.54
1.6148

1. 276.2 − 49.361	**2.** 84.66 − 52.089	**3.** 653.64 − 8.9
4. 2.3004 − .6856	**5.** 375.4 − 72.86	**6.** 351.3 − .562
7. 8.26 − 1.748	**8.** 65.018 − 6.459	**9.** 942.06 − 186.19
10. 427.21 − 98.151	**11.** 1.738 − .6232	**12.** 548.3 − 73.66
13. 12.647 − 6.4273	**14.** 24.663 − 7.218	**15.** 6.8022 − 1.899
16. 333.2 − 42.721	**17.** 12.111 − 6.483	**18.** 2.055 − 1.476

_____
TOTAL

_____
TOTAL

The Complete Book of Challenge Math

Name _____

$= \pi \ \frac{4}{5} \ 2 \div \ ^3A \ - r^2 + 8 \ 1 \times 6mm \ 7 \ 32°F \ 10 \ 63\% \ 8cm \ \frac{7}{8}$

Compare the Harvest

Solve each problem. Write the difference in the correct portion of the Venn diagram. Don't forget to use the outside set.

1.   887.245
       − 265.9
       _____

2.   567.597
       − 541.256
       _____

3.   857.445
       − 256.104
       _____

4.   647.258
       − 321.144
       _____

5.   561.9353
       − 25.8941
       _____

6.   367.996
       − 341.55
       _____

7.   1,132.425
       − 483.125
       _____

8.   461.477
       − 325.446
       _____

9.   847.191
       − 246.25
       _____

10. 234.8315
       − 225.8899
       _____

11. 688.778
       − 542.818
       _____

12. 308.6191
       − 254.3651
       _____

13. 762.96
       − 130.554
       _____

14. 1,021.232
       −   56.1859
       _____

15. 941.509
       − 250.168
       _____

16. 965.415
       − 520.694
       _____

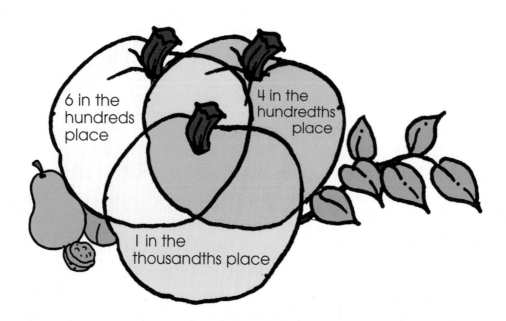

6 in the hundreds place

4 in the hundredths place

1 in the thousandths place

The Complete Book of Challenge Math

$$= \pi \ \frac{4}{5} \ 2 \div {}^{3}A - r^{2} + 8 \ 1 \times 6\text{mm} \ 7 \ 32°F \ 10 \ 63\% \ 8 \text{cm} \ \frac{7}{8}$$

Estimating Decimal Differences

When estimating decimal differences, round to whole numbers to make the subtraction easy to do. This comes in handy when you don't need an exact answer or when you don't have the time or the paper to do the subtraction.

Nearest One		
8.762	→	9
− 4.103	→	− 4
4.659	→	5

Actual = 4.659
Estimated = 5
Difference = .341

Nearest Ten		
63.45	→	60
− 28.86	→	− 30
34.59		30

Actual = 34.59
Estimated = 30
Difference = 4.59

Nearest Hundred		
339.62	→	300
− 93.99	→	− 100
245.63		200

Actual = 245.63
Estimated = 200
Difference = 45.63

Remember, look at the number to the right of the place value you are rounding to. If that number is < 5, the number you are rounding stays the same. If that number is ≥ 5, the number you are rounding goes up by 1.

Estimate.

I. 93.75 → 90
    − 48.12 → − 50
              40

2. 6.54
    − 2.81

3. 925.16
    − 377.77

4. 84.9 − 21.736

5. 9.365 − 2.844

6. 811.56 − 378.53

7. 9.157 − 4.51

8. 762.1 − 445.9

9. 79.12 − 33.6

Name _____

Boxer's Subtraction

Write the estimated difference in the punching bags beneath each problem inside the gloves. Then, draw a line to the correct punching bag.

The Complete Book of Challenge Math

© 2006 American Education Publishing

$= \pi \ \frac{4}{5} \ 2 \div \ ^3A - r^2 + 8 \ 1 \times 6^{mm} \ 7 \ 32°F \ 10 \ 63\% \ 8 \ cm \ \frac{7}{8}$

Robin Hood's Loot

According to legend, Robin Hood stole from the rich and gave to the poor. Follow the path to figure out how much Robin Hood has to give to the poor.

Add numbers in loot bags.

Subtract numbers in gift boxes.

Start Here

25

1.75

2.89

9.95

5.85

.05

.09

18.94

3.81

4.02

End

The Complete Book of Challenge Math

Name _____

$= \pi \ \frac{4}{5} \ 2 \div \ ^3 A - r^2 + 8 \ 1 \times 6^{mm} \ 7 \ 32°F \ 10 \ 63\% \ 8 \ cm \ \frac{7}{8}$

Practice With Decimal Subtraction

Solve each problem. Show your work.

1. 62.42
  − 24.23
  _____

2. 93.56
  − 42.38
  _____

3. 47.32
  − 14.28
  _____

4. 3.25
  − 2.67
  _____

5. 40.05
  − 23.28
  _____

6. 8.621
  − 3.248
  _____

7. 90.5
  − 62.9
  _____

8. 583.7
  − 392.4
  _____

9. 7.642
  − 5.269
  _____

10. 36.49
  − 29.82
  _____

11. 500.6
  − 341.2
  _____

12. 80.94
  − 28.23
  _____

13. 69.48
  − 42.93
  _____

14. 9.302
  − 7.281
  _____

15. 6.94
  − 4.83
  _____

16. 76.4
  − 52.8
  _____

17. 94.53
  − 42.82
  _____

18. 64.07
  − 52.82
  _____

19. 300.2
  − 225.4
  _____

20. 500.5
  − 432.2
  _____

21. 85.245
  − 43.462
  _____

22. 300.24
  − 142.48
  _____

23. 38.325
  − 13.146
  _____

24. 564.02
  − 325.24
  _____

25. 306.95
  − 212.28
  _____

26. 762.14
  − 341.25
  _____

27. 52.432
  − 26.514
  _____

28. 746.34
  − 482.16
  _____

**Success
ahoy!
Just
practice!**

$= \pi \; \frac{4}{5} \; 2 \div \;^3 A - r^2 + 8 \; 1 \times 6mm \; 7 \; 32°F \; 10 \; 63\% \; 8cm \; \frac{7}{8}$

Adding and Subtracting Decimals

Sometimes it is necessary to add and subtract many decimals. An example of this would be balancing a checkbook. There are two ways to do this.

Example: $16.98 - 8.42 + 39.15 - 46.23 + 15.44 - 11.96$

1. Add and subtract from left to right.

A. 16.98
− 8.42
———
8.56

B. 8.56
+ 39.15
———
47.71

C. 47.71
− 46.23
———
1.48

D. 1.48
+ 15.44
———
16.92

E. 16.92
− 11.96
———
4.96

OR

2. A. Add all numbers being added.
B. Add all numbers being subtracted.
C. Subtract B from A.

A. 16.98
39.15
+ 15.44
———
71.57

B. 8.42
46.23
+ 11.96
———
66.61

C. 71.57
− 66.61
———
4.96

Add and subtract.

1. $2.096 - .842 + 3.91 - 4.03 + .008 - 1.141$

2. $143.63 - 98.74 + 65.13 - 104.39 + 71.09 - 12.82$

3. $26.17 + 39.56 + 43.71 - 88.44 - 17.51 + 20.04$

4. $1,596.05 - 800.96 + 3,782.75 - 312.31 + 500.04$

The Complete Book of Challenge Math

Name _____

$= \pi \ \frac{4}{5} \ 2 \div {}^3 \! \sqrt{A} - r^2 + 8 \ 1 \times 6mm \ 7 \ 32°F \ 10 \ 63\% \ 8cm \ \frac{7}{8}$

Charting the Weather

For four months the students in Ms. Forecaster's class charted the weather. The following chart shows their findings to the nearest tenth. Use what you've learned about subtracting decimals to solve the problems below.

MONTH	SUNNY	PARTLY SUNNY	CLOUDY
October	13.4	12.8	4.8
November	7	13.1	9.9
December	6.3	11	13.7
January	8.4	16.7	5.9

1. How many more sunny days did January have than December?

_____

2. In November, how many more cloudy days were there than sunny days?

_____

3. How many more partly sunny days were there than sunny days in January?

_____

4. What is the difference in days between the month with the most cloudy days and the month that had the fewest cloudy days?

_____

5. Which month had the most sunny days? How many more sunny days did it have than the month with the second most?

_____

Which month came in second?

_____

6. Which month had the most cloudy days?

_____

Which month had the fewest cloudy days?

_____

How many total cloudy days were there in these four months?

_____

$= \pi \ \frac{4}{5} \ 2 \div {}^3A - r^2 + 8 \ 1 \times 6 \text{mm} \ 7 \ 32°F \ 10 \ 63\% \ 8 \text{cm} \ \frac{7}{8}$

The Rock Concert

Cindy's older sister took her to see her favorite rock band at the Fox Theater. Read about their evening and answer the questions. Show your work.

1. How old was Cindy? The concert was in July 1995. She was born in June 1984.

_____

2. They left for the concert at 5:30 P.M. They arrived at 7:30 P.M. How long did it take them to drive?

_____

3. There are 3,030 seats in the two-level Fox Theater. If 1,275 of the seats are on the ground level, how many are in the balcony?

_____

4. Earlier that week, her mother had bought Cindy a special outfit to wear to the concert. It cost $43.89. If Mother handed the clerk a $50.00 bill, how much change did she get?

_____

5. They had a wonderful time. The concert lasted from 8:00 P.M. until 11:30 P.M. How long was the concert?

_____

6. The feature band played on the stage for 2 hours and 15 minutes. How much of the total concert time did that band <u>not</u> play?

_____

7. Before the feature band, a "warm-up" band played. How long did the warm-up band play?

_____

8. Cindy bought a souvenir T-shirt after the concert. Of the 3,020 people who attended the concert, 243 bought T-shirts. How many did <u>not</u> buy a T-shirt?

_____

     The Complete Book of Challenge Math

Name _____

The Value of Money

Ms. Moneybags liked to use coins in her classroom to help with problem solving.

I. Use **six coins** to make each amount given in the chart. Indicate how many of each coin you would need.

	Amount	50¢	25¢	10¢	5¢	I¢
a.	$1.41					
b.	$ .87					
c.	$ .50					
d.	$1.20					
e.	$ .96					

2. Figure the amount of change you would receive for each transaction. Then, chart the **five coins** that could be used for change.

	Amount of Money	Amount of Purchase	Coin Received as Change				
			50¢	25¢	10¢	5¢	I¢
a.	$3.42	$2.79					
b.	$7.65	$6.20					
c.	$4.79	$3.68					
d.	$5.61	$5.15					
e.	$6.12	$5.45					

$$= \pi \; \frac{4}{5} \; 2 \div {}^3 A - r^2 + 8 \; 1 \times 6^{mm} \; 7 \; 32°F \; 10 \; 63\% \; 8 \, cm \; \frac{7}{8}$$

Holiday Shopping

As an early holiday gift your grandparents gave you a checkbook and $100. You have decided that you will use the money to purchase all of your holiday gifts. Balance the checkbook by adding deposits and subtracting debits. Keep a running total.

Date	Check #	Transaction and Reason	Debit	Deposit	Balance
12/1		Deposit—gift from grandparents		$100.00	
12/4		Deposit—babysitting at Smiths'		$16.00	
12/5	101	Clothes House—jacket	$84.32		
12/7	102	Pizza Palace—lunch	$6.46		
12/8	103	Toys and More—craft set for Sammi	$16.89		
12/8		Deposit—shoveling at Cruz's		$15.00	
12/8		Deposit—shoveling at our house and at Grandma T's		$20.00	
12/9		Deposit—shoveling at Cruz's, Vinns', Sniches', Van Dons'		$50.00	
12/10	104	Bath Stuff—gifts for Grandmas T and M	$19.87		
12/10	105	Men's Den—gifts for Corey, Grandpa T, and Grandpa M	$56.82		
12/12		Deposit—babysitting at Smiths'		$24.00	
12/13		Deposit—shoveling at Cruz's, Vinns', Sniches', Van Dons'		$50.00	
12/14	106	Rich's Jewelry Store—gift for Daphne	$26.89		
12/14	107	Hamburger Hut—lunch	$4.77		
12/14	108	Toys and More—art set for Randi	$15.73		
12/15		Deposit—babysitting at Cruz's		$17.50	
12/16		Deposit—shoveling at our house and at Grandma T's		$20.00	
12/17		Deposit—shoveling at Cruz's, Vinns', Sniches', Van Dons'		$50.00	
12/19	109	Steele's Steaks—gift certificate for piano teacher	$30.00		
12/19	110	Pizza Palace—slumber party with friends	$23.88		

The Complete Book of Challenge Math

= π $\frac{4}{5}$ 2 ÷ ^3A – r^o + 8 1 × 6ᵐᵐ 7 32°F 10 63% 8cm $\frac{7}{8}$

Shopping for Gifts

A group of friends went to the mall to look for gifts for their family and friends at the holiday season. Read about their choices and answer the questions. Show your work.

1. Heather looked for a pair of silver earrings for her sister. One pair was $19.95, and the other pair was $12.49. How much less did the second pair cost?

_____

2. Fred chose a mug for his teacher which cost $4.79. How much change did he get from a $10 bill?

_____

3. Since Lani loved music boxes, she bought one for each of her two sisters. One music box cost $18.59, and the other was $16.99. How much did she spend on music boxes?

_____

4. Peggy bought some piano sheet music for the holidays. The first piece was $3.39, the second was $2.95, and the third was $4.49. How much did she pay for the three pieces of sheet music?

_____

5. Bill only brought $20.00 with him. He bought a shirt for his dad for $14.79. Then, he found a sweater for his mother which was on sale for only $9.88. How much would he have to borrow from John to buy the sweater?

_____

6. Barry had 3 ten-dollar bills. He wanted to buy his brother a football for $9.95 and a soccer ball for his sister which cost $14.49. Does he have enough money? How much more does he need, or how much change will he get?

_____

7. While they were shopping, Peggy and Lani stopped for lunch. They each bought a soda at $1.19 each, and they split a hamburger which was $1.49. How much was their lunch bill?

_____

Multiplying and Dividing Decimals

Name _____

Multiplying Decimals

Example A
8.6 × .4

$$\begin{array}{r} 8.6 \\ \times\ .4 \\ \hline 3.44 \end{array}$$

8.6 — 2 decimal places

3.44 — 2 decimal places

1. Put numbers in position to multiply.
2. Multiply.
3. Count number of places to right of decimal(s) in numbers being multiplied.
4. Put decimal point the same number of places in the product.

Example B
9.35 × 2.1

$$\begin{array}{r} 9.35 \\ \times\ 2.1 \\ \hline 935 \\ +1870 \\ \hline 19.635 \end{array}$$

9.35 — 3 decimal places

19.635 — 3 decimal places

Finish this problem:

$$\begin{array}{r} 72.4 \\ \times\ 6.3 \\ \hline 2172 \\ +4344 \\ \hline \end{array}$$

72.4 — 2 decimal places

2 decimal places

Multiply.

1.
$$\begin{array}{r} 6.7 \\ \times\ 3.9 \\ \hline 603 \\ +201 \\ \hline 26.13 \end{array}$$

2.
$$\begin{array}{r} 4.87 \\ \times\ .2 \\ \hline \end{array}$$

3.
$$\begin{array}{r} .23 \\ \times\ .5 \\ \hline \end{array}$$

4. .917 × 4.6

5. 1.03 × .59

6. 8.35 × .66

7. 5.19 × 4.3

8. 4.88 × 6.7

9. 39.3 × 7.3

$= \pi \frac{4}{5} 2 \div {}^3 A - r^2 + 8 \ 1 \times 6^{mm} \ 7 \ 32°F \ 10 \ 63\% \ 8 cm \frac{7}{8}$

Multiplying Decimals (Two-Digit Multiplier)

Example
$.268 \times .17$

$$\begin{array}{r} .268 \leftarrow 3 \text{ places} \\ \times \ .17 \leftarrow 2 \text{ places} \\ \hline 1876 \\ + \ 2680 \\ \hline .04556 \leftarrow 5 \text{ places} \end{array}$$

1. Put numbers in position to multiply.

2. Multiply by ones.

3. Multiply by tens. (Add zero to keep position.)

4. Add.

5. Count the number of places to the right of the decimal points.

6. Put decimal point in product the same number of places from the right. Insert zeros when necessary.

Multiply.

1.
$$\begin{array}{r} 2.38 \\ \times \ 4.5 \\ \hline 1190 \\ + \ 9520 \\ \hline 10.71 \end{array}$$

2.
$$\begin{array}{r} 6.803 \\ \times \quad 9.4 \\ \hline \end{array}$$

3.
$$\begin{array}{r} 75.3 \\ \times \ .28 \\ \hline \end{array}$$

4. $.438 \times .11$

5. 324.6×5.3

6. $86.1 \times .49$

7. 3.981×8.9

8. 162.9×3.7

9. $99.02 \times .45$

The Complete Book of Challenge Math

Name _____

$= \pi \; \frac{4}{5} \; 2 \div \; ^3A - r^2 + 8 \; 1 \times 6^{mm} \; 7 \; 32°F \; 10 \; 63\% \; 8\,cm \; \frac{7}{8}$

Major League Multiplication

Solve each problem. Find the matching answer in the mitt. Then, write the letter on the blanks above the matching numbers to answer the question.

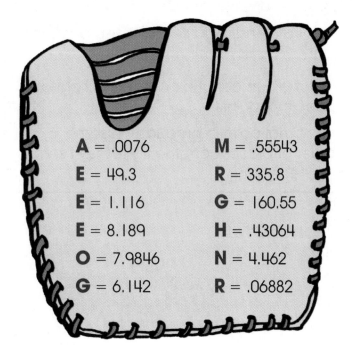

A = .0076   M = .55543
E = 49.3   R = 335.8
E = 1.116   G = 160.55
E = 8.189   H = .43064
O = 7.9846   N = 4.462
G = 6.142   R = .06882

1.   4.65
     × .24

2.   .04
     × .19

3.   .222
     × .31

4.   5.8
     × 8.5

5.   9.7
     × .46

6.   .862
     × 9.5

7.   7.3
     × 46

8.   .829
     × .67

9. 9.62 × .83

10. .769 × .56

11. 24.7 × 6.5

12. 8.3 × .74

What was "Babe" Ruth's real name?

___ ___ ___ ___ ___ ___   ___ ___ ___ ___ ___ ___
12   4   9   7   11   1   10   6   3   8   2   5

$= \pi \ \frac{4}{5} \ 2 \div \ ^3A - r^2 + 8 \ 1 \times 6^{mm} \ 7 \ 32°F \ 10 \ 63\% \ 8_{cm} \ \frac{7}{8}$

Multiplying Decimals (Three-Digit Multiplier)

Example		
.2187 × .306	$\begin{array}{r} .2187 \\ \times \ .306 \\ \hline 13122 \\ 00000 \\ + \ 656100 \\ \hline .0669222 \end{array}$ ← 4 places ← 3 places ← 7 places	**1.** Put numbers in position to multiply. **2.** Multiply by ones. **3.** Multiply by tens. **4.** Multiply by hundreds. **5.** Add. **6.** Count the number of places to the right of the decimal points. **7.** Put decimal point in product the same number of places from the right. Insert zeros when necessary.

Multiply.

1.
$$\begin{array}{r} 4.65 \\ \times \ 78.9 \\ \hline 4185 \\ 37200 \\ + \ 325500 \\ \hline \end{array}$$

2.
$$\begin{array}{r} 28.8 \\ \times \ 3.74 \\ \hline \end{array}$$

3.
$$\begin{array}{r} 6.033 \\ \times \ .858 \\ \hline \end{array}$$

4. $438 \times .111$

5. 324.6×5.32

6. $86.1 \times .496$

7. 72.72×8.61

8. $4.93 \times .505$

9. 5.513×7.33

The Complete Book of Challenge Math

$$= \pi \; \tfrac{4}{5} \; 2 \div {}^{3}A - r^{2} + 8 \; 1 \times 6^{mm} \; 7 \; 32°F \; 10 \; 63\% \; 8\,cm \; \tfrac{7}{8}$$

Solving for Touchdowns

Tackle this number puzzle! An entire box should be used for a decimal point.

Across

5. 6.35
    × .841

7. 5.88
    × 1.97

9. 60.4
    × .525

10. .712
    ×42.5

11. 24.6 × 69.8

12. 8.94 × 84.9

Down

1. 8.52
    × .007

2. 25.73
    × .289

3. 2.887
    × .009

4. 43.7
    × 36.9

6. 9.564 × 70.8

8. .145 × 8.66

Name _____

Multiplying and Dividing Decimals

Estimating Decimal Products

When estimating decimal products, round to a whole number to make the multiplication easy. For example, your neighbor asked you to babysit for 4.75 hours and pays $3.25 per hour. You'd want to figure out how much you'd earn before accepting by doing the multiplication mentally by rounding to the nearest one.

Nearest One

$$4.75 \rightarrow 5$$
$$\times\ 3.25 \rightarrow \times\ 3$$
$$15$$

*Nearest Ten

$$28.623 \rightarrow 30$$
$$\times 43.799 \rightarrow \times\ 40$$
$$1200$$

*Nearest Ten and One

$$88.43 \rightarrow 90$$
$$\times\ 3.45 \rightarrow \times\ 3$$
$$270$$

*Multiply the non-zero numbers first. Then, count the number of zeros in the rounded numbers and add that number of zeros to the product.

Estimate.

1. $65.43 \rightarrow 70$
   $\times\ 4.59 \rightarrow \times\ 5$

2. 2.86
   $\times\ 5.13$

3. 33.6
   $\times\ 29.7$

4. 93.78
   $\times\ 78.99$

5. 8.9645
   $\times\ 5.1663$

6. 44.04
   $\times\ 48.08$

189

© 2006 American Education Publishing

The Complete Book of Challenge Math

Name _____

Planting Products

Write the estimated products in the flowers beneath each problem in the watering cans. Then, draw a line from the watering can to the correct flower.

Name _____

Mogul Multiplication

Help the skier get down this difficult mogul course by checking the multiplication problems. Start at the top and draw a line down the page for her path by connecting the answers that are correct. Then, correct the answers to the problems that are wrong.

$$\begin{array}{r} .52 \\ \times\ 7.3 \\ \hline 37.96 \end{array}$$

$$\begin{array}{r} 30.4 \\ \times\ .3 \\ \hline 9.12 \end{array}$$

$$\begin{array}{r} 16.4 \\ \times\ .7 \\ \hline 11.48 \end{array}$$

$$\begin{array}{r} 6.4 \\ \times\ .81 \\ \hline 5.184 \end{array}$$

$$\begin{array}{r} 34.2 \\ \times\ .15 \\ \hline 4.13 \end{array}$$

$$\begin{array}{r} 8.7 \\ \times\ .6 \\ \hline 52.2 \end{array}$$

$$\begin{array}{r} .51 \\ \times\ .51 \\ \hline .2601 \end{array}$$

$$\begin{array}{r} 8.03 \\ \times\ .3 \\ \hline 2.609 \end{array}$$

$$\begin{array}{r} .12 \\ \times\ 3.6 \\ \hline .532 \end{array}$$

$$\begin{array}{r} 66.1 \\ \times\ .8 \\ \hline 52.88 \end{array}$$

$$\begin{array}{r} 2.49 \\ \times\ .2 \\ \hline 2.498 \end{array}$$

$$\begin{array}{r} 14.3 \\ \times\ .44 \\ \hline 62.92 \end{array}$$

$$\begin{array}{r} 22.2 \\ \times\ .22 \\ \hline 4.884 \end{array}$$

$$\begin{array}{r} 8.5 \\ \times\ .9 \\ \hline 7.65 \end{array}$$

$$\begin{array}{r} 72.1 \\ \times\ .33 \\ \hline 27.393 \end{array}$$

$$\begin{array}{r} 6.1 \\ \times\ .2 \\ \hline 12.2 \end{array}$$

$$\begin{array}{r} 82.1 \\ \times\ .4 \\ \hline 32.84 \end{array}$$

$$\begin{array}{r} .955 \\ \times\ .4 \\ \hline .482 \end{array}$$

$$\begin{array}{r} 3.3 \\ \times\ .3 \\ \hline 9.99 \end{array}$$

$$\begin{array}{r} 51 \\ \times\ .19 \\ \hline 8.79 \end{array}$$

$$\begin{array}{r} .23 \\ \times\ .4 \\ \hline .092 \end{array}$$

$$\begin{array}{r} .142 \\ \times\ 2.1 \\ \hline .9228 \end{array}$$

The Complete Book of Challenge Math

Elf Power

Have you seen any elves or gnomes today? Treat them kindly and they may reward you with a pocketful of gold.

Multiply. Then, write the letters on the blanks above the matching answers to solve the riddle.

13 × 0.7	2.1 × 0.3	4.5 × 3	.67 × 5	.21 × 0.7
E	**G**	**O**	**E**	**T**

22 × 0.4	2.13 × 0.3	41.3 × 0.02	67 × 0.2	.87 × 3
N	**W**	**M**	**S**	**G**

Where does an elf live?

"___ ___ ___ ___ ___   ___ ___ ___ ___ ___
 0.63 8.8 13.5 0.826 3.35   13.4 0.639 3.35 9.1 0.147

                                         ___ ___ ___ ___ ___ "
                                         2.61 8.8 13.5 0.826 9.1

IT'S A SWEET PLACE!

$= \pi \ \frac{4}{5} \ 2 \div \ ^3A - r^2 + 8 \ 1 \times 6^{mm} \ 7 \ 32°F \ 10 \ 63\% \ 8 \, cm \ \frac{7}{8}$

Halloween Treats

Harvey is cooking a pot of Halloween treats to serve with his holiday feast. The recipe calls for some unusual ingredients.

DON'T FORGET THE GOPHER GUTS!

Treats	Cooking Time
Bat wings	15 minutes per pound
Spider eggs	21 minutes per pound
Snake eyes	12 minutes per pound
Fang-furters	16 minutes per pound
Toad warts	26 minutes per pound
Spook-etti	6 minutes per pound

Harvey has a problem. He doesn't know how long he should cook each of his special treats. To find out how long Harvey must cook 3.2 pounds of fang-furters, multiply the amount of fang-furters by the cooking time. **Example:**

$$
\begin{array}{r}
16 \\
\times \ 3.2 \\
\hline
32 \\
48 \ \ \\
\hline
51.2 \text{ minutes}
\end{array}
$$

How long must Harvey cook . . .

2.3 pounds of spider eggs? _____

3.6 pounds of bat wings? _____

5.8 pounds of spook-etti? _____

2.8 pounds of snake eyes? _____

1.2 pounds of toad warts? _____

Remember to show your work on a sheet of scratch paper and label your answers.

The Complete Book of Challenge Math

Name _____

Practice Multiplying Decimals

Practice hard. You'll win!

Find the products. Show your work.

I. 36.5
× 8.4

2. 516.24
× 0.3

3. 3.614
× 0.57

4. 516.4
× 0.04

5. 462.3
× 7.1

6. 742.01
× 3.4

7. 0.316
× 1.7

8. 486.1
× 5.6

9. 56.01
× 0.8

10. 20.147
× 3.8

11. 43.4
× 0.67

12. 64.8
× 3.2

13. 1.015
× 0.3

14. 61.3
× 5.4

15. 4,621.4
× 0.42

16. 874.7
× 4.3

17. 0.148
× 0.7

18. 23.52
× 7.8

19. 51.6
× 4.9

20. 8.64
× 3.4

21. 6.454
× 5.6

22. 1.462
× 0.83

23. 21.362
× 5.7

24. 7.218
× 0.68

25. 6.145
× 7.4

26. 92.32
× 0.94

27. 314.6
× 0.7

28. 864.25
× 8.5

$= \pi \ \frac{4}{5} \ 2 \div \ ^3 A - r^2 + 8 \ 1 \times 6^{mm} \ 7 \ 32°F \ 10 \ 63\% \ 8 \ cm \ \frac{7}{8}$

Valentine's Day Dance

Mr. Spendthrift's class was assigned the job of purchasing all the materials needed for the Valentine's Day dance. Use what you've learned about multiplying decimals to solve the problems below.

1. One group went to the drug store for decorations. They purchased two packages of red construction paper and one package of pink. Each package cost $2.24. They also bought seven rolls of white crepe paper and nine rolls of red which cost $1.79 each. They needed 125 fancy white hearts. Each package of 24 cost $3.19. How much did everything cost all together?

_____

2. Another group was sent to buy the snacks. They bought two large sheet cakes, each costing $28.95. They also bought 68 cans of punch for $1.49 each. How much did they spend all together?

_____

3. The third group was in charge of napkins, paper plates, paper cups, and plastic forks. They needed enough for 415 people. The napkins came in packages of 60 for $1.95. The paper plates came in packages of 36 for $3.79, the paper cups cost $2.24 for 16, and the plastic forks were $3.16 for 48. How much was spent for each different item?

napkins_____   plates_____   cups _____   forks _____

How much did they cost all together?

_____

4. What was the total cost of this Valentine's Day dance?

_____

5. Figure what the cost of this dance would be if they needed three sheet cakes, 102 cans of punch, and enough paper plates, napkins, paper cups, and plastic forks for 600 people.

_____

The Complete Book of Challenge Math

Name _____

Delivering Encyclopedias

Scott's big brother, Leon, works as a delivery person for an encyclopedia company. Answer each question below about his work.

1. A small box of books weighs 8.3 pounds. A large box weighs 3 times as much. How much does the large box weigh?

_____

2. When someone buys a set of encyclopedias, the books come in 7 large boxes and 3 small boxes. How much does the whole set weigh?

_____

3. In five days last week, Leon drove an average of 46.5 miles each day. How many total miles did he drive last week?

_____

4. Leon uses his own van to make deliveries, and the company pays him $.30 a mile to cover expenses. How much money was paid to Leon for his travel expenses last week?

_____

5. The five grade schools in Scottsdale each ordered a new set of the encyclopedias. Using the weight from problem 2, calculate how many pounds of encyclopedias Leon delivered to the school warehouse.

_____

6. The company awarded five unabridged dictionaries as a free bonus for ordering 5 sets of the encyclopedias. Each dictionary weighed 5.48 pounds. How much weight did the 5 dictionaries add to the delivery?

_____

7. On days when he is not making deliveries, Leon works in the warehouse getting orders ready to ship out of town. One day he boxed 27 sets of encyclopedias. Using the weight from problem two, how much did the 27 sets weigh?

_____

$$= \pi \ \frac{4}{5} \ 2 \div \ ^3A - r^2 + 8 \ 1 \times 6^{mm} \ 7 \ 32°F \ 10 \ 63\% \ 8\,cm \ \frac{7}{8}$$

Dividing Decimals by Whole Numbers

Example
$185.61 \div 23$

$23\overline{)185.61}$ ↑

$23\overline{)185.61}$

```
      8.07
23)185.61
  -184
 ───────
     16
    - 0
    ────
    161
   -161
   ────
      0
```

1. Bring decimal point directly up.
2. Decide where to place the first digit in the quotient.
3. Divide. Then, multiply.
   a. $185 \div 23 = 8$
   b. $8 \times 23 = 184$
4. Subtract and compare.
   a. $185 - 184 = 1$
   b. Is 1 less than 23? Yes.
5. Bring down. Repeat the steps.
   a. Bring down 6.
   b. 23 cannot go into 16.
   c. Bring down 1.
   d. $161 \div 23 = 7$
   e. $7 \times 23 = 161$
   f. $161 - 161 = 0$
6. Check.
   a. $8.07 \times 23 = 185.61$

Divide.

1.
```
    921
  ↑
8)7.368
 -72
 ────
  16
 -16
 ───
   8
  -8
  ──
   0
```

2. $14\overline{).4998}$

3. $7\overline{)583.8}$

4. $9\overline{)399.78}$

5. $21\overline{)121.8}$

6. $6\overline{)438.06}$

The Complete Book of Challenge Math

Multiplying and Dividing Decimals

Name _____

The Perfect Sweet Treat Solution

Solve each division problem. Then, draw a line from the popcorn to the correct drink.

$3)\overline{7.95}$

6.84

$11)\overline{3.322}$

$5)\overline{.31}$

2.65

.905

$9)\overline{2.196}$

.395

.302

$2)\overline{.016}$

$7)\overline{47.88}$

.063

$5)\overline{11.4}$

.244

$4)\overline{15.48}$

1.135

$8)\overline{7.24}$

.008

$2)\overline{.79}$

3.87

2.28

$8)\overline{.504}$

.062

$6)\overline{6.81}$

$= \pi \ \frac{4}{5} \ 2 \div \ ^3A - r^2 + 8 \ 1 \times 6^{mm} \ 7 \ 32°F \ 10 \ 63\% \ 8\,cm \ \frac{7}{8}$

Decimal Trivia

Solve each problem. Find the matching answers in the $5 bill. Then, write the letters on the blanks above the matching numbers to answer the question.

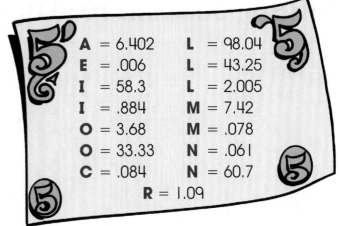

A = 6.402   L = 98.04
E = .006   L = 43.25
I = 58.3   L = 2.005
I = .884   M = 7.42
O = 3.68   M = .078
O = 33.33   N = .061
C = .084   N = 60.7
             R = 1.09

1. $12\overline{)44.16}$ **2.** $8\overline{).624}$

3. $5\overline{)37.1}$ **4.** $13\overline{)11.492}$ **5.** $9\overline{)389.25}$ **6.** $6\overline{)349.8}$

7. $7\overline{)686.28}$ **8.** $15\overline{).09}$ **9.** $22\overline{)1335.4}$ **10.** $10\overline{)20.05}$

11. $5\overline{)166.65}$ **12.** $7\overline{).427}$ **13.** $12\overline{)76.824}$ **14.** $9\overline{).756}$

What is pictured on the back of a $5 bill?

15. $13\overline{)14.17}$

___ ___ ___ ___ ___ ___ ___
10   4   9   14   1   7   12

___ ___ ___ ___ ___ ___ ___ ___
3   8   2   11   15   6   13   5

The Complete Book of Challenge Math

Dividing Decimals (One-Digit Divisor)

Example A	$$\begin{array}{r} 8.07 \\ .6\overline{)\,4.8\uparrow4\,2} \\ -4\,8 \\ \hline 4 \\ -\ 0 \\ \hline 4\,2 \\ -\ 4\,2 \\ \hline 0 \end{array}$$
4.842 ÷ .6	

1. Put numbers in position to divide.
2. Move decimal in divisor to the right of number.
3. Move decimal in dividend the same number of places to the right.
4. Bring decimal point directly up to quotient.
5. Divide, adding zeros to dividend when necessary.
6. Check by multiplying.

Example B
294 ÷ .7

$$\begin{array}{r} 4\,2\,0. \\ .7\overline{)\,2\,9\,4.0\uparrow} \\ -\ 2\,8 \\ \hline 1\,4 \\ -\ 1\,4 \\ \hline 0\,0 \end{array}$$

Example C
3.18 ÷ .4

$$\begin{array}{r} 7.9\,5 \\ .4\overline{)\,3.1\uparrow8\,0} \\ -\ 2\,8 \\ \hline 3\,8 \\ -\ 3\,6 \\ \hline 2\,0 \\ -\ 2\,0 \\ \hline 0 \end{array}$$

Divide.

1.
$$\begin{array}{r} .623 \\ .8\overline{)\,.4984} \\ -48 \\ \hline 18 \\ -16 \\ \hline 24 \\ -24 \\ \hline 0 \end{array}$$

2. $.6\overline{)522}$

3. $.9\overline{)5.067}$

4. 2.64 ÷ .5

5. 520.8 ÷ .7

6. 39.04 ÷ .4

$= \pi \quad \frac{4}{5} \quad 2 \div {}^3 A - r^2 + 8 \quad 1 \times 6^{mm} \quad 7 \quad 32°F \quad 10 \quad 63\% \quad 8\,cm \quad \frac{7}{8}$

Sammie Snail's Shell

Check the division problems. Connect the answers that are correct to help Sammie Snail find his shell. Then, correct the answers to the problems that are wrong.

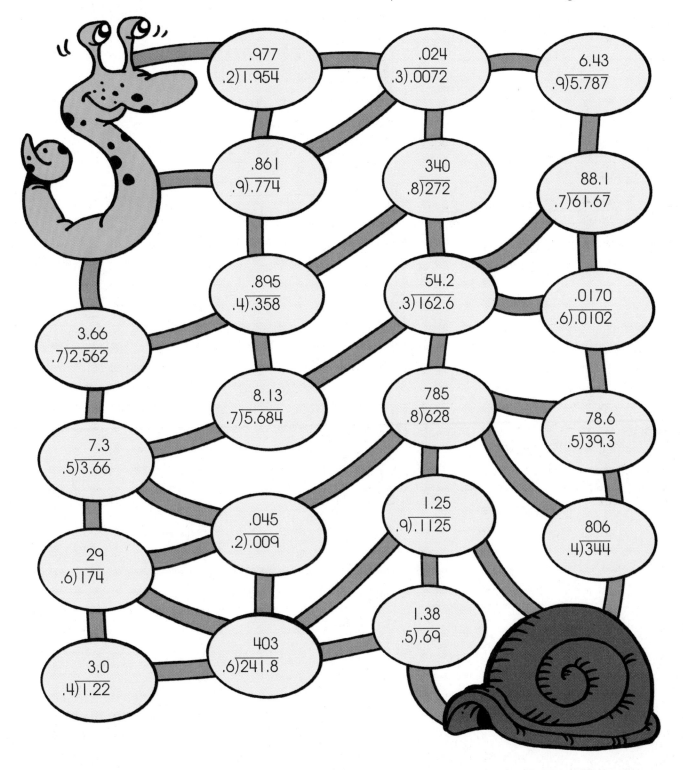

© 2006 American Education Publishing

The Complete Book of Challenge Math

Name _____

$= \pi \; \frac{4}{5} \; 2 \div \; {}^{3}A - r^{2} + 8 \; 1 \times 6^{mm} \; 7 \; 32°F \; 10 \; 63\% \; 8\,cm \; \frac{7}{8}$

Dividing Decimals (Two-Digit Divisor)

| **Example A** |
| 2.352 ÷ .42 |

```
          5.6
.4 2) 2.3 5↑2
     - 2 1 0
       2 5 2
     - 2 5 2
           0
```

1. Put numbers in position to divide.

2. Move decimal in divisor to right of number.

3. Move decimal in dividend the same number of places to the right.

4. Bring decimal point directly up to quotient.

5. Divide, adding zeros to dividend when necessary.

| **Example B** |
| 441 ÷ 6.3 |

```
          7 0.
6.3) 4 4 1.0↑
   - 4 4 1
          0 0
```

| **Example C** |
| 39.69 ÷ 5.4 |

```
          7.3 5
5.4) 3 9.6↑9 0
   - 3 7 8
       1 8 9
     - 1 6 2
         2 7 0
       - 2 7 0
             0
```

Divide.

1.
```
          5.6
.26) 1.456
   - 1 30
     156
   - 156
       0
```

2. 4.5) 1.08

3. .72) 28.80

4. 8.46 ÷ 1.8

5. 18.944 ÷ 3.7

6. 7.531 ÷ .34

Bob Means Business

Does businessman Bob make it up the corporate ladder? Solve the division problems. Shade in the answers on the ladder to find out. If any numbers are not shaded when all the problems have been completed, Bob gets fired. Some answers may not be on the ladder.

1. $.42\overline{)3.192}$

2. $1.5\overline{)1.47}$

3. $.22\overline{)1.936}$

4. $3.6\overline{)2160}$

5. $.53\overline{).3551}$

6. $.34\overline{)1.462}$

7. $360 \div 4.5$

8. $.522 \div .18$

9. $2.325 \div 2.5$

10. $1.976 \div .38$

11. $40.32 \div .63$

12. $6.6 \div 1.2$

| 8.8 |
| 60 |
| 5.2 |
| 7.6 |
| 64 |
| 2.9 |
| 5.6 |
| .98 |
| 80 |
| .67 |
| 4.3 |

Does Bob make it or get fired? _____

The Complete Book of Challenge Math

Multiplying and Dividing Decimals

Name _____

Fill That Basket

Solve each problem. Shade in the answers in the produce baskets to determine which has the largest amount of produce.

1. $6\overline{)13.86}$ **2.** $8\overline{)370.4}$ **3.** $4\overline{)21.264}$ **4.** $24\overline{)8.4}$

5. $36\overline{)60.48}$ **6.** $87\overline{)405.42}$ **7.** $49\overline{)17.64}$ **8.** $.3\overline{)20.772}$

9. $.8\overline{)6.152}$ **10.** $.04\overline{)13.684}$ **11.** $.52\overline{)3.8116}$ **12.** $.86\overline{)2.7735}$

13. $6.2\overline{)380.68}$ **14.** $3.4\overline{)3.468}$ **15.** $.06\overline{)1.9206}$ **16.** $2.1\overline{)118.02}$

17. $4.2\overline{)261.66}$ **18.** $.14\overline{)1.932}$ **19.** $2.9\overline{)21.315}$ **20.** $.013\overline{).37284}$

A

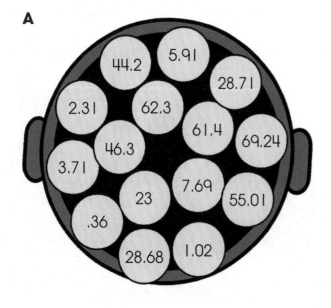

44.2 5.91 28.71 2.31 62.3 61.4 69.24 46.3 3.71 23 7.69 55.01 .36 28.68 1.02

B

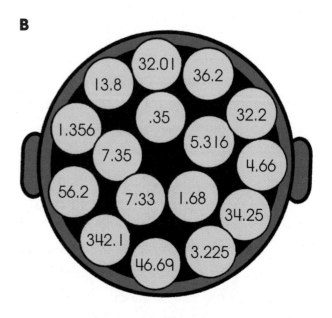

32.01 36.2 13.8 .35 32.2 1.356 5.316 7.35 4.66 56.2 7.33 1.68 34.25 342.1 3.225 46.69

$= \pi \; \frac{4}{5} \; 2 \div \; ^3A - r^2 + 8 \; 1 \times 6^{mm} \; 7 \; 32°F \; 10 \; 63\% \; 8 \, cm \; \frac{7}{8}$

To Market, to Market

At the local grocery store, prices vary greatly. Most items come in a variety of package sizes. A wise shopper finds the unit rate or unit price, then bases purchasing decisions on the best prices. Find the unit rate of each item. Circle the best deal.

Potato Chips—14-oz. package of Brand A for $2.66	14-oz. package of store brand for $1.96
8-oz. package of cream cheese for $1.84	8-oz. package of store brand for $1.36
Ice cream—2 quarts of Brand B for $5.00	2 quarts of Brand C for $3.20
Apple Juice—64 ounces of Brand M for $2.56	64 ounces of Brand T for $1.92
32 ounces of taco chips for $1.76	32 ounces of Brand T for $1.12
Microwave Popcorn—3 packages of Brand P for $3.36	4 packages of Brand S for $1.47
3 packages of snack crackers for $2.07	6 packages of Brand P for $5.76

The Complete Book of Challenge Math

$$= \pi \quad \tfrac{4}{5} \quad 2 \div \quad {}^5 A - r^2 + 8 \quad 1 \times 6^{mm} \quad 7 \quad 32°F \quad 10 \quad 63\% \quad 8\,cm \quad \tfrac{7}{8}$$

Shopping for Soccer Supplies

The soccer team members needed to buy their own shin guards, socks, shoes, and shorts. A couple of the players volunteered to do some comparative shopping to find the store with the best deal. Use their charts to answer the questions below.

SPORTS CORNER	
Socks	3 pairs for $9.30
Shoes	2 pairs for $48.24
Shin Guards	4 pairs for $32.48
Shorts	5 pairs for $60.30

JOE'S SOCCER	
Socks	2 pairs for $6.84
Shoes	3 pairs for $84.15
Shin Guards	5 pairs for $35.70
Shorts	4 pairs for $36.36

1. Which store had the best price for socks? _____

How much less were they per pair? _____

2. Which store had the best price for shin guards? _____

How much would you save per pair? _____

3. How much would one pair of shoes and socks cost at Joe's Soccer? _____

How much at Sports Corner? _____

4. Which store had the best price for shorts? _____

How much less were they per pair? _____

5. Total the price per pair for each item at each store. If you could shop at only one store, which one would give you the best overall deal? _____

How much would you save? _____

$= \pi \ \frac{4}{5} \ 2 \div \ ^3A - r^2 + 8 \ 1 \times 6^{mm} \ 7 \ 32°F \ 10 \ 63\% \ 8\,cm \ \frac{7}{8}$

Eating at Earl's

Lindsey invited six friends to have lunch with her at Earl's Sandwich Shoppe. Each girl ordered a sandwich and a soft drink. When the bill came Lindsey noticed that someone had smeared the lunch check with big blobs of mustard.

Help Lindsey find out what was written under those dried blobs of mustard. Use your problem-solving skills to write the correct numbers or words in the mustard blobs.

Earl's Sandwich Shoppe Menu			
Sandwiches	**Soft drinks**	**Large**	**Small**
Earl's Club............................$2.79	Fruit Juices	$1.25	$1.05
Mort's Meatball.................. $3.29	Lemonade	$0.95	$0.65
Tony's Tuna.........................$2.49	Spring Water	$0.85	$0.55
Chuck's Chicken............... $2.29			
Vick's Veggie......................$2.97			
Frank's Frank.......................$1.49			

YOU WANT FRIES WITH THAT, HON?

Earl's Lunch Check

Quantity	Item	Price
2	Vick's Veggie	$5.58
2		$9.87
	Mort's Meatball	$0.95
		$3.75
1	Large Fruit Juices	$1.10
		$0.85
2		
1		
	Total	$28.04

The Complete Book of Challenge Math

$= \pi \; \frac{4}{5} \; 2 \div {}^3A - r^2 + 8 \; 1 \times 6^{mm} \; 7 \; 32°F \; 10 \; 63\% \; 8 \, cm \; \frac{7}{8}$

Estimating Decimal Quotients

When estimating decimal quotients, round to a whole number to make the division easy. For example, if you had 17.8 milliliters of medicine left and took 3.12 milliliters each day, how many days of medicine would you have left?

Example A

$17.8 \div 3.12 \rightarrow 18 \div 3 = 6$

1. Round the numbers at a place value that makes the division easy.

2. Divide the rounded non-zero numbers.

3. Cancel all zeros in the divisor and the same number of zeros in the dividend.

4. Bring up any remaining zeros.

Example B

$629.48 \div 88.23 \rightarrow 630 \div 90$

$$\begin{array}{r} 7 \\ 9\cancel{0}\overline{)63\cancel{0}} \end{array}$$

Example C

$4{,}489.56 \div 52.6 \rightarrow 4{,}500 \div 50$

$$\begin{array}{r} 90 \\ 5\cancel{0}\overline{)450\cancel{0}} \end{array}$$

Estimate.

1. $14.97 \div 2.73$

$$\begin{array}{r} 5 \\ 3\overline{)15} \end{array}$$

2. $476.92 \div 62.8$

3. $3{,}589.662 \div 88.74$

4. $36.43 \div 5.782$

5. $419.551 \div 72.21$

6. $6{,}389.75 \div 78.57$

Name _____

Put Your Best Foot Forward

Write the estimated quotients shown on the feet beneath each problem inside the socks. Then, draw a line from the sock to the correct foot.

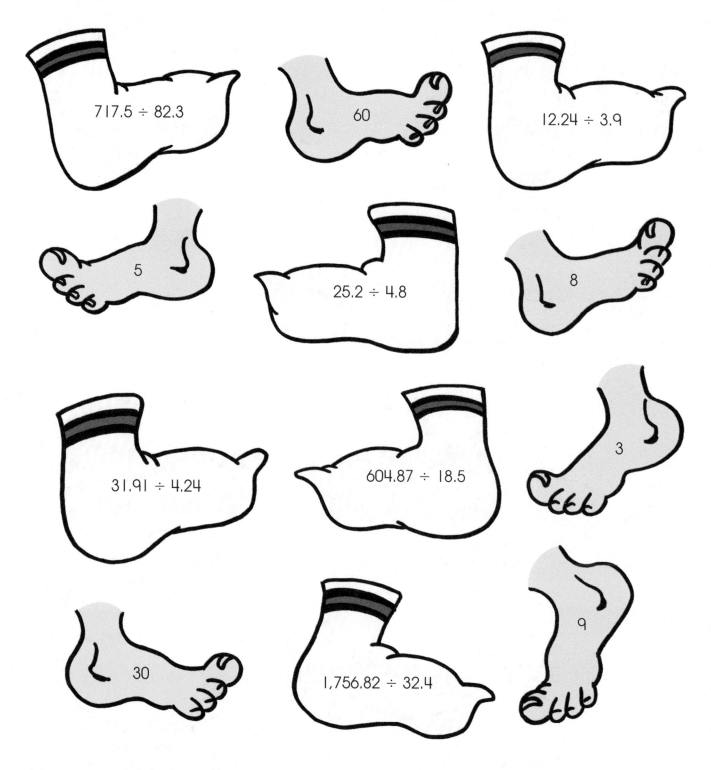

717.5 ÷ 82.3

60

12.24 ÷ 3.9

5

25.2 ÷ 4.8

8

31.91 ÷ 4.24

604.87 ÷ 18.5

3

30

1,756.82 ÷ 32.4

9

The Complete Book of Challenge Math

Name _____

= π $\frac{4}{5}$ 2 ÷ ³A − r^2 + 8 1 × 6mm 7 32°F 10 63% 8 cm $\frac{7}{8}$

Fishing

Multiply the numbers in the small fish. Then, circle each correct answer in the large fish to determine the "keepers."

634.82 × 2.93 =

1,860.0226
18,600.226
386.9394
389.6394
672.20689
21.45196
6.272.06

31.547 × .68 =

8.6291 × 77.9 =

57.81 × 6.74 =

Divide the numbers in each small fish. Then, circle the correct answers in the large fish.

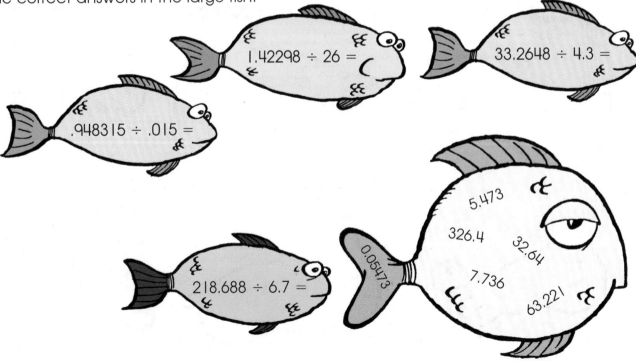

1.42298 ÷ 26 =

33.2648 ÷ 4.3 =

.948315 ÷ .015 =

218.688 ÷ 6.7 =

5.473
326.4
32.64
7.736
63.221
0.05473

Multiplying and Dividing Decimals by Powers of 10

Multiplying by Powers of 10

$1 \times .33 = \quad .33$
$10 \times .33 = \quad 3.3$
$100 \times .33 = \quad 33$
$1,000 \times .33 = 330$

To multiply a decimal by a power of ten, move the decimal point one place to the right for each zero in the power of ten.

Dividing by Powers of 10

$28.6 \div 1 \quad = 28.6$
$28.6 \div 10 \quad = 2.86$
$28.6 \div 100 \quad = .286$
$28.6 \div 1,000 = .0286$

To divide a decimal by a power of ten, move the decimal point one place to the left for each zero in the power of ten.

Multiply or divide.

1. 5.96×100

2. $79.2 \div 10$

3. $.07 \times 1$

4. $55.5 \div 1,000$

5. $.782 \div 1$

6. 322×10

7. $.86 \times 100$

8. $2.87 \div 100$

9. $55 \div 10$

10. 89.6×100

11. $.071 \times 1,000$

12. $3.29 \div 1,000$

Name _____

Wheels of Wonder

Find each product or quotient. Multiply or divide each number by the number in the center. The first one has been started for you.

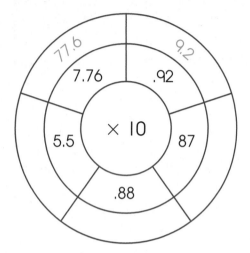

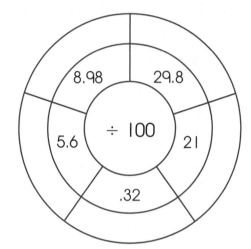

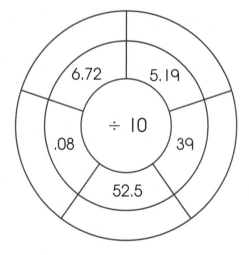

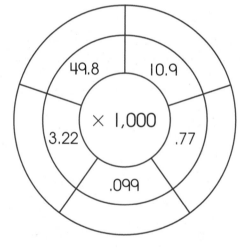

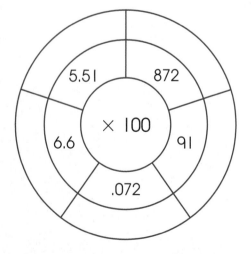

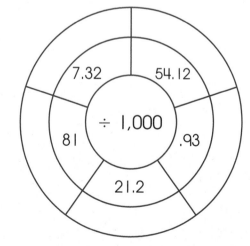

Calculating Percents

Name _____

Writing Decimals as Percents and Percents as Decimals

Decimals as Percents

To write a decimal as a percent, move the decimal point 2 places to the right and add a percent sign (%). You may need to insert zeros.

$$.50 = .50 = 50\%$$
$$.62 = .62 = 62\%$$
$$1.4 = 1.40 = 140\%$$
$$.07 = .07 = 7\%$$

Percents as Decimals

To write a percent as a decimal, move the decimal point 2 places to the left and omit the % sign. You may need to insert zeros.

$$63\% = 63 = .63$$
$$90\% = 90 = .9$$
$$1\% = 01 = .01$$
$$.2\% = 00.2 = .002$$

Write as a percent.

1. .39 _____   **2.** .08 _____   **3.** 1.2 _____   **4.** .6 _____

5. 7 _____   **6.** 2.01 _____   **7.** .002 _____   **8.** 5.67 _____

Write as a decimal.

9. 78% _____   **10.** 50% _____   **11.** 9% _____   **12.** 3.3% _____

13. .01% _____   **14.** 7% _____   **15.** 60.2% _____   **16.** .009% _____

$= \pi \; \frac{4}{5} \; 2 \div {}^3\! A - r^2 + 8 \; 1 \times 6\,mm \; 7 \; 32°F \; 10 \; 63\% \; 8\,cm \; \frac{7}{8}$

Happy Anniversary!

When did the Statue of Liberty celebrate her 100th anniversary? Check each problem. Shade in the true equations to find the answer to the statement at the bottom of the page.

.51 = 51%	84% = .84	17% = .17	.87 = 8.7%	185% = 1.85	.9 = 9%	4.8% = .48
7% = .07	1.6 = 16%	.11 = 11%	2.9% = .29	.09 = 9%	40% = .04	.77 = 7.7%
160% = 1.6	.06 = 6%	222% = 2.22	10.1 = 101%	90% = .9	4.29 = 42.9%	87% = .087
.37 = 37%	93% = 9.3	1.9 = 190%	64% = 6.4	.001 = .1%	12% = .12	65% = .65
2% = .02	3.8 = 38%	30% = .3	.13 = 1.3%	1% = .01	55.5 = 555%	38% = .38
.004 = .4%	.8 = 80%	92% = .92	.02 = 20%	4.4% = .044	.55 = 55%	.2 = 20%

The Statue of Liberty celebrated her 100th anniversary in 19_____.

The Complete Book of Challenge Math

Name _____

Writing Fractions as Percents and Percents as Fractions

Fractions as Percents

$$\frac{3}{8} = 8\overline{)3.000}$$

$$\begin{array}{r} .375 \\ \hline 8\overline{)3.000} \\ -24 \\ \hline 60 \\ -56 \\ \hline 40 \\ -40 \\ \hline 0 \end{array}$$

$.375 = 37.5\%$

1. Divide numerator by denominator.

2. Write this decimal as a percent.

Percents as Fractions

$55\% = .55$

fifty-five hundredths $= \dfrac{55}{100}$

$\dfrac{55 \ (\div 5)}{100 \ (\div 5)} = \dfrac{11}{20}$

1. Write percent as a decimal.

2. Write decimal as a fraction using the place value.

3. Reduce by dividing numerator and denominator by the GCF.

Write as a percent.

1. $\dfrac{3}{4}$ _____

2. $\dfrac{2}{25}$ _____

3. $\dfrac{3}{10}$ _____

4. $\dfrac{1}{2}$ _____

5. $\dfrac{2}{5}$ _____

6. $\dfrac{7}{8}$ _____

7. $\dfrac{1}{4}$ _____

8. $\dfrac{7}{10}$ _____

Write as a reduced fraction.

9. 60% _____

10. 25% _____

11. 44% _____

12. 5% _____

13. 32% _____

14. 64% _____

15. 76% _____

16. 18% _____

$= \pi \ \frac{4}{5} \ 2 \div {}^3\!A - r^2 + 8 \ 1 \times 6^{mm} \ 7 \ 32°F \ 10 \ 63\% \ 8^{cm} \ \frac{7}{8}$

Incredible Inventions

Solve each problem. Find the matching answers in the test tube. Then, write the letters on the blanks above the matching numbers to answer the question.

Write as a percent.

1. $\frac{1}{4}$ **2.** $\frac{5}{8}$ **3.** $\frac{7}{10}$

4. $\frac{13}{100}$ **5.** $\frac{3}{5}$ **6.** $\frac{7}{20}$

$A = \frac{1}{8}$

$E = \frac{23}{100}$

$E = 35\%$

$E = \frac{1}{5}$

$I = \frac{9}{20}$

$O = 45\%$

$U = \frac{4}{5}$

$U = 53.5\%$

$B = \frac{3}{4}$

$C = 60\%$

$D = 13\%$

$G = \frac{7}{50}$

$G = \frac{33}{50}$

$N = 62.5\%$

$M = \frac{3}{20}$

$S = 25\%$

$T = 70\%$

Write as a reduced fraction.

7. 20% **8.** 45% **9.** 14%

10. 75% **11.** 66% **12.** 23%

What did Samuel Benedict invent?

___ ___ ___ ___   ___ ___ ___ ___ ___ ___ ___ ___
12 11 9   1   10 6   2   7   4   8   5   3

The Complete Book of Challenge Math

Name _____

= π $\frac{4}{5}$ 2 ÷ ^3A − r^2 + 8 1 × 6mm 7 32°F 10 63% 8 cm $\frac{7}{8}$

Decimals, Fractions, and Percents

	Decimal	Percent	Fraction
Example A .45	.45	.45 = 45%	forty-five hundredths $\frac{45}{100} = \frac{(\div 5)}{(\div 5)} = \frac{9}{20}$
Example B 61%	61% = .61	61%	sixty-one hundredths $\frac{61}{100}$
Example C $\frac{11}{20}$	.55 20)11.00 −100 100 −100 0	.55 = 55%	$\frac{11}{20}$

Write as a percent.

1. .205 _____

2. $\frac{3}{100}$ _____

3. 1.8 _____

4. $\frac{9}{50}$ _____

5. .43 _____

6. $\frac{4}{5}$ _____

Write as a decimal.

7. 4.6% _____

8. $\frac{4}{5}$ _____

9. 125% _____

10. $\frac{9}{10}$ _____

11. 99% _____

12. $\frac{7}{8}$ _____

Write as a reduced fraction.

13. .12 _____

14. 90% _____

15. .06 _____

16. 4% _____

17. .36 _____

18. 35% _____

= π $\frac{4}{5}$ 2 ÷ ^3A − r^2 + 8 1 × 6^{mm} 7 32°F 10 63% 8cm $\frac{7}{8}$

Mirthful Mugs

Draw the correct eyes and mouths on the faces by finding the decimal and reduced fraction for each percent.

70%

52%

8%

71%

60%

85%

Key:

 = $\frac{13}{25}$  = $\frac{3}{5}$  = $\frac{2}{25}$

 = $\frac{17}{20}$ = $\frac{7}{10}$ = $\frac{71}{100}$

 = .6   = .52   = .08

 = .71    = .7    = .85

The Complete Book of Challenge Math

Name _____

$= \pi \ \frac{4}{5} \ 2 \div {}^3 A - r^2 + 8 \ 1 \times 6^{mm} \ 7 \ 32°F \ 10 \ 63\% \ 8\,cm \ \frac{7}{8}$

Finding Percent of a Number

Example A	80% of 20 is what number?	**1.** Write percent as a decimal.
		2. Multiply the two numbers.

80% = .8

$$\begin{array}{r} 20 \\ \times\ .8 \\ \hline 16.0 \end{array}$$
Answer = 16

Example B   What is 73% of 50?

73% = .73

$$\begin{array}{r} 50 \\ \times\ \ .73 \\ \hline 150 \\ +\ 3500 \\ \hline 36.50 \end{array}$$
Answer = 36.5

Find the percents.

1. 60% of 200

2. 42% of 5

3. 95% of 160

4. 21% of 141

5. 15% of 60

6. 20% of 50

7. 69.2% of 21

8. 33% of 70

9. 80.1% of 200

Name _____

$= \pi \ \frac{4}{5} \ 2 \div \ ^{5}A - r^{2} + 8 \ 1 \times 6^{mm} \ 7 \ 32°F \ 10 \ 63\% \ 8\,cm \ \frac{7}{8}$

Wacky Wanda's Wecipe

Wanda the Witch altered her family recipe for goulash. Make the changes to the recipe. Then, write the letters of the problems in the blanks above the matching answers to find out what Wanda says to her guests.

Gross Goulash

Stir together:
40 worms
70 strands of hair
24 snails
150 toenails
150 rutabagas
600 ants
120 cat whiskers
80 teeth
200 cloves of garlic
40 roaches
Simmer for 6 days.

Wanda likes:

A 5% of the teeth

E 62% of the cloves of garlic

I 150% of the snails

O 125% of the cat whiskers

B 30% of the worms

N 108% of the ants

P 90% of the toenails

P 15% of the roaches

T 20% of the hair

T 2% of the rutabagas

____ ____ ____ ____   ____ ____ ____ ____ ____ ____ ____ !
12   150   648   124   4   6   135   124   14   36   3

The Complete Book of Challenge Math

Name _____

$= \pi \ \frac{4}{5} \ 2 \div \ ^3A = r^2 + 8 \ 1 \times 6^{mm} \ 7 \ 32°F \ 10 \ 63\% \ 8 \ cm \ \frac{7}{8}$

Sales and Discounts

| **Sale Prices** |

$88.75   20% off   100% = full price
          − 20% = discount
          ────
          80% = you pay
          80% = .8

88.75
× .8
──────
71.000
↓
$71 is the
sale price.

88.75
× .2
──────
17.750

OR

88.75
−71.00
──────
17.75
↓
$17.75 is the savings.

| **Discounts** |

Paul the produce peddler gives a 10% discount if you pay your bill within 7 days. Your bill was $212.50, and you paid on the 4th day. What did you pay?

10% = .1

$212.50
×   .1
────────
$21.250
↓
$21.25 is the discount.

You pay Paul:

$212.50
×   .9
────────
$191.250
↓
$191.25

OR

$212.50
−   21.25
────────
$191.25

What is the sale price of a $62 sweater if it is:

1. 30% off   **2.** 25% off   **3.** 15% off   **4.** 80% off

What is your discount if your bill is $49.50 and you get a:

5. 10% discount   **6.** 30% discount   **7.** 4% discount   **8.** 50% discount

The Complete Book of Challenge Math

$$= \pi \quad \tfrac{4}{5} \quad 2 \div \quad {}^{5}A - r^2 + 8 \; 1 \times 6^{mm} \; 7 \; 32°F \; 10 \; 63\% \; 8_{cm} \; \tfrac{7}{8}$$

Bobby's Bargain Basement Bonanza

Bargain Betty loves to get a good deal! She won't buy anything unless it's on sale. Betty decided to go to Bobby's Bargain Basement where everything is on sale.

Bobby's Bargain Basement

skirts	$26.50 → 40% off	sweaters	$32.40 → 20% off
shirts	$24.00 → 25% off	jeans	$18.50 → 10% off
shoes	$28.60 → 15% off	boots	$30.00 → 12% off
socks	$7.20 → 35% off	dresses	$31.90 → 50% off
pants	$27.40 → 30% off	belts	$12.00 → 8% off
coats	$34.00 → 45% off	robes	$28.20 → 5% off

Solve the problems using Bobby's price list. Find the matching answers at the bottom of the page. Then, write the letters on the blanks above the answers to find a word describing Betty. Look up the word in the dictionary.

A What is the discount on shoes?

I What is the sale price for a pair of socks?

I What is the sale price for a pair of pants?

O What is the discount on shirts?

O What is the discount on coats?

U What is the sale price for a skirt?

M What is the discount on boots?

N What is the sale price for a robe?

P What is the sale price for a sweater?

R What is the discount on jeans?

S What is the sale price for a belt?

S What is the discount on dresses?

___ ___ ___ ___ ___ ___ ___ ___ ___ ___ ___ ___

$25.92 $4.29 $1.85 $11.04 $19.18 $3.60 $6.00 $26.79 $4.68 $15.30 $15.90 $15.95

The Complete Book of Challenge Math

Name _____

$= \pi \ \frac{4}{5} \ 2 \div \ ^3 A - r^2 + 8 \ 1 \times 6^{mm} \ 7 \ 32°F \ 10 \ 63\% \ 8 \ cm \ \frac{7}{8}$

After-Holiday Sale!

After the holidays, everything at Big Buys is discounted. Calculate the discounts and subtract from the regular prices. Write the discounted prices on the sale tags.

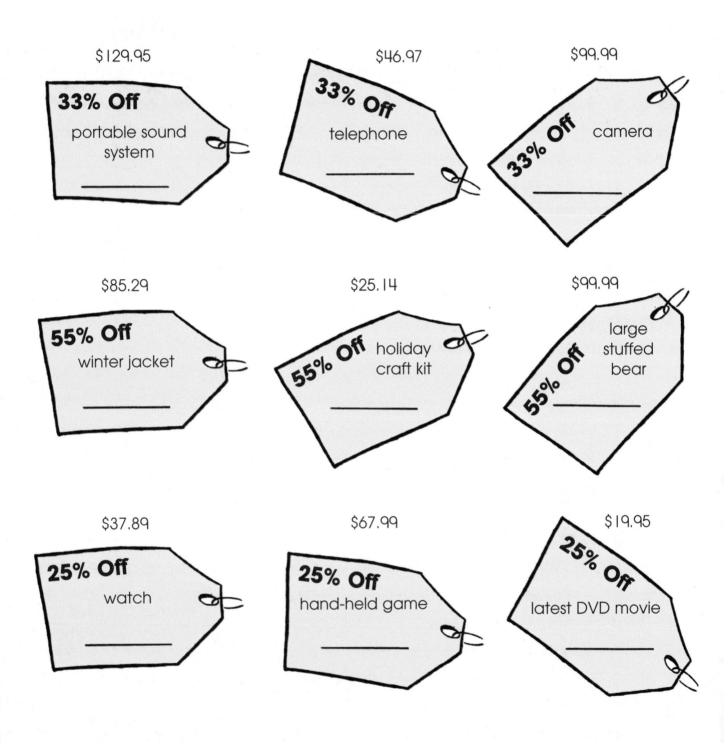

$129.95 — **33% Off** portable sound system _____

$46.97 — **33% Off** telephone _____

$99.99 — **33% Off** camera _____

$85.29 — **55% Off** winter jacket _____

$25.14 — **55% Off** holiday craft kit _____

$99.99 — **55% Off** large stuffed bear _____

$37.89 — **25% Off** watch _____

$67.99 — **25% Off** hand-held game _____

$19.95 — **25% Off** latest DVD movie _____

Holiday Cash

You received a total of $164.00 as gift money during the holiday season. Read each of the following situations and keep a running balance. Notice that each situation begins with the remaining balance of the previous situation; you do not begin with $164.00 each time. Show your work.

Beginning balance: $164.00

1. You have decided that you must put 30% of your gift money into your savings account.

remaining balance: _____

2. You lost your ski boots and you must replace them. They are normally $87.95, but are 35% off with the post-holiday sales.

remaining balance: _____

3. You promised your brother you would buy him an action figure for helping you shovel the driveway. You can buy three for $7.00, but you want to buy only one.

remaining balance: _____

4. Grandpa pays you $6.50 each time you shovel his driveway. You shoveled it four times this week.

remaining balance: _____

5. You went out for pizza with seven friends. You split the cost of two pizzas with all of your friends. The pizzas, without beverages, cost $16.50. You also paid for two large drinks at $1.09 each.

remaining balance: _____

The Complete Book of Challenge Math

Name _____

$= \pi \ \frac{4}{5} \ 2 \div \ ^3A - r^2 + 8 \ 1 \times 6mm \ 7 \ 32°F \ 10 \ 63\% \ 8cm \ \frac{7}{8}$

The Supply Depot

The student-run store sold most of the needed school supplies. Use the store's price guide to solve the problems below.

SUPPLY DEPOT PRICE GUIDE

pencils . . . . .$ .12	paper . . . . .$ .98
pens . . . . . .$ .69	folders . . . . .$ .08
marker sets .$1.29	notebooks . .$3.00

1. Alisha bought two pencils, one folder, and a set of markers.
How much did she spend? _____

2. Ben had $8.00 to purchase his supplies. He bought paper, one pen, two folders, and a notebook.

How much did these supplies cost? _____

How much money did he have left? _____

3. At the end of the year, the Supply Depot had a sale. Everything was 15% off. How much did each item cost then?

pencils _____   pens _____   marker sets _____

folders _____   notebooks _____   paper _____

4. Mica bought three pencils, paper, two pens, and one set of markers during the sale.

How much did she spend? _____

How much was her total savings? _____

5. The Supply Depot ran low on several items and needed to order more from the dealer. The dealer sells at a reduced cost. They ordered three dozen pencils at 40% of their original selling price, two dozen pens at 48% of the selling price, one dozen folders for 55% of the selling price, and six notebooks for 38% of their original selling price. How much did all the supplies cost?

pencils _____   pens _____   folders _____   notebooks _____

Total _____

$= \pi \ \frac{4}{5} \ 2 \div \ ^3A - r^2 + 8 \ 1 \times 6^{mm} \ 7 \ 32°F \ 10 \ 63\% \ 8_{cm} \ \frac{7}{8}$

Percentage Problems

For extra credit, Sally and Gabriel had to write percentage problems. Solve their problems.

1. There were 400 students in the school. If 38% of the students were boys, how many boys were there? _____

2. Out of the 345 sheets of construction paper in Mrs. Rainbow's classroom, 20% were red and 40% were blue.
How many sheets were red? _____
How many sheets were blue? _____

3. Only 19% of the 400 students ate the cafeteria food on Monday. How many students purchased cafeteria food that day? _____

4. 25% of 76 band members can play a clarinet. How many can play a clarinet? _____

5. 35 trees were planted around the school. 60% were maples. How many of the trees planted were maples? _____

6. The local pizza parlor gave the eighth-grade class a 25% discount on pizzas they purchased to sell at the football game. Each pizza originally cost $12.00.
How much did the eighth graders pay per pizza? _____
If they purchased 12 pizzas, how much did they save all together? _____

7. They saw these signs at the sports shop nearby. Figure each sale price.

Sale! 15% off All In-Line Skates! Regularly $97.00	25% Savings All Mitts! Regularly $24.00	Huge Savings! 20% off All Mountain Bikes! Regularly $132.00

_____ _____ _____

The Complete Book of Challenge Math

Name _____

Calculating Interest

In order to teach the concept of interest to his class, Mr. Savemore set up an imaginary bank in his classroom. Each student was given play money which they could put into a savings account. Mr. Savemore then assigned a monthly interest or loan rate to each student to use in their calculations. Solve the problems.

1. Samantha deposited $12.35 into her savings account. She was given 8% as her monthly rate of interest. How much interest would Samantha earn at the end of one month?   _____

What would her savings balance be at the beginning of her second month?   _____

2. David deposited $18.93. He was assigned an 11% monthly interest rate. How much interest would David receive his first month? _____

What would his adjusted total be with the interest figured in? _____

3. Jennifer started her savings account with $9.18 at an interest rate of 12% monthly. Figure what her balance would be at the end of . . .
a. one month.   _____
b. two months.   _____
c. three months.   _____

4. Jeremy decided he would borrow $123.00 for a new mountain bike. His interest rate on the 3-year loan was 18% per year. How much would he pay in interest for his loan?   _____

5. Susie wanted to borrow $89.95 for a CD player. The rate of interest on her $1\frac{1}{2}$-year loan was 17% per year.

How much would she pay in interest?   _____
How much, in total, would her CD player cost? _____

Measurement

Name _____

$= \pi \ \frac{4}{5} \ 2 \div \ \frac{3}{4} \ - r^2 + 8 \ 1 \times 6 \ mm \ 7 \ 32°F \ 10 \ 63\% \ 8 \ cm \ \frac{7}{8}$

What Time Is It?

As the sun rises on the East Coast of the United States, it's still dark on the West Coast. So, clocks in the four standard time zones are set at different times. Use the map to help you figure out the times in the states listed below.

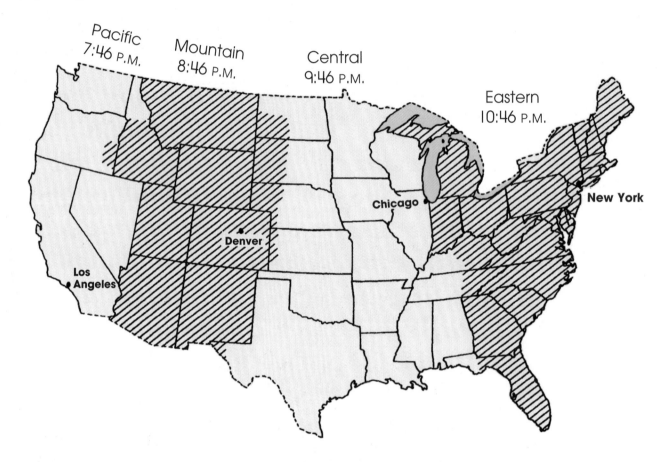

If it's . . .

	what time is it in . . .	
5:00 A.M. in Pennsylvania,	Utah?	_____
9:30 P.M. in Ohio,	California?	_____
3:00 P.M. in Nevada,	Minnesota?	_____
11:00 A.M. in Texas,	Virginia?	_____
3:30 P.M. in Washington,	Illinois?	_____
9:00 A.M. in Georgia,	Montana?	_____
2:30 A.M. in Arkansas,	Utah?	_____

= π 4/5 2 ÷ 3 A − r² + 8 1 × 6ᵐᵐ 7 32°F 10 63% 8 cm 7/8

Ring the Alarm

People rise and shine at all hours of the day and night depending on their work schedules. The alarms have been set on each clock. Complete the chart by giving either the time the alarm will sound, or the amount of time that was added to each time piece.

1.

2.

11 : 05

3.

03 : 24

4.

5.

09 : 25

6.
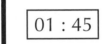
01 : 45

7.

8.

I NEED 24 HOURS OF SLEEP A DAY!

Clock	Amount of time set on the alarm	Time the alarm will ring
1	1 hour 25 min.	
2	2 hours 10 min.	
3	2 hours 30 min.	
4		12:50
5		3:00
6	2 hours 15 min.	
7	$\frac{1}{2}$ hour	
8	12 hours	

The Complete Book of Challenge Math

Name _____

$$= \pi \ \tfrac{4}{5} \ 2 \div {}^3A - r^2 + 8 \ 1 \times 6^{mm} \ 7 \ 32°F \ 10 \ 63\% \ 8_{cm} \ \tfrac{7}{8}$$

It's About Time

Use the information in the chart to answer the questions below. Show your work. Label your answers.

60 seconds	= 1 minute
60 minutes	= 1 hour
24 hours	= 1 day
7 days	= 1 week
52 weeks	= 1 year
365 days	= 1 year

1. A lemon shark grows a new set of teeth every 14 days. If this shark can grow up to 24,000 teeth in a year, about how many teeth are in each set? Explain how you arrived at your answer.

_____

_____

_____

_____

2. If you average 8 hours of sleep a night, how much time do you spend sleeping in 4 weeks? _____ About how many days is this? _____

3. A chimney swift (a type of bird) travels about 217,048 kilometers per year. At this rate, what would its weekly average be? _____

4. One species of bamboo can grow up to 2 feet in 12 hours. If it continued growing at this rate, how many feet tall would it be in 2 weeks? _____ How many yards? _____

$$= \pi \ \tfrac{4}{5} \ 2 \div {}^{3}\!A - r^{2} + 8 \ 1 \times 6^{mm} \ 7 \ 32°F \ 10 \ 63\% \ 8\,cm \ \tfrac{7}{8}$$

As Time Goes By

Read each time given. Each time reads hours, then minutes, then seconds.
Write the elapsed or predicted time and show it on the clock face.

1. It is 5:34:21. What time will it be in
1 hour, 3 minutes, and 45 seconds?   _____

2. It is 10:55:47. What time will it be in
2 hours, 6 minutes, and 34 seconds?   _____

3. It is 8:17:39. What time will it be in
8 hours, 19 minutes, and 54 seconds?   _____

4. It is 6:42:57. What time will it be in
7 hours, 38 minutes, and 49 seconds?   _____

5. It is 4:28:06. What time was it 2 hours,
46 minutes, and 20 seconds ago?   _____

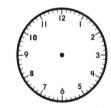

6. It is 11:13:31. What time was it 6 hours,
28 minutes, and 42 seconds ago?   _____

The Complete Book of Challenge Math

Name _____

$= \pi \frac{4}{5} \ 2 \div {}^3 A - r^2 + 8 \ 1 \times 6 \text{mm} \ 7 \ 32°F \ 10 \ 63\% \ 8 \text{cm} \ \frac{7}{8}$

Celsius and Fahrenheit

To change a Celsius temperature to Fahrenheit, use the following formula:
$(1.8 \times °C) + 32 = °F$.

To change a Fahrenheit temperature to Celsius, use the following formula:
$(°F - 32) \div 1.8 = °C$.

Use the formulas to change each temperature below to degrees on the alternate scale. Show your work. Check your answers with an actual thermometer.

1. 25°C = _____ °F

2. 55°C = _____ °F

3. 10°C = _____ °F

4. −5°C = _____ °F

5. 68°F = _____ °C

6. 176°F = _____ °C

7. 95°F = _____ °C

8. 41°F = _____ °C

The Complete Book of Challenge Math

= π 4/5 2 ÷ ³A − r² + 8 1 × 6ᵐᵐ 7 32°F 10 63% 8 cm 7/8

Wacky Weather

Find the temperature on each thermometer. Write the temperature using both the Fahrenheit and Celsius scales. Read the riddle. Figure out the new temperature and show it on the blank thermometer. Write the new temperature in both Fahrenheit and Celsius.

1.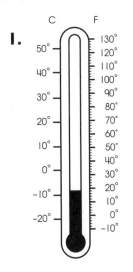

The temperature increased by 5 degrees Celsius, then by 10 degrees Celsius. The Celsius temperature then tripled. The temperature dropped 6 degrees Celsius then plummeted 25 degrees Celsius before warming up 6 degrees Celsius.

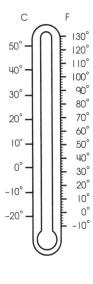

°C   °F

2.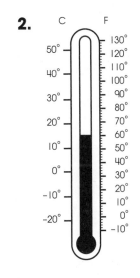

The temperature went up another 4 degrees Fahrenheit before dropping 10 degrees Fahrenheit. It dropped 2 degrees Fahrenheit each of the next 4 hours, then 5 degrees Fahrenheit the next 3 hours before going up 16 degrees. The temperature went up another 11 degrees Fahrenheit, then plummeted 43 degrees Fahrenheit.

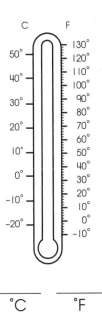

°C   °F

The Complete Book of Challenge Math

Name _____

$= \pi \ \frac{4}{5} \ 2 \div \ ^3A - r^2 + 8 \ 1 \times 6^{mm} \ 7 \ 32°F \ 10 \ 63\% \ 8 \text{cm} \ \frac{7}{8}$

Looking at Thermometers

Look at each thermometer. Write the temperature in both Celsius and Fahrenheit.

I.

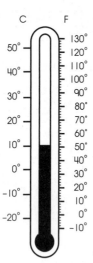

_____   _____
°C   °F

2.

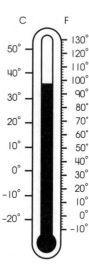

_____   _____
°C   °F

3.

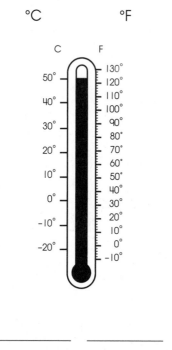

_____   _____
°C   °F

4.

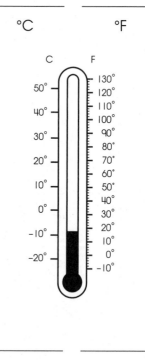

_____   _____
°C   °F

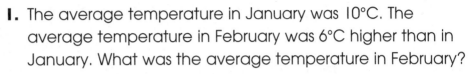

Weather Forecast (Temperature Celsius)

Karla did her science fair project on weather forecasting. She recorded the temperature daily in degrees Celsius. Answer her questions.

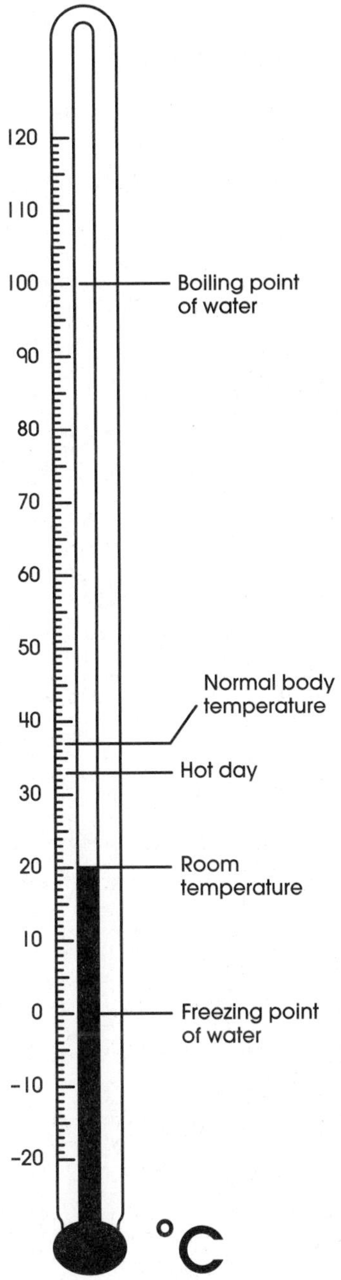

1. The average temperature in January was 10°C. The average temperature in February was 6°C higher than in January. What was the average temperature in February?

_____

2. It was cold enough for Karla to go ice skating outside on January 24. Did she record the temperature as −15°C, or 15°C?

_____

3. Karla filled a hot water bottle with boiling water to take along to warm her hands while she skated. When she started, how many degrees warmer was the water in the bottle than the temperature outside?

_____

4. What clothing should Karla have worn outside when the temperature was −15°C?

_____

5. One day, Karla had a body temperature of 40°C. Was she well or sick?

_____

6. The average temperature in March, according to Karla's weather station, was 22°C. Using the temperatures from problem one, what was the average temperature during January, February, and March?

_____

Thermometer labels:
- 120
- 110
- 100 — Boiling point of water
- 90
- 80
- 70
- 60
- 50
- 40 — Normal body temperature
- Hot day
- 30
- 20 — Room temperature
- 10
- 0 — Freezing point of water
- −10
- −20

°C

The Complete Book of Challenge Math

Name _____

$$= \pi \; \frac{4}{5} \; 2 \div {}^{5}A - r^2 + 8 \; 1 \times 6^{mm} \; 7 \; 32°F \; 10 \; 63\% \; 8\,cm \; \frac{7}{8}$$

Customary Units

Capacity measures how much space a container holds. It is measured in cups, pints, quarts, and gallons. *Length* is a measure of distance. It is measured in inches, feet, yards, and miles. *Weight* measures how heavy an object is. It is measured in ounces, pounds, and tons.

Juan was asked to write the units that he thought would best measure each object.

Juan's Answers: **Your Answers:**

1. amount of flour used to bake a cake   cups   _____

2. single serving of milk   teaspoons   _____

3. liquid baby medicine   tablespoons   _____

4. weight capacity of a bridge   tons   _____

5. distance driven across the country   feet   _____

6. weight of a bunch of bananas   ounces   _____

7. amount of iced-tea in a pitcher   gallons   _____

8. radius of a CD   inches   _____

9. distance of a sprint   miles   _____

10. length of a house   inches   _____

IS THAT CORRECT?

Check each of Juan's answers using the following checklist.
- Did he choose the right *type* of measurement (capacity, length, or weight) for each object?
- Did he choose the most appropriate unit size for each object? Write correct on the line if Juan's answer is correct. Correct any mistakes he might have made.

The Complete Book of Challenge Math

$= \pi \ \frac{4}{5} \ 2 \div {}^{3}A - r^{2} + 8 \ 1 \times 6^{mm} \ 7 \ 32°F \ 10 \ 63\% \ 8 \ cm \ \frac{7}{8}$

Metric Units

> The base units of measurement in the metric system are meters (length), liters (capacity), and grams (mass). The prefixes *milli* and *kilo* in front of a base unit help determine the size of an object.
>
> milli = 1,000 times <u>smaller</u> than the base
>
> kilo = 1,000 times <u>larger</u> than the base

Keoni was asked to write the units that she thought would best measure each object.

Keoni's Answers: **Your Answers:**

1. weight of a penny	<u>grams</u>	_____
2. weight of a paperclip	<u>milligrams</u>	_____
3. liquid baby medicine	<u>liters</u>	_____
4. amount of water in a reservoir	<u>kiloliters</u>	_____
5. carton of milk	<u>kiloliters</u>	_____
6. can of soda	<u>milliliters</u>	_____
7. weight of a woman	<u>grams</u>	_____
8. length of a ruler	<u>centimeters</u>	_____
9. distance between two cities	<u>meters</u>	_____
10. short distance race	<u>meters</u>	_____

IS THAT CORRECT?

Check each of Keoni's answers using the following checklist.

- Did Keoni choose the right type of measurement (capacity, length, or mass) for each object?
- Did Keoni choose the most appropriate unit size for each object? Write correct on the line if Keoni's answer is correct. Correct any mistakes she might have made.

The Complete Book of Challenge Math

Name _____

$= \pi \frac{4}{5} \ 2 \div {}^{3}A - r^{2} + 8 \ 1 \times 6^{mm} \ 7 \ 32°F \ 10 \ 63\% \ 8^{cm} \frac{7}{8}$

Converting Customary Lengths

Make sure you use the correct conversions.

12 inches = 1 foot
3 feet = 1 yard
5,280 feet = 1 mile

Connor found the equivalent measurements and wrote his answers on the lines.

Connor's Answers:

1. 15 yards = <u>5 feet</u>

2. 18 feet = <u>6 yards</u>

3. 42 inches = <u>504 feet</u>

4. 5 miles = <u>26,400 feet</u>

5. 36 feet = <u>12 yards</u>

6. 12 feet = <u>36 yards</u>

7. 4 feet = <u>60 inches</u>

8. 15,840 feet = <u>4 miles</u>

9. 2 miles = <u>10,560 feet</u>

10. 180 inches = <u>15 feet</u>

IS THAT CORRECT?

Mark looked at Connor's answer to the first problem. Here is what he thinks:

"15 yards can't equal 5 feet. A foot is smaller than a yard. You would expect much more than 15 feet in 15 yards. The answer should be more than 15 feet. This answer doesn't make sense."

Check the rest of Connor's answers carefully using the following checklist.
• Did he divide to convert from smaller units to bigger units?
• Did he multiply to convert from bigger units to smaller units?
• Did he multiply or divide by the correct amount?

For each problem, decide whether the number should get bigger or smaller. Put a checkmark next to any answers that are too big or too small. Then, write the correct answers.

$= \pi \frac{4}{5} \ 2 \div {}^3\!A - r^2 + 8 \ 1 \times 6^{mm} \ 7 \ 32°F \ 10 \ 63\% \ 8^{cm} \frac{7}{8}$

Volcanoes and Oceans (U.S. Customary Length)

Use the chart to answer the questions below. Show your work. Label your answers.

I foot (ft.)	= 12 inches (in.)
I yard (yd.)	= 3 feet (ft.)
I mile (mi.)	= 1,760 yards (yd.)

I. Kilauea and Mauna Loa are volcanoes in Hawaii. Kilauea is about 4,090 feet above sea level. Mauna Loa is about 13,677 feet above sea level. Use the conversion chart above to find out if either volcano is more than a mile above sea level.

Step one: Use the conversion chart above to determine the number of feet in a mile. Show your work.

Step two: If a volcano has a height greater than I mile, write its height in miles, yards, and feet. If it is not greater than I mile, write its height in yards and feet. Show your work.

2. Dolphins, porpoises, and humpback whales are members of the whale family. A porpoise can be about 80 inches long. A dolphin can measure up to 360 inches. A humpback whale can measure up to 740 inches. Use the conversion chart to find out if any of these mammals are longer than a yard.

Step one: Use the conversion chart above to determine the number of inches in a yard. Show your work.

Step two: If one of these whales is greater than a yard, write its measure in yards, feet, and inches. If it is less than a yard, write its length in feet and inches. Show your work.

The Complete Book of Challenge Math

Measurement

Name _____

$= \pi \frac{4}{5} 2 \div {}^{3}A - r^2 + 8 \ 1 \times 6mm \ 7 \ 32°F \ 10 \ 63\% \ 8cm \frac{7}{8}$

At the Zoo (U.S. Customary Length)

Animal	Height/ Length	Converted Height	Weight	Converted Weight
1. male ostrich	$7\frac{3}{4}$ feet	2 yd. 1 ft. 9 in	5,520 ounces	345 lb.
2. male Indian elephant	$9\frac{1}{2}$ feet		4 tons	
3. male walrus	12 feet		$1\frac{1}{2}$ tons	
4. female walrus	8 feet		$1\frac{1}{4}$ tons	
5. hippopotamus	60 inches		$1\frac{3}{8}$ tons	
6. male giraffe	17 feet		1 ton 582 pounds	
7. male gorilla	75 inches		7,200 ounces	
8. male wolf	73 inches		1,296 ounces	
9. platypus	26 inches		83 ounces	
10. white rhinoceros	5 feet 7 inches		$3\frac{1}{2}$ tons	
11. Galapagos tortoise	48 inches		$\frac{3}{10}$ ton	
12. condor (wingspan)	$9\frac{1}{2}$ feet		368 ounces	

$$= \pi \quad \frac{4}{5} \quad 2 \div \quad ^3A - r^2 + 8 \quad 1 \times 6^{mm} \quad 7 \quad 32°F \quad 10 \quad 63\% \quad 8 \, cm \quad \frac{7}{8}$$

Football Team Workout (U.S. Customary Length)

As Ms. Parrish's students watched the high school football team, they wrote these math problems about the team and the field. Refer to the chart to answer the questions below.

I mile = 1,760 yards I mile = 5,280 feet I yard = 36 inches 12 inches = I foot	mi. = mile yd. = yard ft. = foot in. = inch

1. Jo Anne's brother threw the ball 27 yds. How many ft. did he throw the ball?

_____

2. The football field was 100 yds. long. How many ft. long was the field?

_____

3. The football field was 162 ft. wide. How many yds. wide was the field?

_____

4. The team missed a first down by $\frac{1}{3}$ of a yd. How many in. was that?

_____

5. The football is 11 in. in length. At least how many footballs would have to be placed end to end to equal more than a yd.?

_____

6. The pass receivers practiced 40-yd. sprints. How many feet did they run each time? How many inches?

_____

Circle the answer that makes the most sense.

7. A baseball bat is about 3 _____ long.

        inches   feet   yards   miles

8. A ball point pen is about 6 _____ long.

        inches   feet   yards   miles

The Complete Book of Challenge Math

Name _____

Converting Customary Measurements of Capacity

> Make sure you use the correct conversions.
>
> 1 pint = 2 cups
> 1 quart = 2 pints
> 1 gallon = 4 quarts

Julia found the equivalent measurements and wrote her answers on the lines.

Julia's Answers:

1. 28 gallons = <u>7 quarts</u>

2. 12 quarts = <u>24 pints</u>

3. 12 cups = <u>6 pints</u>

4. 7 pints = 3   cups

5. 38 pints = <u>19 quarts</u>

6. 28 quarts = <u>112 gallons</u>

7. 4 gallons = <u>16 quarts</u>

8. 44 cups = <u>11 pints</u>

9. 36 quarts = <u>9 gallons</u>

10. 100 pints = <u>50 cups</u>

IS THAT CORRECT?

Erin looked at Julia's answer to the first problem. Here is what she thinks:

> "28 gallons can't equal 7 quarts. Quarts are smaller than gallons. You would expect much more than 28 quarts in 28 gallons. The answer should be more than 28, but it's not. This answer doesn't make sense."

Check the rest of Julia's answers carefully using the following checklist.
- Did she divide to convert from smaller units to bigger units?
- Did she multiply to convert from bigger units to smaller units?
- Did she multiply or divide by the correct amount?

For each problem, decide whether the number should get bigger or smaller.
Put a checkmark next to any answers that are too big or too small. Then, write the correct answers.

$= \pi \frac{4}{5} 2 \div {}^{3}A - r^2 + 8 1 \times 6^{mm} 7 32°F 10 63\% 8\,cm \frac{7}{8}$

In the Grocery Aisle (U.S. Customary Capacity)

Fill in the blanks in the measurement charts. Use the charts to answer the questions below. Show your work.

1 tablespoon = 3 teaspoons
1 cup = 16 tablespoons
1 cup = _____ teaspoons
1 cup = 8 fluid ounces
1 pint = 2 cups
1 pint = _____ fluid ounces
1 quart = _____ cups

1 quart = 2 pints
1 quart = _____ fluid ounces
1 gallon = _____ cups
1 gallon = _____ pints
1 gallon = 4 quarts
1 gallon = _____ fluid ounces

1. Pia bought a 1-pint 8-ounce bottle of syrup. The label states that it is 2% real maple syrup. About how many ounces of real maple syrup are in the bottle?

_____

2. Jade's family bought a canister of drink mix powder that will make 8 gallons. How many quarts is this? _____ How many ounces is it?

_____

There are 5 people in Jade's family. Each person drinks two 16-ounce glasses a day. How much does the family drink in one day? _____
At this rate, how many days will one canister of drink mix last?

_____

3. George is making a salad that calls for $1\frac{1}{2}$ cups of olive oil. The measuring cups are dirty, but not the measuring spoons. How many tablespoons of olive oil should he use for this recipe? _____ What if he used teaspoons instead?

_____

George bought a 16-ounce bottle of olive oil. Will he have enough olive oil for the salad? Explain.

_____

_____

The Complete Book of Challenge Math

= π $\frac{4}{5}$ 2 ÷ ^3A − r^2 + 8 1 × 6mm 7 32°F 10 63% 8cm $\frac{7}{8}$

Liquid Refreshment (U.S. Customary Capacity)

Kerri is in charge of the fruit punch at the PTO thank-you tea. She has only a one-cup measure. Using the chart, help her change the recipe to cups.

1 gallon = 4 quarts 1 quart = 2 pints 1 pint = 2 cups 1 cup = 8 ounces	gal. = gallon qt. = quart pt. = pint oz. = ounce c. = cup

1. The recipe calls for 2 quarts of water. How many cups of water should she use?

_____

2. It calls for 16 ounces of frozen lemonade and 8 oz. frozen orange juice. How many total cups of lemonade and orange juice are in the recipe?

_____

3. The water and frozen juice are mixed with 2 quarts of pineapple juice. How many cups of pineapple juice will she mix in?

_____

4. Next, she must add 4 quarts of ginger ale. How many cups are in 4 qts.?

_____

5. How many cups of carbonated water should she add if the recipe calls for 2 quarts?

_____

6. Finally, 2 cups of sugar are added to the mixture. How many total cups of ingredients have been used in the punch?

_____

7. Kerri added ice and poured the punch into $4\frac{1}{4}$-quart pitchers. If each person at the tea was served about $\frac{1}{2}$ cup of punch, how many people will this recipe serve? (Remember, the sugar dissolves.)

_____

The Complete Book of Challenge Math

$= \pi \; \frac{4}{5} \; 2 \div {}^{3}A - r^2 + 8 \; 1 \times 6^{mm} \; 7 \; 32°F \; 10 \; 63\% \; 8\,cm \; \frac{7}{8}$

Converting Customary Measurements of Weight

> Make sure you use the correct conversions.
>
> 1 pound = 16 ounces
> 1 ton = 2,000 pounds

Karen found the equivalent measurements and wrote her answers on the lines.

Karen's Answers:

1. 128 ounces = <u>2,048 pounds</u>

2. 4 tons = <u>8,000 pounds</u>

3. 96 pounds = <u>6 ounces</u>

4. 80 ounces = <u>5 pounds</u>

5. 12,000 pounds = <u>5 tons</u>

6. 30 pounds = <u>480 ounces</u>

7. 144 ounces = <u>9 pounds</u>

8. 7 tons = <u>7,000 pounds</u>

9. 16 pounds = <u>4 ounces</u>

10. 240 ounces = <u>15 pounds</u>

IS THAT CORRECT?

Daniel looked at Karen's answer to the first problem. Here is what he thinks:

> "128 ounces can't equal 2,048 pounds. Pounds are larger than ounces. You would expect much less than 128 pounds in 128 ounces. The answer should be less than 128, but it's not. This answer doesn't make sense."

Check the rest of Karen's answers carefully using the following checklist.
- Did she divide to convert from smaller units to bigger units?
- Did she multiply to convert from bigger units to smaller units?
- Did she multiply or divide by the correct amount?

For each problem, decide whether the number should get bigger or smaller. Put a checkmark next to any answers that are too big or too small. Then, write the correct answers.

The Complete Book of Challenge Math

Name _____

= π $\frac{4}{5}$ 2 ÷ ^3A – r^2 + 8 1 × 6mm 7 32°F 10 63% 8cm $\frac{7}{8}$

Fresh Fruit (U.S. Customary Weight)

1 pound (lb.)	= 16 ounces (oz.)
1 ton (t.)	= 2,000 pounds (lb.)

Use the chart above to convert each measurement to ounces, then to pounds and ounces.

1. apples: $2\frac{1}{2}$ lb. 8 oz.   _____   _____

2. blueberries: 2 lb. 20 oz   _____   _____

3. bananas: $1\frac{1}{2}$ lb. 12 oz.   _____   _____

4. peaches: $2\frac{3}{4}$ lb. 6 oz.   _____   _____

5. plums: $1\frac{3}{4}$ lb. 13 oz.   _____   _____

6. Use the clues to draw the baskets of produce from above in order. The first basket of fruit is on the left. The fruit with the most weight is not first or last. None of the baskets with a weight greater than 47 ounces are next to each other. The basket with the least weight is not second. The basket with 52 ounces of fruit in it is after the basket with 41 ounces of fruit. The first basket has a weight that is equal to 3 pounds.

$= \pi \frac{4}{5}\ 2 \div \ ^3A - r^2 + 8\ 1 \times 6\text{mm}\ 7\ 32°\text{F}\ 10\ 63\%\ 8\text{cm}\ \frac{7}{8}$

Vegetable Stand (U.S. Customary Weight)

Cary worked at the farmers' market last summer, weighing and selling fruits and vegetables. Using the chart, answer the questions below.

1 ton = 2,000 pounds 1 pound = 16 ounces	ton = t. pound = lb. ounce = oz.

1. Cary's father drove a truck to the farmers' market that could carry 2,000 lbs. of fruits and vegetables. How many tons could his truck carry?

_____

2. Green beans were $1.19 per pound. If a woman bought 4 pounds, how much change would she get back from a $5 bill?

_____

3. One man bought $\frac{1}{2}$ pound of lettuce. How many ounces did he buy?

_____

4. Cary's dad had a special on cantaloupe at $.25 per pound. Cary's friend bought 2 cantaloupes. If his total was $1, how many pounds of cantaloupe did he buy?

_____

5. On Saturday, Cary gave away a free recycling sticker for every customer who brought her or his own bag. He gave away 263 stickers. If the average customer who recycles buys 4 pounds of produce, how many pounds of food did Cary probably sell?

_____

6. Cary's dad recently put a new top and cover on the stand. The top and cover weigh $\frac{1}{2}$ ton. How many pounds do the top and cover weigh?

_____

The Complete Book of Challenge Math

Name _____

$$= \pi \ \frac{4}{5} \ 2 \div \ ^{3}A - r^{2} + 8 \ 1 \times 6^{mm} \ 7 \ 32°F \ 10 \ 63\% \ 8_{cm} \ \frac{7}{8}$$

Converting Metric Lengths

> Make sure you use the correct conversion factors.
>
> 10 millimeters (mm) = 1 centimeter (cm)
> 100 centimeters (cm) = 1 meter (m)
> 1,000 meters (m) = 1 kilometer (km)

Barbara found the equivalent measurements and wrote her answers on the lines.

Barbara's Answers:

1. 35 cm = <u>3,500 mm</u>

2. 49 m = <u>4,900 cm</u>

3. 7 m = <u>700 cm</u>

4. 8,200 mm = <u>82 cm</u>

5. 100 mm = <u>10 cm</u>

6. 600 cm = <u>6 mm</u>

IS THAT CORRECT?

Lucita looked at Barbara's answer to the first problem. Here is what she thinks:

> "It seems reasonable to think 35 centimeters is equal to 3,500 millimeters. Centimeters are larger than millimeters. You would expect there to be more than 35 millimeters in 35 centimeters. The answer should be more than 35, which it is."

Then, Lucita looked at the first answer more closely.

> "Converting from bigger units to smaller units means multiply.
> There are 10 millimeters in a centimeter.
> 35 cm × 10 mm/cm = 350 mm
> The answer should be 350 mm, not 3,500 mm."

Check the rest of Barbara's answers carefully using the following checklist.
- Did she divide to convert from smaller units to bigger units?
- Did she multiply to convert from bigger units to smaller units?
- Did she multiply or divide by the correct amount?

For each problem, decide whether the number should get bigger or smaller. Put a checkmark next to any answers that are too big or too small. Then, write the correct answers.

$$= \pi \ \frac{4}{5} \ 2 \div {}^{3}\!A - r^{2} + 8 \ 1 \times 6^{mm} \ 7 \ 32°F \ 10 \ 63\% \ 8 \, cm \ \frac{7}{8}$$

Around the Room (Metric Length)

Look at the data collected in the table below. Fill in the missing columns. The first row is done for you.

1 meter	=	100 centimeters
1 decimeter	=	10 centimeters
1 centimeter	=	10 millimeters

Table One

Object	Millimeters	Centimeters	Decimeters	Meters
1. 6 dm	600	60	6	0.6
2. 23 mm				
3. 7.2 dm				
4. 54 cm				

Choose three objects of your own to fill in the chart below. Measure each object and fill in the first column. Use your measurement to fill in the remaining columns.

Table Two

Object	Millimeters	Centimeters	Decimeters	Meters
1.				
2.				
3.				

The Complete Book of Challenge Math

Name _____

$= \pi \frac{4}{5} 2 \div {}^{3}A - r^2 + 8 \ 1 \times 6^{mm} \ 7 \ 32°F \ 10 \ 63\% \ 8_{cm} \frac{7}{8}$

How Far? How Long? (Metric Length)

Ms. Martinez made the chart below about metric length for her class. Refer to the chart to answer the questions.

1 kilometer = 1,000 meters 1 meter = 100 centimeters 1 centimeter = 10 millimeters	km = kilometer m = meter cm = centimeter mm = millimeter

1. Eric can throw a ball about 2,300 cm. How many meters can he throw the ball?

_____

2. Barbara's book is 30 mm thick. How many centimeters thick is the book?

_____

3. Delores can reach 2 meters high. How many centimeters can she reach?

_____

4. Holly can take a giant step of 960 mm. How many centimeters can she step?

_____

5. We walked 3,000 meters in the shopping mall. How many kilometers did we walk?

_____

6. Rae Ann is 1,540 mm tall. How many centimeters tall is she?

_____

Circle the answer that makes the most sense.

7. On our trip downtown and back, we drove the car 40 _____ .

         mm   cm   m   km

8. A city block is 120 _____ long.

         mm   cm   m   km

9. My 8-year-old sister, Diana, is 143 _____ tall.

         mm   cm   m   km

The Complete Book of Challenge Math

$= \pi \ \frac{4}{5} \ 2 \div \ ^3A - r^2 + 8 \ 1 \times 6^{mm} \ 7 \ 32°F \ 10 \ 63\% \ 8_{cm} \ \frac{7}{8}$

Metric Length Conversions

Fill in the blanks. Use the information to answer the questions below.

1 centimeter (cm)	=	10 millimeters (mm)
1 decimeter (dm)	=	10 centimeters (cm)
1 meter (m)	=	_____ millimeters (mm)
1 meter (m)	=	_____ centimeters (cm)
1 meter (m)	=	10 decimeters (dm)
1 decameter (dkm)	=	_____ centimeters (cm)
1 decameter (dkm)	=	_____ decimeters (dm)
1 decameter (dkm)	=	10 meters (m)
1 hectometer (hm)	=	100 meters (m)
1 hectometer (hm)	=	_____ decameters (dkm)
1 kilometer (km)	=	1,000 meters (m)
1 kilometer (km)	=	_____ decameters (dkm)
1 kilometer (km)	=	_____ hectometers (hm)

1. Sydney's house is two houses away from the corner. She wants to measure the distance from her house to the corner. Which unit of measure should she use and why?

2. Dillon needs to measure the height of his dog. Which unit of measure should he use and why?

3. Anya is making a 5-meter paper chain. The chain is currently 34.3 decimeters long. How many more decimeters are needed? How many centimeters? How many meters?

4. Blake is biking to his grandmother's house. Her house is 7 kilometers away. He has already gone 210.7 decameters. How many more decameters must he pedal? How many meters? How many kilometers?

The Complete Book of Challenge Math

Name _____

$= \pi \ \frac{4}{5} \ 2 \div \ ^3A - r^2 + 8 \ 1 \times 6mm \ 7 \ 32°F \ 10 \ 63\% \ 8cm \ \frac{7}{8}$

Awesome Town (Metric Length)

Mrs. Longameter's class was working on metric measurement. Help them solve their problems.

1. The students' desks are .75 meters wide. If 15 desks were placed side to side, how wide would they be all together? _____

2. Underline the items which would be best measured using meters:

   a. the distance between two universities

   b. the length of a lawn chair

   c. the height of a mountain

   d. the length of three trucks

   e. the width of a putting green

3. Which might be the length of a driveway—5 km *or* 50 m? _____

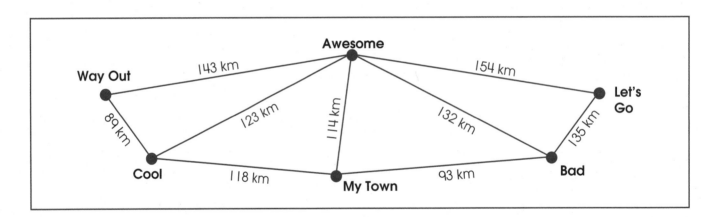

4. Use the map above to answer the following questions.

   a. What is the total distance from Way Out
   to Let's Go passing through Awesome?   _____

   b. How many kilometers is it from Cool to My Town
   to Awesome to Bad?   _____

The Complete Book of Challenge Math

$$= \pi \ \tfrac{4}{5} \ 2 \div {}^3 A - r^2 + 8 \ 1 \times 6\,\text{mm} \ 7 \ 32°F \ 10 \ 63\% \ 8\,\text{cm} \ \tfrac{7}{8}$$

Converting Metric Measures of Capacity

Make sure you use the correct conversion factors.

10 milliliters (mL) = I centiliter (cL)
100 centiliters (cL) = I liter (L)
1,000 liters (L) = I kiloliter (kL)

Jose found the equivalent measurements and wrote his answers on the lines.

Jose's Answers:

I. 200 cL = <u>20 L</u>

2. 8 kL = <u>8,000 L</u>

3. 500 cL = <u>5 mL</u>

4. 4 L = <u>400 cL</u>

5. 34 L = <u>3,400 cL</u>

6. 2,800 cL = <u>28 L</u>

IS THAT CORRECT?

Miguel looked at Jose's answer to the first problem. Here is what he thinks:

> "It seems reasonable to think 200 centiliters is equal to 20 liters. Liters are larger than centiliters. You would expect there to be less than 200 liters in 200 centiliters. The answer should be less than 200, which it is."

Then Miguel looked at the first answer more closely.

> "Converting from smaller units to bigger units means divide.
> There are 100 centiliters in a liter.
> 200 cL ÷ 100 cL/L = 2 L
> The answer should be 2 L, not 20 L."

Check the rest of Jose's answers carefully using the following checklist.
- Did Jose divide to convert from smaller units to bigger units?
- Did he multiply to convert from bigger units to smaller units?
- Did he multiply or divide by the correct amount?

For each problem, decide whether the number should get bigger or smaller. Put a checkmark next to any answers that are too big or too small. Then, write the correct answers.

The Complete Book of Challenge Math

Name _____

= π $\frac{4}{5}$ 2 ÷ ^3A − r^2 + 8 1 × 6mm 7 32°F 10 63% 8 cm $\frac{7}{8}$

How Much? How Full? (Metric Capacity)

Jana and her friends wrote some problems about capacity in metric terms. Refer to the chart to answer the questions below.

1 kiloliter = 1,000 liters 1 liter = 1,000 milliliters	kL = kiloliter L = liter mL = milliliter

1. Jana found that the fish tank in her classroom held about 20 liters of water. How many milliliters of water did it hold?

_____

2. Her teacher asked her to give the fish some vitamins each day. If she gave them 35 milliliters each day, how many milliliters would she give them in a week (Monday through Friday)?

_____

3. Terri waters 6 plants in the classroom. She gives each of the plants 500 milliliters of water. How many milliliters of water does she need to water all of the plants? How many liters does she use?

_____

4. Susan took 5 milliliters of cough medicine 4 times a day for one week. How many milliliters of medicine did she take in a day? In seven days?

_____

5. The school stores fuel oil in a 12-kiloliter tank. How many liters does the tank hold when it is full?

_____

Circle the answer that makes the most sense.

6. A drop of water is about 1 _____ of water.

        milliliter   liter   kiloliter

7. A water cooler holds about 15 _____ of water.

        milliliters   liters   kiloliters

$$= \pi \ \tfrac{4}{5} \ 2 \div {}^3A - r^2 + 8 \ 1 \times 6^{mm} \ 7 \ 32°F \ 10 \ 63\% \ 8 \, cm \ \tfrac{7}{8}$$

Converting Metric Measures of Mass

Make sure you use the correct conversion factors.

10 milligrams (mg) = 1 centigram (cg)
100 centigrams (cg) = 1 gram (g)
1,000 grams (g) = 1 kilogram (kg)

Shawn found the equivalent measurements and wrote his answers on the lines.

Shawn's Answers:

1. 3 kg = <u>3,000 g</u>

2. 4 g = <u>400 cg</u>

3. 75 g = <u>7,500 cg</u>

4. 300 cg = <u>30 g</u>

5. 60 kg = <u>6 g</u>

6. 4,900 mg = <u>49 cg</u>

IS THAT CORRECT?

Jason looked at Shawn's answer to the first problem. Here is what he thinks:

"It seems reasonable to think 3 kilograms is equal to 3,000 grams. Grams are much smaller than kilograms. You would expect there to be much more than 3 grams in 3 kilograms. The answer should be much more than 3, which it is."

Then, Jason looked at the first answer more closely.

"Converting from bigger units to smaller units means multiply.
There are 1,000 grams in a kilogram.
3 kg × 1,000 g/kg = 3,000 g
The answer is correct."

Check each of Shawn's answers carefully using the following checklist.
• Did he divide to convert from smaller units to bigger units?
• Did he multiply to convert from bigger units to smaller units?
• Did he multiply or divide by the correct amount?

For each problem, decide whether the number should get bigger or smaller.
Put a checkmark next to any answers that are too big or too small. Then, write the correct answers.

The Complete Book of Challenge Math

= π $\frac{4}{5}$ 2 ÷ ^3A − r^2 + 8 1 × 6^{mm} 7 32°F 10 63% 8 cm $\frac{7}{8}$

How Much Does It Weigh? (Metric Mass)

The students in Mrs. Penny's fifth-grade classroom brought in a collection of things to weigh. Using the chart, answer the questions below.

1 kilogram = 1,000 grams 1 gram = 1,000 milligrams	kilogram = kg gram = g milligram = mg

1. Beverly brought a tennis ball to school. If it weighed 60 grams, how many milligrams would 3 tennis balls weigh?

_____

2. Aaron brought a can of chicken soup that weighed 360 grams. Would 3 cans of soup weigh over or under 1 kilogram?

_____

3. Rachel brought a troll doll that weighed 100 grams. About how many from her collection would make a kilogram of troll dolls?

_____

4. Steven's hair comb weighed 35 grams. How many mg does his comb weigh?

_____

5. Emily brought a peanut that weighed 8 grams. How many grams would 100 peanuts weigh?

_____

6. One of Harold's shoes weighed about 500 grams. How many kg would both of his shoes weigh?

_____

Circle the answer that makes the most sense.

7. A city phone book probably weighs about 2 _____.

　　　　milligrams　　　　grams　　　　kilograms

8. A medium-sized apple has the mass of about 175 _____.

　　　　milligrams　　　　grams　　　　kilograms

$= \pi \frac{4}{5} 2 \div ^3A - r^2 + 8 \ 1 \times 6^{mm} \ 7 \ 32°F \ 10 \ 63\% \ 8_{cm} \frac{7}{8}$

Metric Measurements

Use the metric units to answer the following spring gardening questions.

thousands	hundreds	tens	ones	tenths	hundredths	thousandths
kilo-	hecto-	deka-	base unit	deci-	centi-	milli-

1. a kilogram = _____ grams

2. a milliliter = _____ liters

3. a centimeter = _____ meters

4. a hectoliter = _____ liters

5. a decigram= _____ grams

6. a dekameter = _____ meters

7. Antonio needs a plant stake that is 1 meter high. The store measures them by the centimeter. How many centimeters long is the plant stake that Antonio needs to buy? _____

8. Jenna wants to buy 2.36 kilograms of seed. The seed comes in 20-gram packages. How many packages does she need to buy? _____

9. Tangie planted 100 grams of seed. Tell how many of each she planted:

_____ mg   _____ cg   _____ hg   _____ kg

10. The plants grew an average of 25 centimeters in 2 weeks. Convert to the following:

_____ mm   _____ dm   _____ m   _____ km

11. Each plant needs 2.5 liters of water. Sue has a deciliter container. How many deciliter containers does she need to fill for each plant? _____

12. Each row has 8 plants. Each plant needs 2.5 liters of water. How many dekaliters of water are needed per row? _____

The Complete Book of Challenge Math

Name _____

$= \pi \frac{4}{5} 2 \div {}^{3}A = r^2 + 8 \ 1 \times 6^{mm} \ 7 \ 32°F \ 10 \ 63\% \ 8 \ cm \ \frac{7}{8}$

Pounds and Kilograms

U.S. Customary System

I pound (lb.)	= 16 ounces (oz.)
I ton (t.)	= 2,000 pounds (lb.)

Metric System

I gram (g)	= 1,000 milligrams (mg)
I kilogram (kg)	= 1,000 grams (g)
I metric ton (t)	= 1,000 kilograms (kg)

Use the measurement tables above to complete the word problems. Show your work.

I. A full-grown gray wolf can weigh 1,508 ounces. How many pounds is this?

_____

2. A worker bee collects enough nectar to make about 45 grams of honey in its lifetime. If a colony of bees can have about 24,286 worker bees, how many

kilograms of honey could these bees make? _____

Convert to metric tons. _____

3. An ostrich egg weighs about 3 pounds. How many ounces is this? _____

How many ounces is an egg that weighs $2\frac{3}{4}$ pounds? _____

How many ounces is a $3\frac{1}{8}$ -pound egg? _____

4. A whale shark can weigh about 39,897 pounds. Convert this to tons and pounds.

_____

Average this to the nearest ton. _____

5. A male African elephant weighs about 5,426 kilograms. A male Indian elephant weighs about 3.6 metric tons. How much more does the African elephant weigh?

Give the answer in both metric tons and kilograms. _____ or

_____

Finding Perimeter

To find the *perimeter* (*P*) of a figure, add the lengths of its sides.

1.

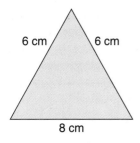

6 cm   6 cm

8 cm

P = ___20 cm___

10.5 m

8 m   8 m

10.5 m

P = _____

8 yd.

6 yd.

2 yd.
2 yd.

7 yd.

P = _____

2.

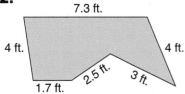

7.3 ft.

4 ft.   4 ft.

2.5 ft.   3 ft.

1.7 ft.

P = _____

4.3 mi.   4.3 mi.

6.2 mi.   6.2 mi.

P = _____

9 dm   8 dm

7 dm   8 dm

15 dm

P = _____

3.

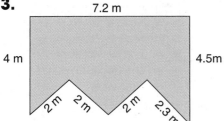

7.2 m

4 m   4.5m

2 m 2 m   2 m 2.3 m

P = _____

2 cm

2 cm

3 cm

3 cm

P = _____

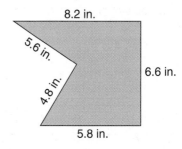

8.2 in.

5.6 in.

4.8 in.   6.6 in.

5.8 in.

P = _____

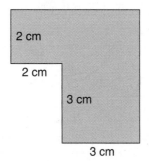

Name _____

Area Exponent

An *exponent* is a number that tells how many times the base is used as a factor.
An exponent can be used to find the area of a square.

$4 \times 4 = 4^2 = 16$ square units

Look at each figure. Write a multiplication problem to find the area.

I.   7 ft.

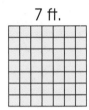

_____

2.   4 m

_____

3.   9 in.

_____

4.   5 yd.

_____

5.   11 mm

_____

6.   15 dm

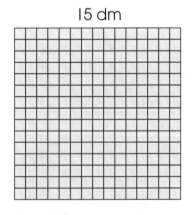

_____

Name _____

Measurement

Exploring Rectangular Area

Use the dimensions to find the area of each figure. Write the area on the line.

1. length _____ height _____ area _____

2. length _____ height _____ area _____

3. length _____ height _____ area _____

4. length _____ height _____ area _____

5. length _____ height _____ area _____

6. length _____ height _____ area _____

7. length _____ height _____ area _____

8. length _____ height _____ area _____

The Complete Book of Challenge Math

Name _____

$= \pi \; \frac{4}{5} \; 2 \div {}^3A - r^2 + 8 \; 1 \times 6^{mm} \; 7 \; 32°F \; 10 \; 63\% \; 8\,cm \; \frac{7}{8}$

Finding the Area of Rectangles and Squares

To find the *area* (*A*) of any rectangle, multiply its length times its width. (A square is a rectangle.)

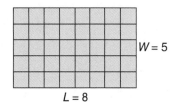

$W = 5$

$L = 8$

$A = \text{length} \cdot \text{width}$

$A = 8 \cdot 5$

$A = 40 \; u^2$

Find the area of each square or rectangle. Write your answers in square units.

1.

6 in.

15 in.

$A = \underline{\;\; 90 \; in.^2 \;\;}$

2.

12.2 yd.

8 yd.

$A = \underline{\qquad\qquad}$

3.

7.4 m

$A = \underline{\qquad\qquad}$

4.

6.2 ft.

8.7 ft.

$A = \underline{\qquad\qquad}$

5.

8.9 m

$A = \underline{\qquad\qquad}$

6.

3.8 dm

12.6 dm

$A = \underline{\qquad\qquad}$

Finding the Area of Combined Shapes

Sometimes you have to separate a figure into smaller figures before you can find the area. Find the area of the smaller figures and add their areas to find the total area.

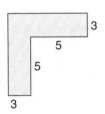

$$A = (5 \cdot 5) + (5 \cdot 1)$$
$$A = 25 + 5$$
$$A = 30 \ u^2$$

Find the total area of each figure. First, draw lines to show the smaller figures. Then, write an equation for finding the area. Give the area in square units (u^2).

1.

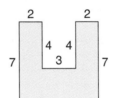

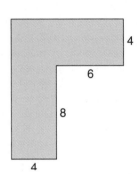

Area = _____   Area = _____   Area = _____

2.

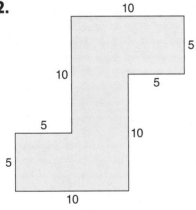

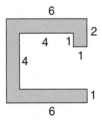

Area = _____   Area = _____   Area = _____

The Complete Book of Challenge Math

Name _____

Finding the Area of Parallelograms

To find the area of a parallelogram, multiply its base times its height.

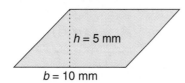

$A = b \cdot h$
$A = 10 \text{ mm} \cdot 5 \text{ mm}$
$A = 50 \text{ mm}^2$

$h = 5 \text{ mm}$
$b = 10 \text{ mm}$

Find the area of each parallelogram. Write your answers in square units.

1.

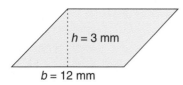

$h = 3 \text{ mm}$
$b = 12 \text{ mm}$

$A = $ _____

2.

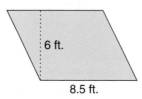

6 ft.

8.5 ft.

$A = $ _____

3.

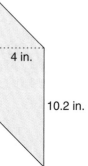

4 in.

10.2 in.

$A = $ _____

4.

1.8 cm

12.2 cm

$A = $ _____

5.

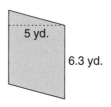

5 yd.

6.3 yd.

$A = $ _____

6.

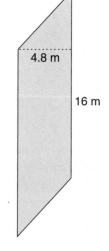

4.8 m

16 m

$A = $ _____

7.

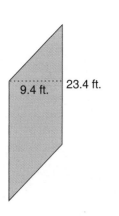

9.4 ft. 23.4 ft.

$A = $ _____

8.

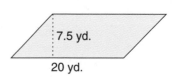

7.5 yd.

20 yd.

$A = $ _____

The Complete Book of Challenge Math

Finding the Area of Triangles

To find the area of a triangle, multiply $\frac{1}{2}$ its base times its height.

$$A = \frac{1}{2} \cdot b \cdot h$$

$$A = \frac{1}{2} \cdot 10 \cdot 3$$

$$A = \frac{1}{2} \cdot 30$$

$$A = 15 \text{ cm}^2$$

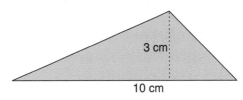

Find each area using the formula $A = \frac{1}{2} \cdot b \cdot h$. Write your answers in square units.

1.

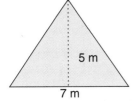

5 m

7 m

$A = $ _____

2.

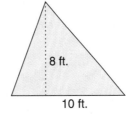

8 ft.

10 ft.

$A = $ _____

3.

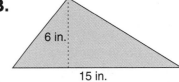

6 in.

15 in.

$A = $ _____

4.

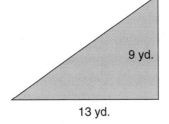

9 yd.

13 yd.

$A = $ _____

5.

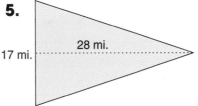

28 mi.

17 mi.

$A = $ _____

6.

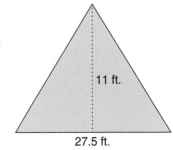

11 ft.

27.5 ft.

$A = $ _____

Name _____

$= \pi \frac{4}{5} \ 2 \div ^3 A - r^2 + 8 \ 1 \times 6^{mm} \ 7 \ 32°F \ 10 \ 63\% \ 8_{cm} \ \frac{7}{8}$

Finding the Area of Trapezoids

To find the area of a trapezoid, use the formula $\frac{1}{2}$ (base$_1$ + base$_2$) • height.

$$A = \frac{1}{2} (b_1 + b_2) • h$$

$$A = \frac{1}{2} (10 + 12) • 6$$

$$A = \frac{1}{2} (22 • 6)$$

$$A = 66 \text{ ft.}^2$$

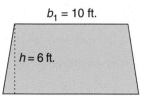

$b_1 = 10$ ft.
$h = 6$ ft.
$b_2 = 12$ ft.

Write an equation using the formula $\frac{1}{2}$ ($b_1 + b_2$) • h. Use it to find the area of each trapezoid. Show your work. Write your answers in square units.

1.

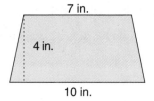

7 in.
4 in.
10 in.

$A =$ _____

2.

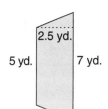

2.5 yd.
5 yd.   7 yd.

$A =$ _____

3.

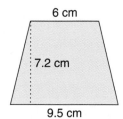

6 cm
7.2 cm
9.5 cm

$A =$ _____

4.

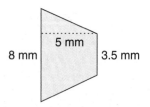

5 mm
8 mm   3.5 mm

$A =$ _____

5.

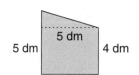

5 dm
5 dm   4 dm

$A =$ _____

6.

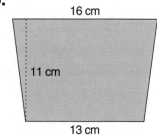

16 cm
11 cm
13 cm

$A =$ _____

Name _____

$= \pi \frac{4}{5} 2 \div {}^{3}A - r^{2} + 8 \; 1 \times 6^{mm} \; 7 \; 32°F \; 10 \; 63\% \; 8_{cm} \frac{7}{8}$

Finding the Circumference of a Circle

Circumference (C) is the distance around a circle. There are two formulas you can use to find circumference. Each formula uses pi (π). Let π = 3.14.

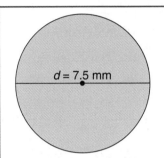

$C = \pi \cdot d$

$C = 3.14 \cdot 7.5$

$C = 23.55 \text{ mm}$

The diameter (*d*) of a circle is a line segment passing through the circle's center with both endpoints on the circle.

$C = \pi \cdot 2 \cdot r$

$C = 3.14 \cdot 2 \cdot 3$

$C = 18.84 \text{ m}$

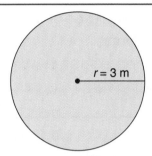

The radius (*r*) of a circle is one-half the circle's diameter.

Find the circumference of each circle. Round to the nearest tenth. You may use a calculator.

1.

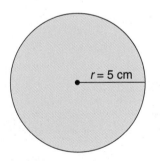

C = _____

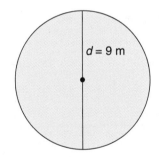

C = _____

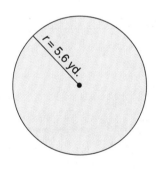

C = _____

2.

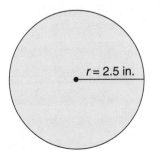

C = _____

C = _____

C = _____

© 2006 American Education Publishing

The Complete Book of Challenge Math

Name _____

$= \pi \frac{4}{5} \ 2 \div {}^3 A - r^2 + 8 \ 1 \times 6\text{mm} \ 7 \ 32°F \ 10 \ 63\% \ 8\text{cm} \ \frac{7}{8}$

Finding the Area of a Circle

To find the area of a circle, use the formula πr^2. Work with a calculator or on scratch paper. Round your answers to the nearest tenth. Write your answers in square units.

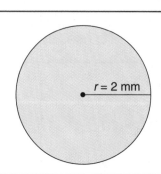

$A = \pi r^2$
$A = 3.14 \cdot (2)^2$
$A = 3.14 \cdot 4$
$A = 12.56 \text{ mm}^2$

1.

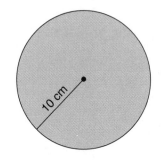

10 cm

$A = \underline{\quad 3.14 \cdot (10)^2 \quad}$
$A = \underline{\quad 3.14 \text{ cm}^2 \quad}$

4.5 mm

$A = \underline{\qquad\qquad}$
$A = \underline{\qquad\qquad}$

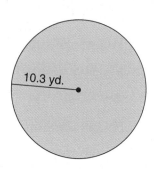

10.3 yd.

$A = \underline{\qquad\qquad}$
$A = \underline{\qquad\qquad}$

2.

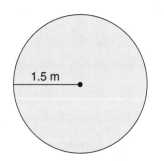

1.5 m

$A = \underline{\qquad\qquad}$
$A = \underline{\qquad\qquad}$

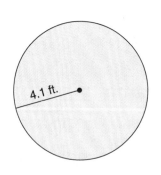

4.1 ft.

$A = \underline{\qquad\qquad}$
$A = \underline{\qquad\qquad}$

14.5 in.

$A = \underline{\qquad\qquad}$
$A = \underline{\qquad\qquad}$

The Complete Book of Challenge Math

$$= \pi \ \tfrac{4}{5} \ 2 \div {}^{3}\!A - r^2 + 8 \ 1 \times 6^{mm} \ 7 \ 32°F \ 10 \ 63\% \ 8\,cm \ \tfrac{7}{8}$$

Planning Gardens (Finding Area and Perimeter)

Hy plans gardens. He needs to know the area and perimeter of each plot to determine the number of plants he needs and the amount of edging or fencing needed. Help him calculate the perimeter and area of the following plots.

1. area _____

perimeter _____

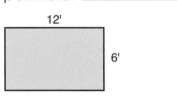

2. area _____

perimeter _____

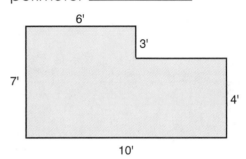

3. area _____

perimeter _____

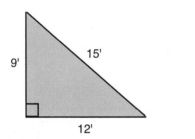

4. area _____

perimeter _____

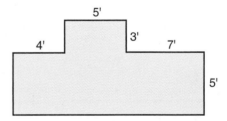

5. area _____

perimeter _____

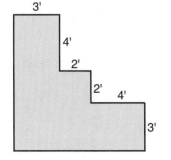

6. area _____

perimeter _____

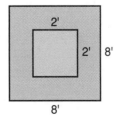

The Complete Book of Challenge Math

Name _____

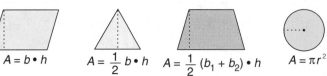

Mixed Practice Finding Area

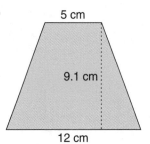

$A = l \cdot w$ $A = l \cdot w$ $A = b \cdot h$ $A = \frac{1}{2} b \cdot h$ $A = \frac{1}{2}(b_1 + b_2) \cdot h$ $A = \pi r^2$

Use the correct formula to find the area of each figure below. Work with a calculator or on scratch paper. Round to the nearest tenth. Write your answers in square units.

1.

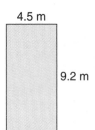

4.5 m

9.2 m

$A = $ _____4.5 • 9.2_____

$A = $ _____41.4 m²_____

2.

5 cm

9.1 cm

12 cm

$A = $ _____

$A = $ _____

3.

14 yd.

8.1 yd.

$A = $ _____

$A = $ _____

4.

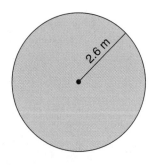

2.6 m

$A = $ _____

$A = $ _____

5.

15.5 mm

21 mm

$A = $ _____

$A = $ _____

6.

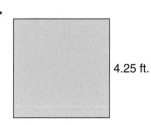

4.25 ft.

$A = $ _____

$A = $ _____

Probability, Statistics, and Graphing

$= \pi \ \frac{4}{5} \ 2 \div \ ^3A - r^2 + 8 \ 1 \times 6^{mm} \ 7 \ 32°F \ 10 \ 63\% \ 8^{cm} \ \frac{7}{8}$

The Probability Ratio

Probability is the likelihood that a particular event or occurrence will take place. Probability is expressed as a ratio in fraction form. A *ratio* is a comparison of two numbers by division. The probability ratio compares the number of favorable outcomes to the total possible outcomes.

Example	What is the probability of a coin landing heads up on one toss? There are **two** sides to the coin so there are **two** possible outcomes to the toss. There is **one** favorable outcome—heads! The probability is 1 out of 2 **or** $\frac{1}{2}$.

The letters of the word "probability" are put in a bag. Find the probability of picking each letter.

1. P _____   **6.** I _____

2. R _____   **7.** L _____

3. O _____   **8.** T _____

4. B _____   **9.** Y _____

5. A _____

10. Find the sum of the probabilities in 1–9 above. What do you notice? Explain.

_____

_____

_____

$= \pi \ \frac{4}{5} \ 2 \div {}^{3}A - r^2 + 8 \ 1 \times 6mm \ 7 \ 32°F \ 10 \ 63\% \ 8cm \ \frac{7}{8}$

Calculating Probability

The following chart displays statistics based on a class of 26 students. The teacher has asked students to respond to a question. Using the chart, what is the probability that the following students will raise their hands?

Classroom Statistics

Groups	Out of 26 Students
Girls	14
Boys	12
Boys wearing tennis shoes	6
Girls wearing tennis shoes	9
Students wearing glasses	5
Students wearing watches	12

1. a girl   _____

2. a boy   _____

3. a boy wearing tennis shoes   _____

4. a girl wearing tennis shoes   _____

5. a student wearing glasses   _____

6. a student wearing a watch   _____

7. a student not wearing tennis shoes   _____

8. Find the sum of the probabilities in numbers 1 and 2 above. What do you notice? Explain.

_____

_____

9. Which has the greater probability of happening, a student wearing tennis shoes answering the question, or a student not wearing tennis shoes answering the question? Explain.

_____

_____

The Complete Book of Challenge Math

Name _____

Probability Using a Spinner

Look at the spinner. What is the probability that the arrow will land on each of the following? Emma wrote her answers as fractions in lowest terms on the lines.

Emma's Answers:

1. The number 3? $\dfrac{1}{6}$

2. A number? $\dfrac{1}{2}$

3. A shape? $\dfrac{3}{8}$

4. A quadrilateral? $\dfrac{1}{4}$

5. A triangle? $\dfrac{1}{6}$

6. An odd number? $\dfrac{8}{3}$

7. An even number? $\dfrac{1}{8}$

8. A shape or a number? 1

Ask the following questions to check Emma's answers.

9. Into how many equal parts is the spinner divided? _____

    Where should this number go in the fraction? _____

10. What does the numerator of the fraction represent in terms of the spinner?

    _____

11. For problems 1–8, decide what numbers should be in the numerator and denominator of each fraction. Reduce your fraction to lowest terms. Compare your answer to Emma's. Correct any of her mistakes. Write your corrected answers in the space below.

For practice, look at the spinner below. What is the probability that the arrow will land on each of the following? Write the probability as a fraction in lowest terms.

12. Yellow? _____

13. Yellow or green? _____

14. Yellow or red? _____

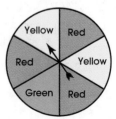

The Complete Book of Challenge Math   © 2006 American Education Publishing

$= \pi \quad \frac{4}{5} \quad 2 \div {}^{3}A - r^2 + 8 \quad 1 \times 6\text{mm} \quad 7 \quad 32°F \quad 10 \quad 63\% \quad 8\text{cm} \quad \frac{7}{8}$

Tree Diagrams and Compound Events

Possible outcomes can be illustrated as *trees* to determine probabilities in compound events or occurrences. Assume that the two spinners below are spun at the same time. What is the probability that each combination will be spun? Complete the *tree diagram,* then list all the possible outcomes of the two spinners and the probability of each outcome. The first two have been done for you.

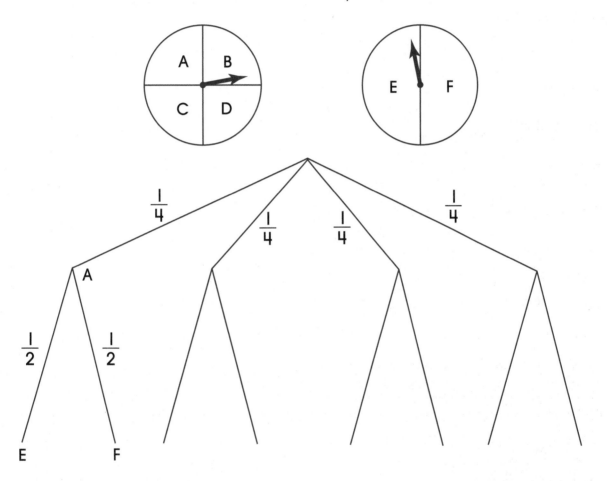

Possible Combinations: ___AE, AF,_____

Probabilities: ___$\frac{1}{8}$, $\frac{1}{8}$,_____

Name _____

$= \pi \frac{4}{5} \ 2 \div \frac{3}{4} - r^2 + 8 \ 1 \times 6^{mm} \ 7 \ 32°F \ 10 \ 63\% \ 8_{cm} \frac{7}{8}$

Tree Diagrams and Compound Events (continued)

Draw a tree diagram to illustrate each probability.

1. Each high school student must sign up for one foreign language course and one music course. The language choices are French, Spanish, German, or Latin. The music choices are choir, symphony, or band. List all the possible outcomes.

Possible Outcomes: _____

What is the probability that Latin and band will be chosen? _____

2. You have a coin and a spinner with the colors red, white, and blue. What is the probability of tossing heads with the color blue?   _____

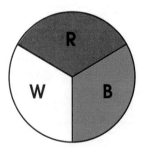

$= \pi \; \frac{4}{5} \; 2 \div {}^{3}A - r^{2} + 8 \; 1 \times 6\,mm \; 7 \; 32°F \; 10 \; 63\% \; 8\,cm \; \frac{7}{8}$

Tree Diagrams and Compound Events (continued)

Mary's family is looking at new cars. They have narrowed it down to the following choices. The tree diagram below shows the possible outcomes.

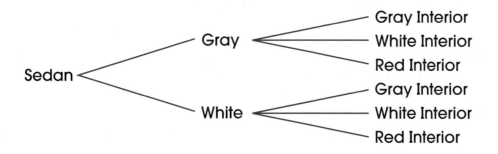

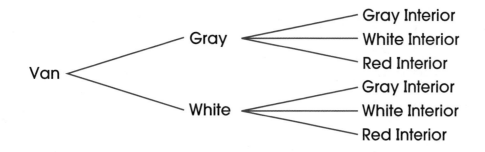

1. The compound event described above
has how many possible outcomes?   _____

2. What is the probability that Mary's family
will select a gray sedan with a black interior?   _____

3. What is the probability that they will select
a gray van?   _____

4. What is the probability that they will select
a white van with red interior?   _____

The Complete Book of Challenge Math

Name _____

$= \pi \ \frac{4}{5} \ 2 \div \ ^{3}A - r^{2} + 8 \ 1 \times 6^{mm} \ 7 \ 32°F \ 10 \ 63\% \ 8 \, cm \ \frac{7}{8}$

Take a Class

Use the data given on this page to answer the questions about summer school experiences.

1. On a sheet of scratch paper, make a tree diagram to show all of the possible combinations for advanced summer classes.

Health	Academic	Application
swimming	adv. mathematics	internship
hiking	adv. science	lab
golf	adv. writing	computer
		partnership

2. How many choices are there? _____

3. What is the probability that Julie will take golf and lab? _____

4. What is the probability that August will take advanced science? _____

5. What is the probability that May will take hiking and internship or hiking and computer? _____

6. What is the probability that June will take advanced mathematics? _____

The advanced science class measured trees in a lot. They make the following stem-and-leaf plot. Answer the questions regarding this data.

Tree Height in Feet

4	0 3 3 5 6 7 7 8
3	1 1 1 2 2 4 5 5 5 7 9 9 9 9
2	0 0 2 2 6 8 8 9
1	1 2 5 5 5 6 8
0	2 2 2 3 3 4 5 5 6 7 7 8 9

7. How many trees grew in the lot? _____

8. What is the range of tree heights? _____ The mode? _____

9. What percent of trees are over 34 feet tall? _____

10. What is the probability that a tree was less than or equal to 12 feet? _____

$= \pi \frac{4}{5} 2 \div ^3 A - r^2 + 8 \ 1 \times 6^{mm} \ 7 \ 32°F \ 10 \ 63\% \ 8 cm \frac{7}{8}$

Understanding Statistics

Using statistics is a helpful way to study various situations. The *mean* (or average) is found by dividing the sum of all possibilities by the number of possibilities. When the possibilities are arranged in numerical order, the middle one is the *median*. The possibility that occurs most frequently is the *mode*. The *range* is the difference between the greatest and the least possibility.

Mike's test scores in spelling were 94, 88, 72, 90, 70, 89, and 70.

1. What was his mean score?   _____

2. What was his median score?   _____

3. What was his mode score?   _____

4. Which score (mean, median, mode) do you think he would like to see on his report card? Why?

_____

5. What was the range of Mike's spelling scores? _____

The chef at Bistro Cafe found it challenging to satisfy all his diners. The ages of the diners one evening were as follows: 87, 58, 54, 61, 3, 35, 31, 28, 3, 16, and 68.

6. What is the mean age?   _____

7. What is the median age?   _____

8. What is the mode?   _____

9. Based on the mean age, what should the chef serve, steak and lobster or macaroni and cheese?   _____

10. Based on the mode, what should be served?   _____

11. What is the range of the diners' ages?   _____

The Complete Book of Challenge Math

Name _____

Mean, Mode, Median, and Range

Twelve students at Park High School were asked how many books they read in the past year.

They responded with the following totals:
45, 38, 25, 59, 101, 49, 87, 75, 77, 59, 48, 81

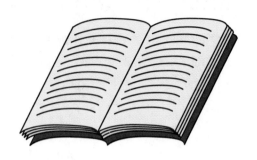

Use the students' totals to complete the activities.

1. What is the mean of these numbers?

_____

2. Write these numbers in order from least to greatest in the chart to the right.

3. What is the mode? _____

4. What is the median? _____

5. What is the range of these numbers?

_____

6. Why do you think the range of these numbers is so great?

_____

_____

7. How many books do you read in a year?

_____

Order	Number of Books
1	
2	
3	
4	
5	
6	
7	
8	
9	
10	
11	
12	

Name _____   Probability, Statistics, and Graphing

First Report Card

Find the mean, or average, of each student's scores. Round to the nearest whole number and record the scores in the last column. Answer the questions below based on this table.

Asia	93	88	97	100	100	97	100	
Dunn	55	60	56	72	43	52	60	
Jorge	88	90	95	100	85	90	90	
Meg	100	100	92	80	100	100	95	
Payne	78	83	79	99	87	92	99	
Shae	97	95	88	100	91	93	98	
Zia	95	100	100	98	95	100	100	

Use the students' cumulative scores to answer the following questions.

1. What is the mean of these cumulative scores? _____

2. What is the range of these scores? _____

3. What is the mode of these scores? _____

4. What is the median of these scores? _____

5. Who had the median score? _____

Use individual student's scores to answer the following questions.

6. What is the range of Dunn's scores? _____

7. What is the mode of Payne's scores? _____

8. What is the median of Meg's scores? _____

THAT'S ONE MEAN REPORT CARD, DUDE!

The Complete Book of Challenge Math

Name _____

$= \pi \frac{4}{5} \ 2 \div ^3 A - r^2 + 8 \ 1 \times 6^{mm} \ 7 \ 32°F \ 10 \ 63\% \ 8_{cm} \frac{7}{8}$

Report Card Time

Ms. Phreye grades on improvement. Before determining semester grades, she eliminates the lowest of the first four test scores. Then, she places the highest of the last three scores in the highest score column. Using Ms. Phreye's system, find the mean, or average, of each student's scores. Use the eight unmarked scores, including the one in the highest score column, to find the mean. Round the mean score to the nearest whole number and record it in the last column. The first one has been done for you. Answer the questions based on this table.

	Weekly Test Scores								Highest Score	Mean Score
Edrea	78	93	62	92	86	89	91	96	96	90
Nevin	75	80	89	75	95	86	90	89		
Philippa	50	87	93	87	87	87	98	94		
Quinn	95	100	100	98	95	96	100	89		
Ramiro	87	94	35	64	50	100	36	50		
Tessa	89	93	88	97	100	100	97	100		
Zedra	55	60	56	72	43	52	60	70		

Use the students' cumulative scores to answer the following questions.

I. What is the mean of all the cumulative scores? _____

2. What is the range of these scores? _____

3. What is the mode of these scores? _____

4. What is the median of these scores? _____

Use individual student's scores to answer the following questions.

5. What is the range of Ramiro's scores? _____

6. What is the mode of Philippa's scores? _____

7. What is the median of Nevin's scores? _____

$= \pi \ \frac{4}{5} \ 2 \div {}^3A - r^2 + 8 \ 1 \times 6mm \ 7 \ 32°F \ 10 \ 63\% \ 8cm \ \frac{7}{8}$

Interpreting Statistics

Find the mean, mode, median, and range of the information in each graph below.
Round the answer to the hundredths place.

Mile Relay Practice Times	
DAY	TIMES
Monday	3.29 minutes
Tuesday	3.24 minutes
Wednesday	3.48 minutes
Thursday	3.24 minutes
Friday	3.89 minutes

mean: _____

mode: _____

median: _____

range: _____

Candy Bars Sold	
DAY	NUMBER OF BARS
Monday	127
Tuesday	225
Wednesday	93
Thursday	82
Friday	111
Saturday	137
Sunday	82

mean: _____

mode: _____

median: _____

range: _____

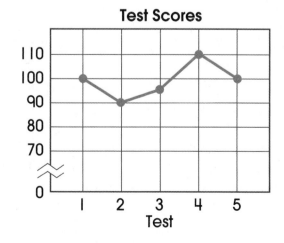

Test Scores

mean: _____

mode: _____

median: _____

range: _____

The Complete Book of Challenge Math

$= \pi \frac{4}{5} 2 \div {}^3A - r^2 + 8 1 \times 6^{mm} 7 32°F 10 63\% 8cm \frac{7}{8}$

Working With Frequency Tables

A *frequency table* is a good way to show information. Frequency tables show how often something has occurred.

Answer the following questions using the frequency table below.

Books Checked Out by Students					
Type	Monday	Tuesday	Wednesday	Thursday	Friday
Nonfiction	23	20	26	18	12
Fairy Tales	11	14	8	15	7
Adventure	29	21	32	24	16
Mystery	32	20	26	36	30

1. How many nonfiction books were checked out during this week? _____

2. How many fairy tale books were checked out during this week? _____

3. How many adventure books were checked out during this week?

   _____

4. How many mystery books were checked out during this week?

   _____

5. What kind of book was checked out most often during this week? _____

6. What kind of book was checked out least often during this week? _____

$= \pi \frac{4}{5} 2 \div {}^3A - r^2 + 8 \ 1 \times 6^{mm} \ 7 \ 32°F \ 10 \ 63\% \ 8_{cm} \frac{7}{8}$

Hair Colors

Relative frequency states the actual frequency of an event related to the total number possible.

The following chart shows the results of a classroom survey that a teacher took.

Classroom Survey	
Groups	Out of 24 Students
Boys	11
Girls	13
Girls with blond hair	4
Girls with dark hair	9
Boys with blond hair	6
Boys with dark hair	5

Using the chart above, find the following relative frequencies.

1. Boys with dark hair   5 out of 24, or $\frac{5}{24}$
_____

2. Girls with dark hair   _____

3. Girls with blond hair   _____

4. Boys with blond hair   _____

5. Students with dark hair   _____

6. Students with blond hair   _____

7. Boys in the classroom   _____

8. Girls in the classroom   _____

9. Boys and girls in the classroom   _____

10. Boys with red hair   _____

The Complete Book of Challenge Math

Probability, Statistics, and Graphing   Name _____

Probability and Relative Frequency

The relative frequency of an outcome is the ratio:

$$\frac{\text{frequency of the outcome}}{\text{total frequencies of outcomes}}$$

1. Make a table to show the relative frequencies from the following car survey.

A car dealer surveyed 200 recent car buyers. Seventy-six of his customers bought red cars, fifty-two customers bought blue cars, forty customers bought gray cars, and the rest purchased white cars.

Color of Cars Purchased	
Color	Relative Frequency

2. Using the table you made, find the probability (*P*) that each car will be chosen in the future.

a. *P* (red) _____   **c.** *P* (blue) _____

b. *P* (grey) _____   **d.** *P* (white) _____

3. Based on the relative frequency shown on the table, what color cars should his business buy the most of next year? Explain.

_____

_____

4. What color cars should he buy the least of next year? Explain.

_____

_____

_____

The Complete Book of Challenge Math   © 2006 American Education Publishing

$= \pi \frac{4}{5} \ 2 \div \frac{3}{} \ A - r^2 + 8 \ 1 \times 6^{mm} \ 7 \ 32°F \ 10 \ 63\% \ 8^{cm} \frac{7}{8}$

Calculating Relative Frequency

Solve the following.

1. Mike is an excellent offensive soccer player. On any given scoring attempt, the probability that Mike will score a soccer goal is $\frac{4}{5}$. He has attempted to score 20 times. How many goals has he probably scored?

_____

2. The probability that Mary will run the mile in under 5 minutes is $\frac{6}{10}$. During the season, she has run the mile 150 times. How many times has she probably run the mile in under 5 minutes?

_____

3. The probability that Sue's dog will catch a ball when thrown is $\frac{8}{12}$. One evening, the ball was thrown 204 times. How many times did the dog probably catch the ball?

_____

4. At the movie theater, the probability that a ticket will be purchased for an action-thriller is $\frac{5}{6}$. If 360 people go to the movie theater, how many will probably see an action-thriller?

_____

5. The probability that a cardinal will land at the bird feeder is $\frac{2}{12}$. Ninety-six birds have landed at the feeder today. Probably how many were cardinals?

_____

6. The probability that a band member will play a cornet is $\frac{5}{8}$. There are 128 band members. How many probably play a cornet?

_____

The Complete Book of Challenge Math

Name _____

$= \pi \ \frac{4}{5} \ 2 \div \ ^3A \ - r^2 + 8 \ 1 \times 6^{mm} \ 7 \ 32°F \ 10 \ 63\% \ 8_{cm} \ \frac{7}{8}$

Working With Picture Graphs

The school newspaper editors at Bluebird Lane School encouraged students to take part in after-school activities. They published this picture graph. Refer to the graph to answer each question.

Students Taking Part in After-School Activities						
Band	🚹	🚹	🚹	🚹		
Student Council	🚹	🚹				
School Paper	🚹	🚹	🚹			
Sports	🚹	🚹	🚹	🚹	🚹	🚹
Clubs	🚹	🚹	🚹	🚹	🚹	🚹
Each 🚹 stands for 10 students						

Source: *Bluebird School Paper,* 2005

1. How many total students take part in after-school activities?

_____

2. In which two activities do the greatest number of students take part?

_____

3. How many more students take part in sports than in the band?

_____

4. Which activity represented has the least participation?

_____

5. How many fewer students take part in the student council than the school paper?

_____

6. How many more students take part in band than in the school paper?

_____

$= \pi \frac{4}{5} 2 \div ^3 A - r^2 + 8 \ 1 \times 6^{mm} \ 7 \ 32°F \ 10 \ 63\% \ 8_{cm} \frac{7}{8}$

Class Elections

Picture graphs can use symbols to represent large numbers. Before making a picture graph, you must first round the numbers to a convenient place. In the chart below, round each number of votes to the nearest tens place. Write the new numbers in the chart.

School Elections		
Grade Level	Total Votes	Votes (Rounded)
Fourth Grade	89	
Fifth Grade	62	
Sixth Grade	76	

To make a picture graph with the information from the chart, let a smiling face equal 10 votes. Draw smiling faces in the picture graph below to represent the total votes of each grade.

School Elections	☺ = 10 votes
Grade Level	**Total Votes (Rounded)**
Fourth Grade	
Fifth Grade	
Sixth Grade	

Use the picture graph to answer these questions.

1. Which grade level cast the most votes? _____

2. Which grade level cast the fewest votes? _____

    The Complete Book of Challenge Math

Name _____

Line and Bar Graphs

A graph compares information in a visual manner. A *line graph* shows changes over time.

Daily
Temperature

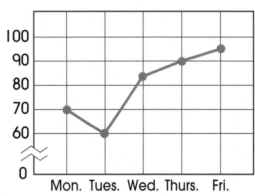

A *bar graph* shows a comparison of two or more quantities.

Average Summer
Temperature

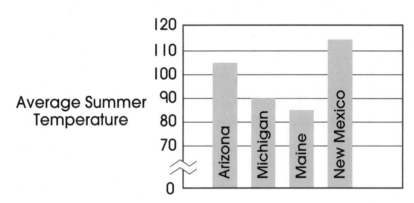

Which kind of graph would be the best way to display the following information? Explain your choice.

1. The average monthly rainfall of Austria

_____

2. A comparison of the sales profits of five insurance companies

_____

3. A meteor count for the month of July

_____

4. A comparison of the different depths at which 10 sea species live

_____

Interpreting Line Graphs

Graphs have a *vertical axis* and a *horizontal axis*. The axes are labeled to show what is being compared.

Average Number of Rainy Days in Miami, Florida

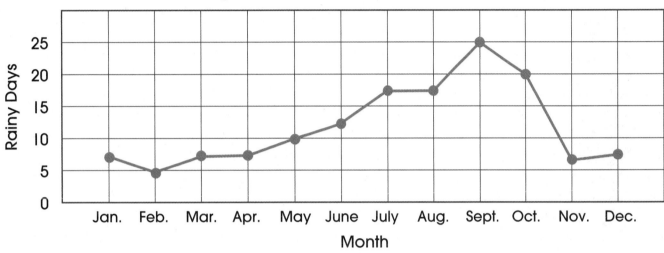

Using the data plotted on the graph, answer the following questions.

1. What is the title of the graph?

_____

2. How is the vertical axis labeled?

_____

3. What is contained in the horizontal axis?

_____

4. Which month had the greatest number of rainy days?

_____

5. Which two-month period shows the greatest change in the number of rainy days?

_____

6. Which month was the driest?

_____

Using the graph, fill in the blanks below. (Hint: When finding the median of an even number of numerals, divide by two the sum of the two numerals in the middle.)

7. range: _____   **8.** mean: _____   **9.** median: _____   **10.** mode: _____

The Complete Book of Challenge Math

Name _____

Basketball Games

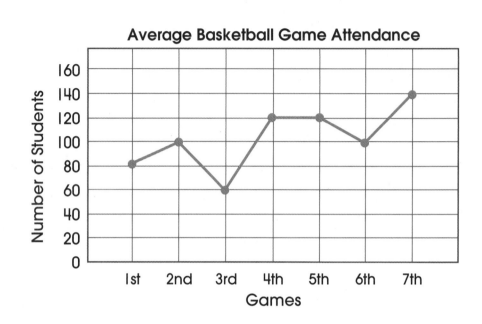

Refer to the line graph above to answer the following questions.

1. Which game had the greatest attendance? _____

2. Which game had the lowest attendance? _____

3. Between which two games was there the greatest increase in attendance?

_____

4. How many students attended the fifth basketball game? _____

5. What was the increase in attendance from the first to the seventh game?

_____

6. Between which two games was there no change in the number of students

attending? _____

7. Between which two games was there the smallest increase in attendance?

_____

Creating Line Graphs

Use the following information and the boxes to create three line graphs. Make sure to label the vertical axis, horizontal axis, and title the graphs themselves.

I. High temperatures for July 1–7:

Mon.	78°
Tues.	88°
Wed.	92°
Thurs.	96°
Fri.	96°
Sat.	98°
Sun.	92°

2. Cars sold in 1994:

Jan.	86
Feb.	143
Mar.	135
Apr.	152
May	201
Jun.	270
Jul.	186
Aug.	157
Sept.	164
Oct.	169
Nov.	135
Dec.	101

3. Meteor count for one week:

Mon.	17
Tues.	3
Wed.	0
Thurs.	7
Fri.	9
Sat.	8
Sun.	11

The Complete Book of Challenge Math

Name _____

= π $\frac{4}{5}$ 2 ÷ ³A − r² + 8 1 × 6mm 7 32°F 10 63% 8cm $\frac{7}{8}$

Interpreting Double Line Graphs

Double line graphing can be used to display two sets of data that will be compared over a period of time.

Example	Chris cuts lawns during the summer to earn money. Each week he cuts five lawns of different sizes, each of which takes a different amount of time. He tried to decrease his time spent on each lawn. The following chart and double line graph show his progress from week one to week four.

Lawn	Week 1	Week 4
1	1.5	1
2	3	2.5
3	1	1
4	4	3.5
5	2	.5

Week 1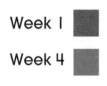

Week 4

Answer the following questions using the information above.

1. Which lawn did not show a decrease in time?   _____

2. Which lawn showed the greatest decrease in time?   _____

3. What was the range of his time spent mowing lawns in week 4? _____

4. What was his mean time spent mowing lawns during week 1? _____

5. What was his mean time spent mowing lawns during week 4? _____

The Complete Book of Challenge Math

$$= \pi \ \frac{4}{5} \ 2 \div \ ^3\! A - r^2 + 8 \ 1 \times 6^{mm} \ 7 \ 32°F \ 10 \ 63\% \ 8_{cm} \ \frac{7}{8}$$

Creating Double Line Graphs

The volleyball players at Newhall High School were working on improving their serves. Each team member was required to practice serving 100 times each week. The table below gives the frequency of successful serves for each team member for weeks one and six. Use the frequency table to fill in the relative frequency table showing each girl's successful serves in weeks one and six.

FREQUENCY		
Name	**Week 1**	**Week 6**
Susan	38	95
Mary	72	95
Jody	40	60
Jessica	52	73
Carrie	34	72
Natasha	78	86

RELATIVE FREQUENCY		
Name	Week 1	Week 6
Susan		
Mary		
Jody		
Jessica		
Carrie		
Natasha		

Construct a double line graph showing the number of each girl's successful serves during the first and sixth weeks of practice. Remember to make a legend indicating the weeks.

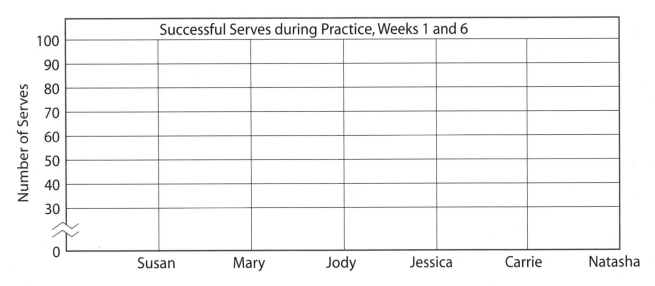

The Complete Book of Challenge Math

Name _____

Interpreting Bar Graphs

Bar graphs are used to compare things. Using the graph below, answer the following questions.

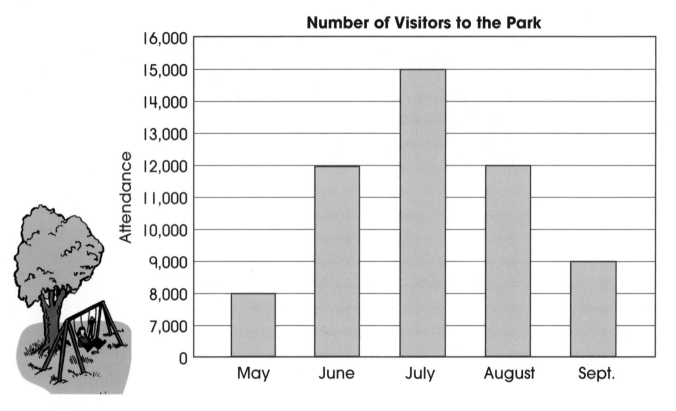

Number of Visitors to the Park

1. Which month has the greatest attendance number? _____

2. Which month has the lowest attendance number? _____

3. Which month has the greater attendance number, September or June? _____

4. Which two months have the same attendance numbers? _____

5. Which month should have the greatest number of park employees working? _____

Why do you think this? _____

_____

$= \pi \frac{4}{5} \ 2 \div \ ^3 A - r^2 + 8 \ 1 \times 6^{mm} \ 7 \ 32°F \ 10 \ 63\% \ 8_{cm} \frac{7}{8}$

Snack Time

Graphs have two axes. Look at the graph below. The vertical axis tells us the number of students and the horizontal axis tells us the types of snacks.

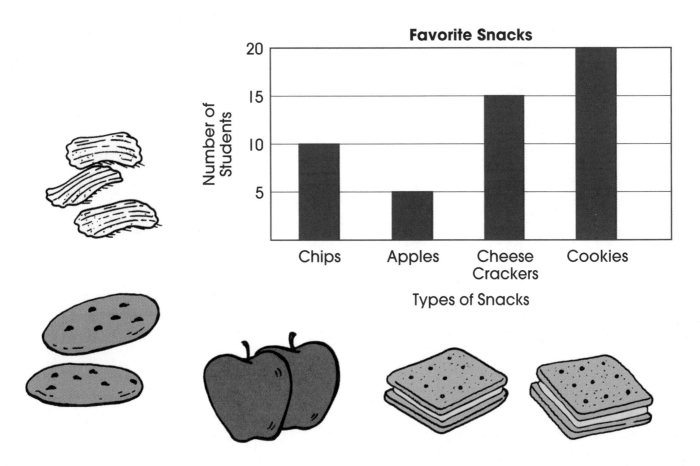

Refer to the graph to answer the following questions.

1. Which type of snack is the favorite of the most students? _____

2. Which type of snack is the favorite of the least number of students? _____

3. How many students like chips the best? _____

4. How many more students chose chips than apples as their favorite snack?

_____

5. How many fewer students chose apples than cheese crackers? _____

6. How many students in all were questioned? _____

The Complete Book of Challenge Math

$= \pi \frac{4}{5} 2 \div {}^3A - r^2 + 8 \ 1 \times 6^{mm} \ 7 \ 32°F \ 10 \ 63\% \ 8\,cm \ \frac{7}{8}$

Creating Bar Graphs

Brian kept track of his science test scores for six weeks in a row. The table to the right shows his scores over this time period.

Using the information from the table, make a bar graph showing Brain's weekly scores. Label your graph. Then, answer the questions at the bottom of the page.

Brian's Weekly Test Scores	
Week 1	70%
Week 2	85%
Week 3	75%
Week 4	90%
Week 5	90%
Week 6	95%

1. In which week did Brian earn his best score? _____

2. In which week did he have his worst score? _____

3. What was the difference between Brian's highest and lowest scores? _____

4. If Brian needs 90% or better to earn an A, in which weeks did he earn an A?

_____

= π 4/5 2 ÷ 3 A − r² + 8 1 × 6 mm 7 32°F 10 63% 8 cm 7/8

Tube Time

Try to get along for a whole week without watching TV. Do some planning for the time you would usually spend watching TV.

Complete this chart during the coming week. Use different colors to create a bar graph showing the kinds of activities that you do during your free time.

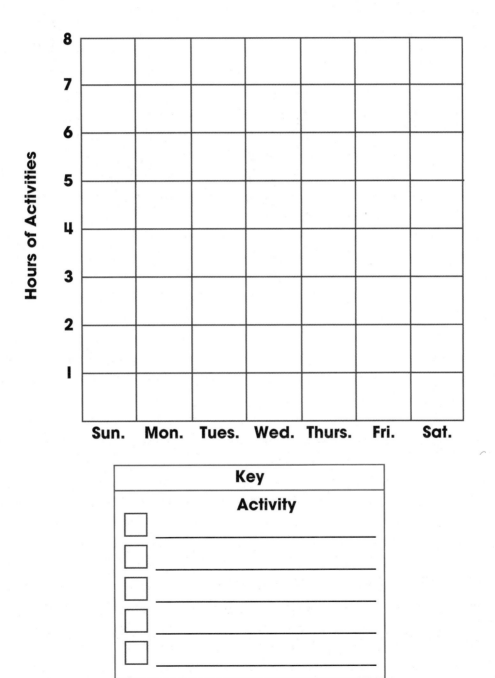

Hours of Activities

8
7
6
5
4
3
2
1

Sun.   Mon.   Tues.   Wed.   Thurs.   Fri.   Sat.

Key		
Activity		
☐	_____	
☐	_____	
☐	_____	
☐	_____	
☐	_____	

The Complete Book of Challenge Math

Name _____

$= \pi \; \frac{4}{5} \; 2 \div {}^{3}A - r^{2} + 8 \; 1 \times 6^{mm} \; 7 \; 32°F \; 10 \; 63\% \; 8 cm \; \frac{7}{8}$

Interpreting Double Bar Graphs

Double bar graphs allow more than one set of data to be compared. The following double bar graph compares the growth between two states. (The data is rounded to the nearest half million.)

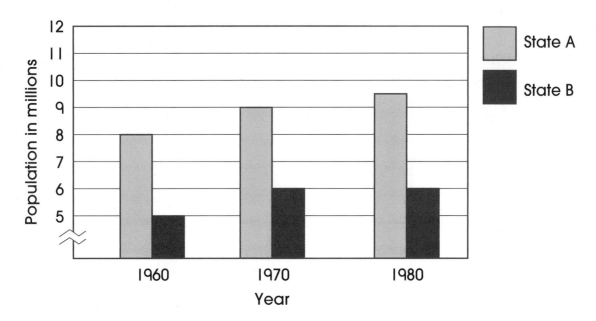

Use the double bar graph above to answer the following questions.

1. What was the population of State A in 1960?

_____

2. What was the population of State B in 1960?

_____

3. Which state experienced the greatest growth in population from 1970 to 1980?

_____

4. What was the growth of State A from 1960 to 1970?

_____

5. What was State B's population gain from 1960 to 1970?

_____

6. Which state had the greatest population growth from 1960 to 1980? What was it?

_____

The Complete Book of Challenge Math

$$= \pi \; \frac{4}{5} \; 2 \div \; ^3A - r^2 + 8 \; 1 \times 6^{mm} \; 7 \; 32°F \; 10 \; 63\% \; 8_{cm} \; \frac{7}{8}$$

Ice Cream Flavors

Double bar graphs allow more than one set of data to be compared. The following double bar graph compares favorite ice cream flavors of fourth- and fifth-grade students.

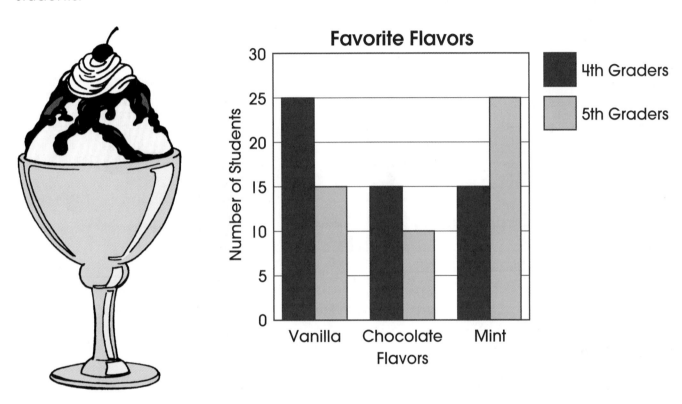

Use the double bar graph above to answer the following questions.

1. Did more fourth graders or fifth graders choose vanilla as their favorite flavor?

_____

2. Was mint chosen by more fourth graders or fifth graders?

_____

3. How many more fourth graders than fifth graders chose chocolate as their favorite flavor?

_____

4. How many fewer fourth-grade students than fifth-grade students chose mint?

_____

     The Complete Book of Challenge Math

= π 4/5 2 ÷ ³A − r² + 8 1 × 6ᵐᵐ 7 32°F 10 63% 8cm 7/8

Bar Graphs and Predictions

City Hall is considering a proposal to build a new shopping mall in a wooded area within the city boundaries. Before it is put to a vote, City Hall decided to run a survey. Out of 4,250 residents and 182 local businesses, 1,000 people were surveyed. The results are graphed below.

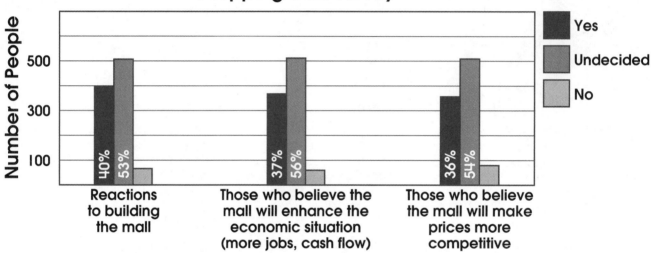

Based on the information in the graph, answer the following questions.

1. Should the mall be built? Explain.

_____

_____

2. Give two reasons why City Hall should vote in favor of the shopping mall proposal.

_____

_____

3. Give two reasons why City Hall should vote against the shopping mall proposal.

_____

_____

4. What is the mean of the percentage who voted yes on the three questions?

_____

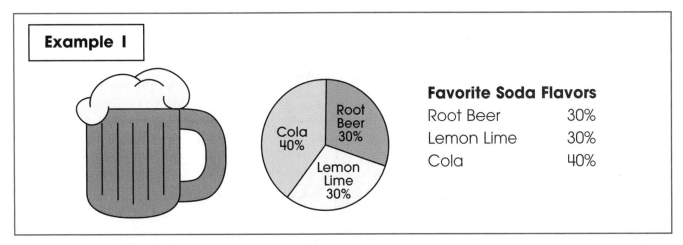

Creating Circle Graphs

Circle graphs (also called pie charts) are best to use when a total amount has been divided into parts. Each part illustrates a ratio of the whole.

Example 1

Favorite Soda Flavors

Root Beer	30%
Lemon Lime	30%
Cola	40%

Use the following information to complete the circle graphs.

1. Birthplaces of the first ten U.S. presidents:

Virginia	60%
Massachusetts	20%
New York	10%
South Carolina	10%

2. Trash collected on Ecology Day:

paper	50%
aluminum cans	15%
plastic	15%
rubber	10%
glass	10%

3. Pizza preferences:

cheese	30%
cheese/pepperoni	20%
cheese/mushroom	10%
deluxe	40%

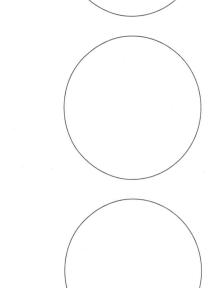

The Complete Book of Challenge Math

Name _____

$= \pi \ \frac{4}{5} \ 2 \div \ ^3 A - r^2 + 8 \ 1 \times 6^{mm} \ 7 \ 32°F \ 10 \ 63\% \ 8 \ cm \ \frac{7}{8}$

A Slice of the Pie

Mr. Armstrong's class earned $482.00 during the school year in order to purchase new books for the library. The graph shows what percentage of the money was earned from each activity. Use the graph to answer the questions.

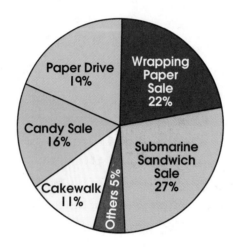

1. Which fundraiser earned the most money?   _____

   How much money did it make? $_____

2. How much money was earned selling candy? $_____

3. How much money was earned from the cakewalk? $_____

4. How much more did the class earn from
   the candy sale than from the cakewalk? $_____

5. How much money was made selling wrapping paper? $_____

6. On a sheet of scratch paper, make a pie graph showing
   percentages of the information in the table from
   a bake sale held the following year.

Goods Sold	350 items
Cupcakes	30
Layer Cakes	15
Brownies	35
Carrot Cakes	20
Oatmeal Cookies	100
Chocolate Chip Cookies	150

$= \pi \ \frac{4}{5} \ 2 \div \ ^3 A - r^2 + 8 \ 1 \times 6^{mm} \ 7 \ 32°F \ 10 \ 63\% \ 8_{cm} \ \frac{7}{8}$

What's Your Favorite?

Circle graphs are best used to display parts of a whole. For example, here are the results when 100 students were surveyed about their favorite school subject.

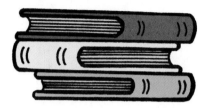

Favorite School Subject	
Math	30
Literature	25
Spelling	45

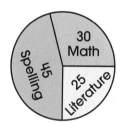

A total of 100 students were surveyed for their favorite in each of the topics below. Show the same information in the circle graphs.

1.

Favorite Jelly Bean Flavor	
Cherry	55
Lime	25
Grape	20

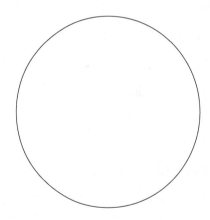

2.

Favorite Pet	
Cats	50
Dogs	30
Fish	10
Rabbits	10

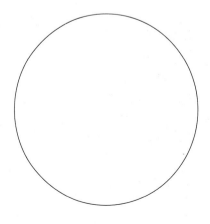

The Complete Book of Challenge Math

Name _____

$= \pi \ \frac{4}{5} \ 2 \div {}^3A - r^2 + 8 \ 1 \times 6\,\text{mm} \ 7 \ 32°\text{F} \ 10 \ 63\% \ 8\,\text{cm} \ \frac{7}{8}$

At the Movies

One hundred third graders were surveyed about their favorite type of movie. The survey results are in the chart below. Show the same data in the circle graph. Then, answer the questions below.

Favorite Movies

Types of Movies	Votes
Cartoons	50
Action	30
Scary	20
Musicals	0

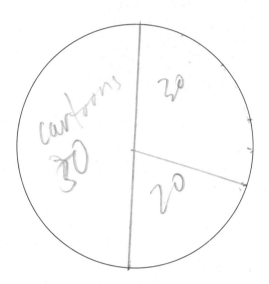

I. List the types of movies in order from the one that received the most votes to the one that received the least votes.

_____

2. What type of movie should the third graders get for their Friday afternoon movie this week? Why?

_____

3. If they can't get their first choice, what should be their second choice? Why?

_____

4. Do you think the graph would look the same if eighth graders voted for their favorite type of movie? Why or why not?

_____

_____

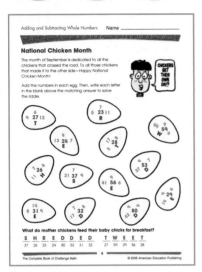

Page 6

Page 7

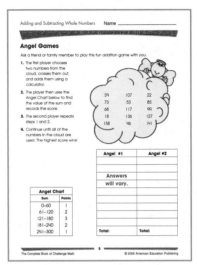

Page 8

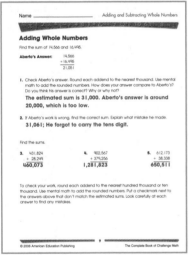

Page 9

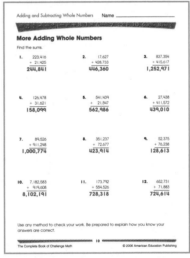

Page 10

Page 11

Page 12

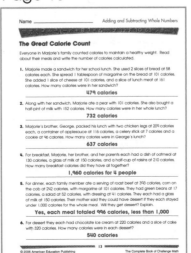

Page 13

Page 14

The Complete Book of Algebra and Geometry

Answer Key

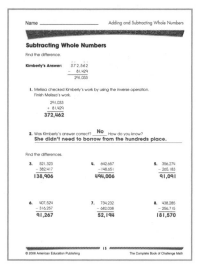

Page 15

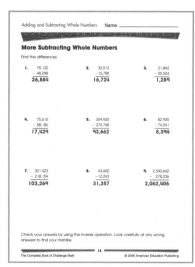

Page 16

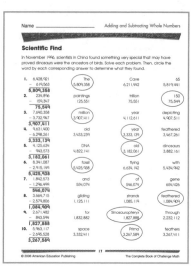

Page 17

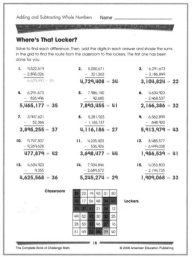

Page 18

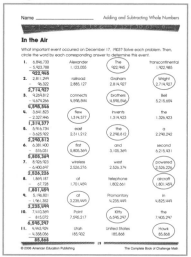

Page 19

Page 20

Page 21

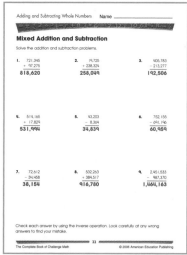

Page 22

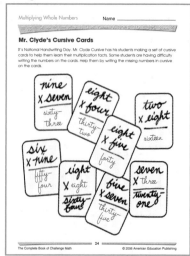

Page 24

The Complete Book of Algebra and Geometry

© 2006 American Education Publishing

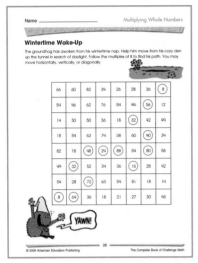

Page 25

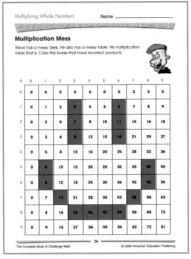

Page 26

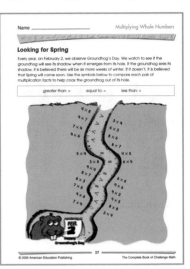

Page 27

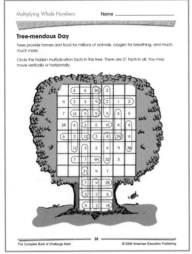

Page 28

Page 29

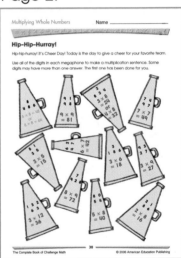

Page 30

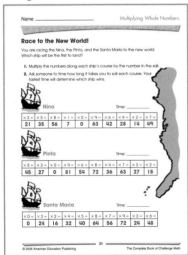

Page 31

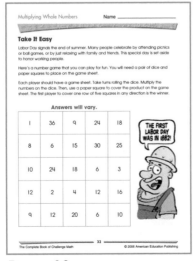

Page 32

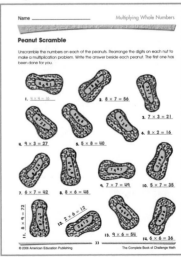

Page 33

The Complete Book of Algebra and Geometry

Answer Key

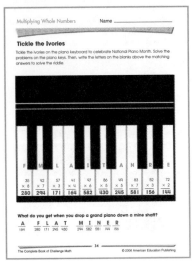

Page 34

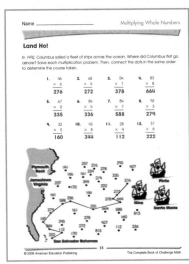

Page 35

Page 36

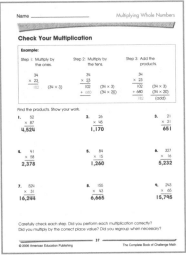

Page 37

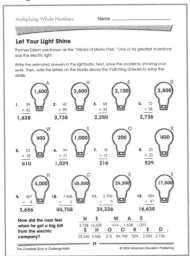

Page 38

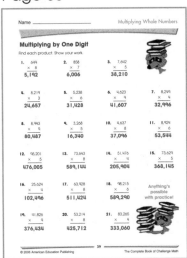

Page 39

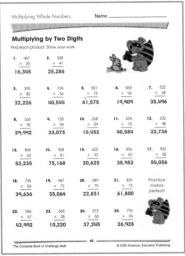

Page 40

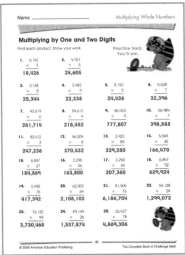

Page 41

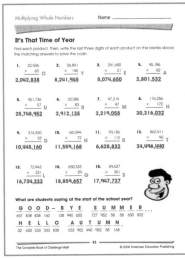

Page 42

The Complete Book of Algebra and Geometry

Page 43

Multiplying Whole Numbers

Multiplying by Three Digits

Find each product. Show your work.

With practice, you can do it!

#		Product
1.	325 × 614	199,550
2.	463 × 527	244,001
3.	265 × 921	244,065
4.	429 × 304	130,416
5.	724 × 630	456,120
6.	512 × 825	422,400
7.	189 × 432	81,648
8.	382 × 265	101,230
9.	361 × 543	196,023
10.	465 × 734	341,310
11.	412 × 398	163,976
12.	252 × 726	182,952
13.	736 × 413	303,968
14.	425 × 817	347,225
15.	832 × 625	520,000
16.	923 × 542	500,266
17.	234 × 489	114,426
18.	564 × 820	462,480
19.	713 × 256	182,528
20.	468 × 375	175,500

43

Page 44

Multiplying Whole Numbers

Multiplying by Four Digits

Find each product. Show your work.

#		Product
1.	5,406 × 2,142	11,579,652
2.	2,482 × 4,321	10,724,722
3.	2,042 × 9,123	18,629,166
4.	2,489 × 4,300	10,702,700
5.	4,364 × 5,127	22,374,228
6.	1,481 × 6,824	10,106,344
7.	1,348 × 3,421	4,611,508
8.	3,901 × 4,612	17,991,412
9.	3,842 × 3,615	13,888,830
10.	3,246 × 1,482	4,810,572
11.	1,498 × 8,003	11,988,494
12.	2,514 × 3,486	8,763,804
13.	3,628 × 2,749	9,973,372
14.	4,215 × 1,321	5,568,015
15.	1,347 × 5,621	7,571,487
16.	1,541 × 2,824	4,351,784
17.	3,045 × 9,120	27,770,400
18.	1,423 × 6,215	8,843,945
19.	2,653 × 5,214	13,832,742
20.	1,434 × 8,172	11,718,648

Anything's possible with practice!

44

Page 45

Multiplying Whole Numbers

Teamwork

Mr. Muscles, the physical education teacher, asked his class to help organize the equipment after gym class. Use multiplication to answer the following questions. Show your work.

1. There were eight stations in the gym. Each station had six small rubber balls and four large ones. How many balls were there all together?
$(6 + 4) \times 8 = 80$ balls

2. Mr. Muscles stores the jump ropes in boxes. The students collected six boxes with seven ropes, nine boxes with four, and 12 boxes with three. How many jump ropes were there all together?
$42 + 36 + 36 = 114$ jump ropes

3. The class used 68 cones during gym. The students put away the cones in several places. There were four stacks of seven in one spot, three stacks of nine in another, and six stacks of two in yet another place. _____ 28 + 27 + 12
Did the students find all 68 cones? __no__
How many, if any, were missing? __1 missing__

4. Mr. Muscles divided the class into groups of five. He wanted to see which group could collect the most baseballs. In Group A, two students collected three, one collected five, and the other two collected two. In Group B, four students collected four and one collected one. In Group C, two students collected four, one collected six, and two collected one. In Group D, four students collected one, and one collected two. In Group E, one student collected four, three collected three, and one student collected two.
Which group collected the most baseballs? __group B__
How many baseballs did each group collect?
Group A __15__   Group D __6__
Group B __17__   Group E __15__
Group C __16__

45

Page 46

Multiplying Whole Numbers

Running a Truck Farm

Mark and his family live on a farm. They raise fruits and vegetables and ship them to market by truck. Read about the farm and answer the questions. Show your work.

1. They planted 98 rows of corn with 125 plants in each row. How many corn plants did they plant?
$98 \times 125 = 12,250$ plants

2. While picking peaches, they filled 742 bushel baskets. Each basket held 45 peaches. How many peaches did they pick?
$742 \times 45 = 33,390$ peaches

3. 41 plums were packed in 1-peck cartons. If there were 237 cartons, how many plums were packed?
$41 \times 237 = 9,717$ plums

4. The truck made deliveries in a 191-kilometer route each day for 23 days of the busiest month. How many total kilometers did the truck travel in that one month?
$191 \times 23 = 4,393$ kilometers

5. The family picked 15 cartons of green beans. If each carton held 300 green beans, how many green beans did they pick?
$15 \times 300 = 1,500$ green beans

6. When the cantaloupes were ripe, they shipped 430 cases each day. If a case held 12 cantaloupes, how many cantaloupes were shipped each day?
$430 \times 12 = 5,160$ cantaloupes each day

7. Mark's father works an average of 48 hours a week. If he works 45 weeks a year, about how many hours does he work in a year?
$48 \times 45 = 2,160$ hours per year

46

Page 48

Dividing Whole Numbers

Gobble These Facts

These wild turkeys are displaying division facts. Solve each division problem and find the quotient that does not match the others. Shade this feather. Unscramble the letters from the shaded feathers to write a Thanksgiving word.

THANKS

48

Page 49

Dividing Whole Numbers

Domino Dots

Write multiplication and division facts for each domino. The first one has been done for you.

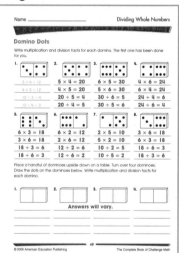

1.	2.	3.	4.
3 × 4 = 12	5 × 4 = 20	6 × 5 = 30	4 × 6 = 24
(3 × 4 = 12)	4 × 5 = 20	5 × 6 = 30	6 × 4 = 24
12 ÷ 3 = 4	20 ÷ 4 = 5	30 ÷ 6 = 5	24 ÷ 4 = 6
12 ÷ 4 = 3	20 ÷ 5 = 4	30 ÷ 5 = 6	24 ÷ 6 = 4

5.	6.	7.	8.
6 × 3 = 18	6 × 2 = 12	5 × 2 = 10	6 × 3 = 18
3 × 6 = 18	2 × 6 = 12	2 × 5 = 10	6 × 3 = 18
18 ÷ 3 = 6	12 ÷ 6 = 2	12 ÷ 2 = 6	18 ÷ 6 = 3
18 ÷ 6 = 3	12 ÷ 6 = 2	10 ÷ 5 = 2	18 ÷ 3 = 6

Place a handful of dominoes upside down on a table. Turn over four dominoes. Draw the dots on the dominoes below. Write multiplication and division facts for each domino.

Answers will vary.

49

Page 50

Dividing Whole Numbers

Domino Trivia

Divide and show your work. Then, cross out the matching answers in the letter grid below. The remaining letters will answer the trivia question.

1. 16 r1   3)49
2. 14 r1   6)85
3. 18 r3   6)93
4. 23 r2   3)71
5. 13 r6   7)97
6. 29 r1   3)88
7. 22 r3   4)91
8. 24 r2   3)74

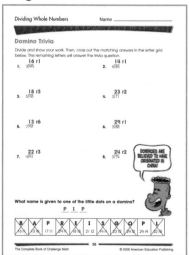

DOMINOES ARE BELIEVED TO HAVE ORIGINATED IN CHINA!

What name is given to one of the little dots on a domino?
P I P

R	A	P	R	E	I	S	G	O	P	L

50

Page 51

Dividing Whole Numbers

Sick Bunny

Divide and show your work. Then, cross out the boxes with the matching answers in the letter grid below. The remaining letters will answer the riddle.

1. 28 r2   3)86
2. 16 r3   4)67
3. 10 r7   4)47
4. 23 r1   4)93
5. 17 r1   4)69
6. 26 r1   3)79
7. 18 r1   2)37
8. 13 r1   7)92
9. 26 r4   7)186
10. 64 r1   3)193
11. 42 r2   7)296
12. 52 r3   4)471

I DON'T FEEL SO HOT.

What do you give sick rabbits?
H A R E   T O N I C !

R	U	H	T	A	B	A	R	V	C	E
B	X	D	O	T	O	N	A	I	C	!

51

Page 52

Dividing Whole Numbers

Mary's Thanksgiving

Thanksgiving Day wasn't always celebrated in the U.S. In 1863, Sarah Josepha Hale, a well-known writer and editor, convinced President Abraham Lincoln to declare the last Thursday in November a National Day of Thanksgiving. Since then, the U.S. celebrates a National Thanksgiving Day each November.

Sarah Josepha Hale is also famous for writing a well-known children's poem. What is it?

Divide and show your work. Then, write each letter in the blank above the matching answer to name the poem.

1. 36 R   6)216
2. 48 A   7)336
3. 37 D   5)185
4. 42 B   4)378
5. 83 I   4)332
6. 67 E   6)536
7. 78 S   9)546
8. 74 T   6)444
9. 35 L   6)210
10. 76 M   8)608
11. 77 Y   4)308

M	A	R	Y		H	A	D	A
76	48	36	77		78	48	37	48

L	I	T	T	L	E		L	A	M	B
35	83	74	74	35	67		35	48	76	42

52

The Complete Book of Algebra and Geometry

Answer Key

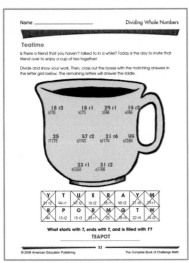

Page 53

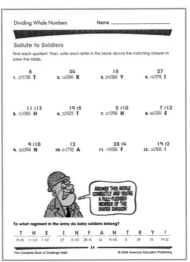

Page 54

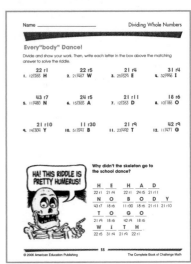

Page 55

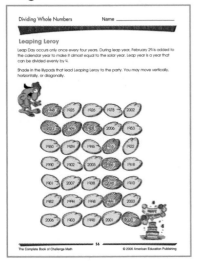

Page 56

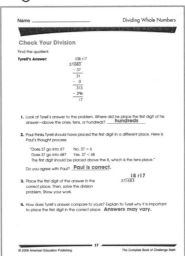

Page 57

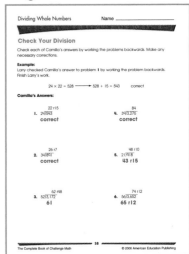

Page 58

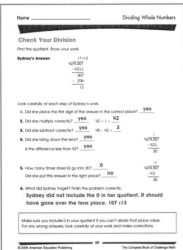

Page 59

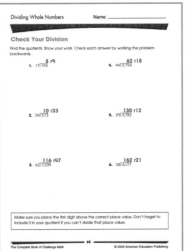

Page 60

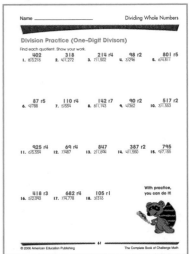

Page 61

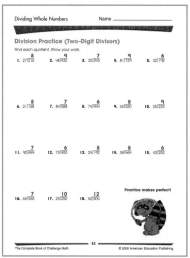

Page 62

Dividing Whole Numbers — Name ___

Division Practice (Two-Digit Divisors)
Find each quotient. Show your work.

1. 8 27)216
2. 9 48)432
3. 7 35)245
4. 9 81)729
5. 6 32)192

6. 8 21)168
7. 7 84)588
8. 6 74)444
9. 8 65)520
10. 9 25)225

11. 7 92)644
12. 6 75)450
13. 7 24)192
14. 8 58)464
15. 6 42)252

16. 7 65)455
17. 10 25)250
18. 12 42)504

Practice makes perfect!

The Complete Book of Challenge Math — © 2006 American Education Publishing — 62

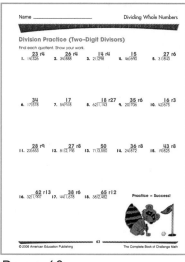

Page 63

Name ___ — Dividing Whole Numbers

Division Practice (Two-Digit Divisors)
Find each quotient. Show your work.

1. 23 r4 14)326
2. 26 r4 34)888
3. 14 r4 21)298
4. 15 46)690
5. 27 r6 31)843

6. 34 17)578
7. 17 54)918
8. 18 r27 62)1,143
9. 35 r6 20)706
10. 16 r3 42)675

11. 28 r9 23)653
12. 27 r8 81)2,195
13. 50 71)3,550
14. 36 r8 24)872
15. 43 r8 19)825

16. 62 r13 32)1,997
17. 38 r6 44)1,678
18. 65 r12 38)2,482

Practice = Success!

© 2006 American Education Publishing — 63 — The Complete Book of Challenge Math

---

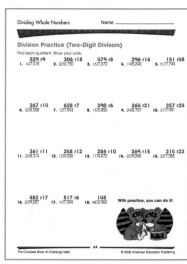

Page 64

Dividing Whole Numbers — Name ___

Division Practice (Two-Digit Divisors)
Find each quotient. Show your work.

1. 529 r9 14)7,415
2. 306 r18 22)6,750
3. 479 r8 16)7,672
4. 296 r16 19)5,640
5. 151 r48 51)7,749

6. 267 r14 32)8,558
7. 628 r7 12)7,543
8. 390 r6 15)5,856
9. 364 r21 24)8,757
10. 257 r24 31)7,991

11. 361 r11 23)8,314
12. 348 r12 13)4,536
13. 286 r10 17)4,872
14. 369 r15 25)9,240
15. 214 r23 33)7,085

16. 482 r17 20)9,657
17. 517 r6 14)7,244
18. 145 48)6,960

With practice, you can do it!

© 2006 American Education Publishing — 64 — The Complete Book of Challenge Math

---

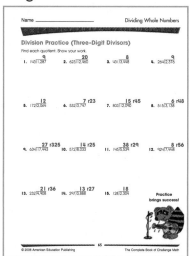

Page 65

Name ___ — Dividing Whole Numbers

Division Practice (Three-Digit Divisors)
Find each quotient. Show your work.

1. 9 143)1,287
2. 20 623)12,460
3. 8 431)3,448
4. 9 264)2,376

5. 12 172)2,064
6. 7 r23 532)3,747
7. 15 r45 803)12,090
8. 6 r48 515)3,138

9. 27 r325 634)17,443
10. 14 r25 572)8,033
11. 38 r29 145)5,539
12. 8 r56 924)7,448

13. 21 r36 232)4,908
14. 13 r27 297)3,888
15. 18 128)2,304

Practice brings success!

© 2006 American Education Publishing — 65 — The Complete Book of Challenge Math

---

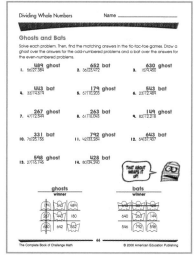

Page 66

Dividing Whole Numbers — Name ___

Ghosts and Bats
Solve each problem. Then, find the matching answers in the tic-tac-toe games. Draw a ghost over the answers for the odd-numbered problems and a bat over the answers for the even-numbered problems.

1. 489 ghost 56)27,384
2. 652 bat 36)23,472
3. 630 ghost 15)9,450

4. 443 bat 33)14,619
5. 179 ghost 57)10,203
6. 543 bat 23)12,489

7. 267 ghost 47)12,549
8. 263 bat 61)16,043
9. 149 ghost 82)12,218

10. 331 bat 76)25,156
11. 792 ghost 42)33,264
12. 643 bat 54)37,437

13. 598 ghost 27)16,146
14. 428 bat 80)34,240

THAT ABOUT WRAPS IT UP!

ghosts winner | bats winner

© 2006 American Education Publishing — 66 — The Complete Book of Challenge Math

---

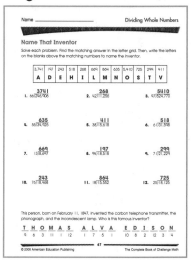

Page 67

Name ___ — Dividing Whole Numbers

Name That Inventor
Solve each problem. Find the matching answer in the letter grid. Then, write the letters on the blanks above the matching numbers to name the inventor.

3,741	197	243	518	268	669	864	635	5,410	725	299	411
A	D	E	H	I	L	M	N	O	S	T	V

1. 3741 66)246,906
2. 268 42)11,256
3. 5410 47)254,270

4. 635 55)34,925
5. 411 38)15,618
6. 518 61)31,598

7. 669 13)8,697
8. 197 94)18,518
9. 299 71)21,229

10. 243 76)18,468
11. 864 18)15,552
12. 725 25)18,125

This person, born on February 11, 1847, invented the carbon telephone transmitter, the phonograph, and the incandescent lamp. Who is this famous inventor?

T H O M A S   A L V A   E D I S O N
9 6 3 11 11 12   1 7 5 1   10 8 2 12 3 4

© 2006 American Education Publishing — 67 — The Complete Book of Challenge Math

---

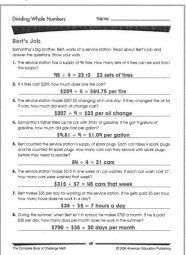

Page 68

Dividing Whole Numbers — Name ___

Bert's Job
Samantha's big brother, Bert, works at a service station. Read about Bert's job and answer the questions. Show your work.

1. The service station has a supply of 95 tires. How many sets of 4 tires can be sold from this supply?
   95 ÷ 4 = 23 r3   23 sets of tires

2. If 4 tires cost $259, how much does one tire cost?
   $259 ÷ 4 = $64.75 per tire

3. The service station made $207.00 changing oil in one day. If they changed the oil for 9 cars, how much did each oil change cost?
   $207 ÷ 9 = $23 per oil change

4. Samantha's father filled up his car with $9.81 of gasoline. If he got 9 gallons of gasoline, how much did gas cost per gallon?
   $9.81 ÷ 9 = $1.09 per gallon

5. Bert counted the service station's supply of spark plugs. Each car takes 4 spark plugs, and he counted 84 spark plugs. How many cars can they service with spark plugs before they need to reorder?
   84 ÷ 4 = 21 cars

6. The service station made $315 in one week on car washes. If each car wash cost $7, how many cars were washed that week?
   $315 ÷ $7 = 45 cars that week

7. Bert makes $35 per day for working at the service station. If he gets paid $5 per hour, how many hours does he work in a day?
   $35 ÷ $5 = 7 hours a day

8. During the summer, when Bert isn't in school, he makes $700 a month. If he is paid $35 per day, how many days does he work in the summer?
   $700 ÷ $35 = 20 days per month

The Complete Book of Challenge Math — 68 — © 2006 American Education Publishing

---

Page 69

Name ___ — Dividing Whole Numbers

Preparing for the Prom
Wayne helped his sister who was on the prom preparation committee. Read about the preparations and answer the questions. Show your work.

1. The committee hired a band for the dance for $500. If the dance lasts from 8 P.M. until 12 A.M., how much will the band be paid per hour?
   $500 ÷ 4 = $125 per hour

2. The dance band has 5 members. How much does each band member get paid per hour?
   $125 ÷ 5 = $25 per hour

3. The committee rented 4 special-effects lights for $100. How much would it cost to rent one light?
   $100 ÷ 4 = $25 per light

4. The committee will rent 256 chairs for the dance. If 4 chairs fit around one table, how many tables will they need to rent?
   256 ÷ 4 = 64 tables

5. There is a fountain in the middle of the dance floor that holds 150 gallons of water. The committee has a 5-gallon bucket. How many buckets of water will it take to fill the fountain?
   150 ÷ 5 = 30 buckets

6. The committee has ordered 192 flowers to be put in vases on the tables. If 3 flowers go in each vase, how many vases will they need?
   192 ÷ 3 = 64 vases

7. Wayne helped his sister put crepe paper around the walls of the room. Each wall was 20 yards long. They used 40 yards of crepe paper per wall. Will 160 yards of crepe paper be enough to decorate the square room?
   yes. 160 ÷ 4 = 40 yards per wall

8. After the prom was over, a cleanup crew of 7 people worked a total of 21 hours to get the room back to order. How many hours did they each work?
   21 ÷ 7 = 3 hours each

© 2006 American Education Publishing — 69 — The Complete Book of Challenge Math

---

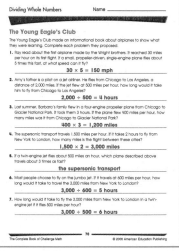

Page 70

Dividing Whole Numbers — Name ___

The Young Eagle's Club
The Young Eagle's Club made an informational book about airplanes to show what they were learning. Complete each problem they proposed.

1. Ray read about the first airplane made by the Wright brothers. It reached 30 miles per hour on its first flight. If a small, propeller-driven, single-engine plane flies about 5 times this fast, at what speed can it fly?
   30 × 5 = 150 mph

2. Amy's father is a pilot on a jet airliner. He flies from Chicago to Los Angeles, a distance of 2,000 miles. If the jet flew at 500 miles per hour, how long would it take him to fly from Chicago to Los Angeles?
   2,000 ÷ 500 = 4 hours

3. Last summer, Barbara's family flew in a four-engine propeller plane from Chicago to Glacier National Park. It took them 3 hours. If the plane flew 400 miles per hour, how many miles was it from Chicago to Glacier National Park?
   400 × 3 = 1,200 miles

4. The supersonic transport travels 1,500 miles per hour. If it takes 2 hours to fly from New York to London, how many miles is the flight between these cities?
   1,500 × 2 = 3,000 miles

5. If a twin-engine jet flies about 500 miles an hour, which plane described above travels about 3 times as fast?
   the supersonic transport

6. Most people choose to fly on the jumbo jet. If it travels at 600 miles per hour, how long would it take to travel the 3,000 miles from New York to London?
   3,000 ÷ 600 = 5 hours

7. How long would it take to fly the 3,000 miles from New York to London in a twin-engine jet if it flies 500 miles per hour?
   3,000 ÷ 500 = 6 hours

The Complete Book of Challenge Math — 70 — © 2006 American Education Publishing

---

The Complete Book of Algebra and Geometry

Answer Key

Page 72

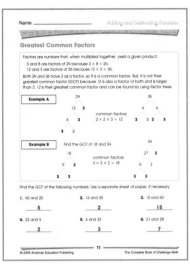

Page 73

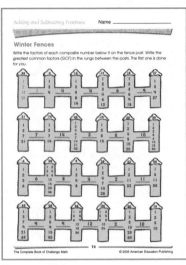

Page 74

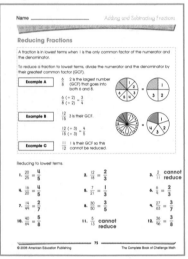

Page 75

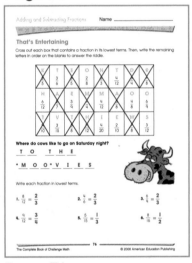

Page 76

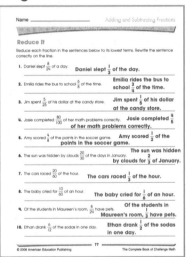

Page 77

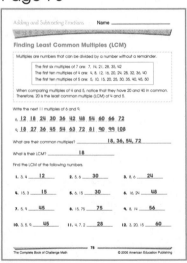

Page 78

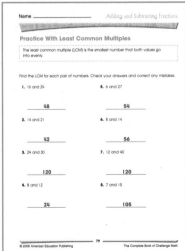

Page 79

Page 80

Answer Key

Page 81

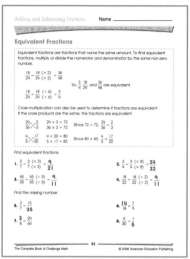

Page 82

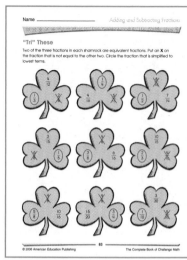

Page 83

Page 84

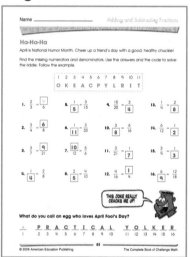

Page 85

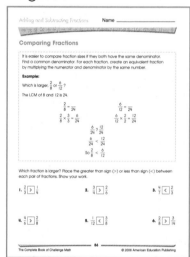

Page 86

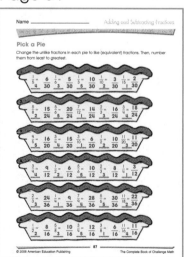

Page 87

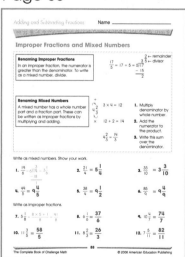

Page 88

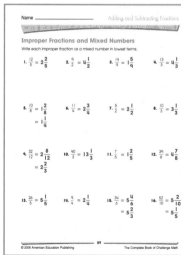

Page 89

© 2006 American Education Publishing

The Complete Book of Algebra and Geometry

Answer Key

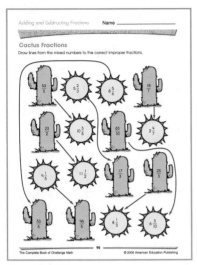

Page 90

Page 91

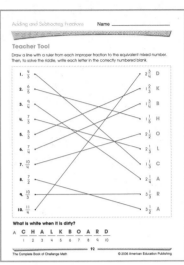

Page 92

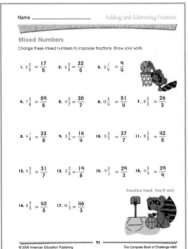

Page 93

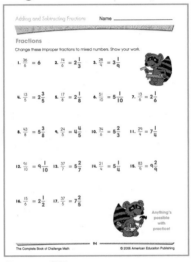

Page 94

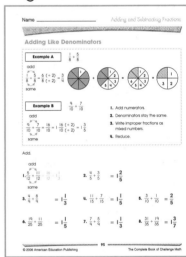

Page 95

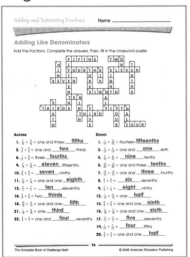

Page 96

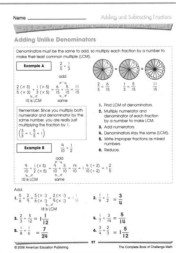

Page 97

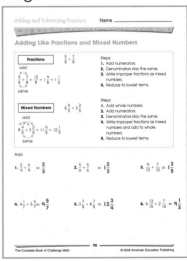

Page 98

The Complete Book of Algebra and Geometry

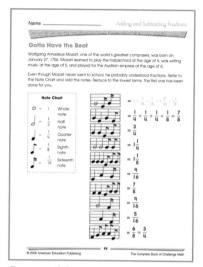

Page 99

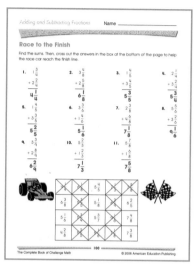

Page 100

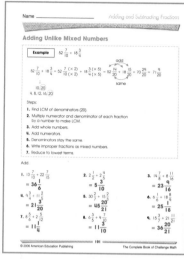

Page 101

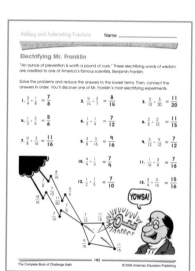

Page 102

Page 103

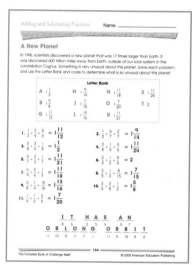

Page 104

The Complete Book of Algebra and Geometry

Answer Key

Page 105

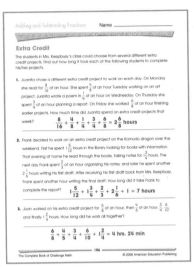

Page 106

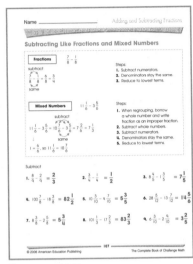

Page 107

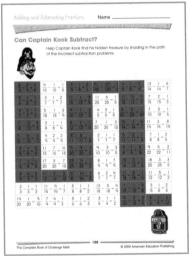

Page 108

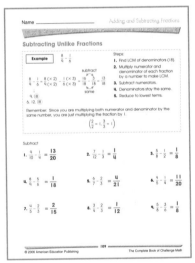

Page 109

Page 110

The Complete Book of Algebra and Geometry

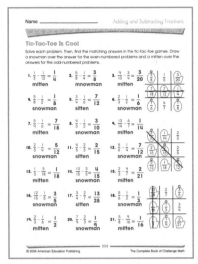

Page 111

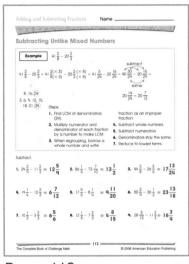

Page 112

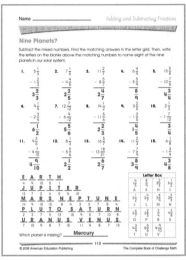

Page 113

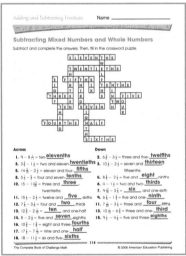

Page 114

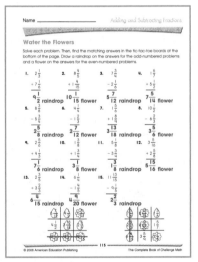

Page 115

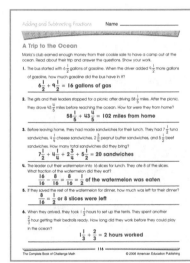

Page 116

The Complete Book of Challenge Math

Answer Key

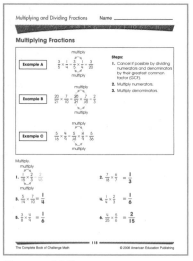

Page 118

Page 119

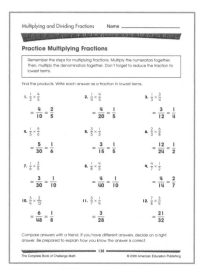

Page 120

Page 121

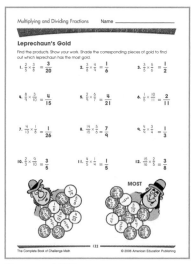

Page 122

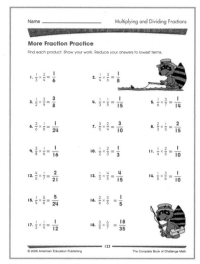

Page 123

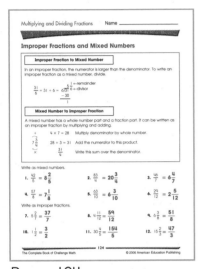

Page 124

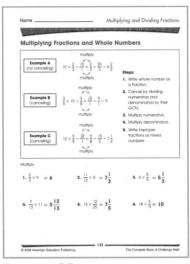

Page 125

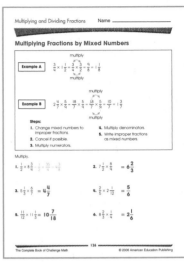

Page 126

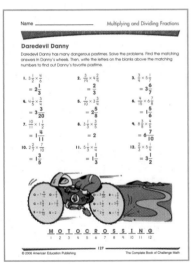

Page 127

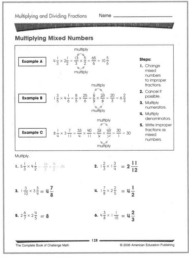

Page 128

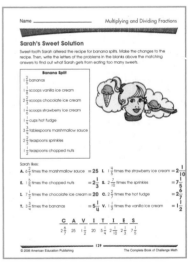

Page 129

The Complete Book of Challenge Math

Answer Key

Page 130

Page 131

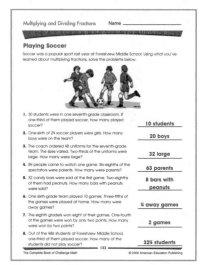

Page 132

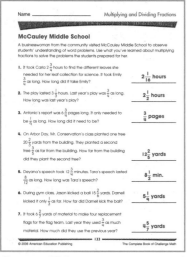

Page 133

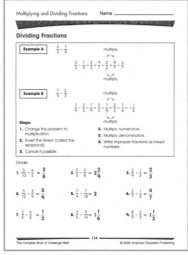

Page 134

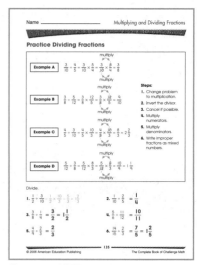

Page 135

Page 136

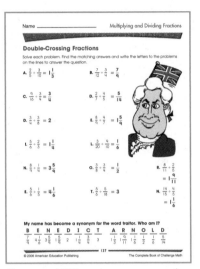

Page 137

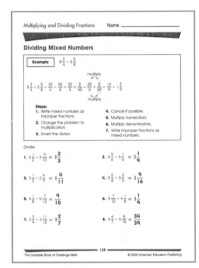

Page 138

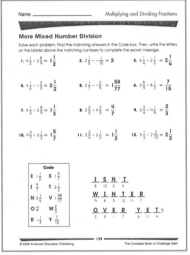

Page 139

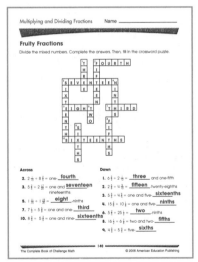

Page 140

Page 141

The Complete Book of Challenge Math

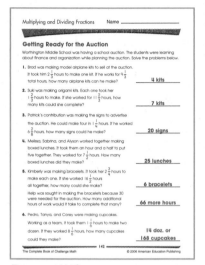

Page 142

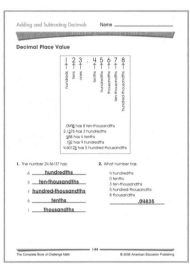

Page 144

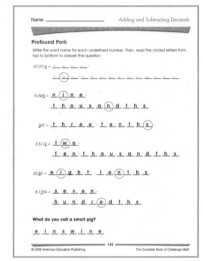

Page 145

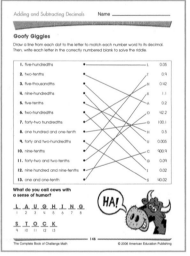

Page 146

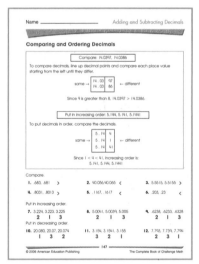

Page 147

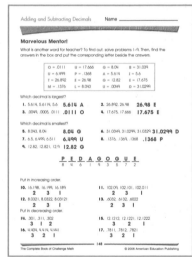

Page 148

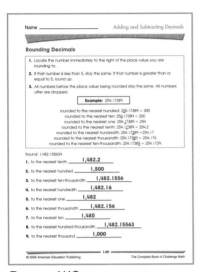

Page 149

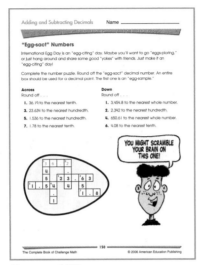

Page 150

Page 151

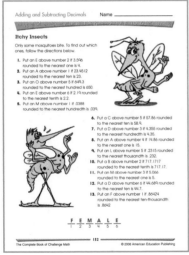

Page 152

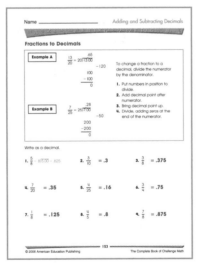

Page 153

Page 154

The Complete Book of Challenge Math

Answer Key

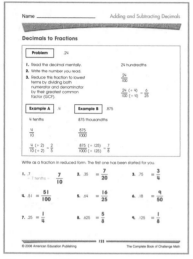

Page 155

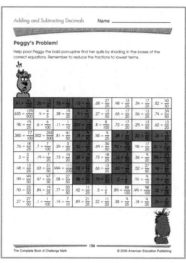

Page 156

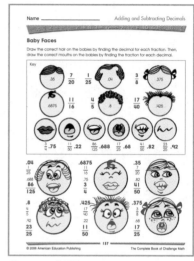

Page 157

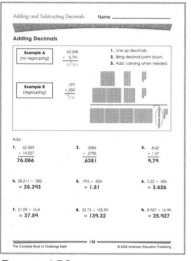

Page 158

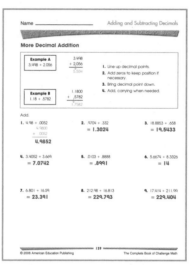

Page 159

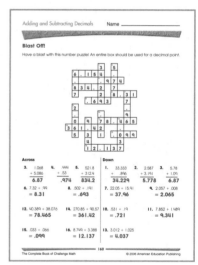

Page 160

Page 161

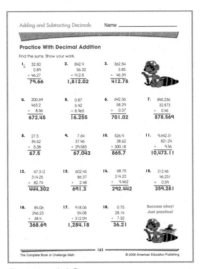

Page 162

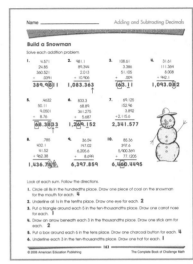

Page 163

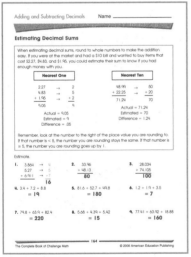

Page 164

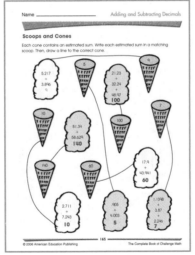

Page 165

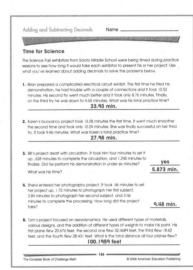

Page 166

The Complete Book of Challenge Math

Answer Key

Page 167

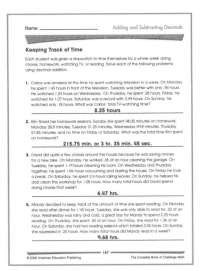

Name _____ *Adding and Subtracting Decimals*

Keeping Track of Time

Each student was given a stopwatch to time themselves for a whole week doing chores, homework, watching TV, or reading. Solve each of the following problems using decimal addition.

1. Carlos was amazed at the time he spent watching television in a week. On Monday he spent 1.45 hours in front of the television. Tuesday was better with only .54 hours. He watched 1.24 hours on Wednesday. On Thursday, he spent .28 hours. Friday, he watched for 1.07 hours. Saturday was a record with 3.49 hours. On Sunday, he watched only .18 hours. What was Carlos' total TV-watching time?

8.25 hours

2. Kim timed her homework sessions. Sunday she spent 48.05 minutes on homework, Monday 28.8 minutes, Tuesday 31.25 minutes, Wednesday 49.8 minutes, Thursday 57.85 minutes, and no time on Friday or Saturday. What was the total time Kim spent on homework?

215.75 min. or 3 hr. 35 min. 45 sec.

3. David did quite a few chores around the house because he was saving money for a new bike. On Monday, he worked .36 of an hour cleaning the garage. On Tuesday, he spent 1.19 hours cleaning his room. On Wednesday and Thursday together, he spent 1.44 hours vacuuming and dusting the house. On Friday he took a break. On Saturday, he spent 2.4 hours raking leaves. On Sunday, he helped his dad clean the workshop for 1.08 hours. How many total hours did David spend doing chores that week?

6.47 hrs.

4. Mandy decided to keep track of the amount of time she spent reading. On Monday she read after dinner for 1.45 hours. Tuesday, she was only able to read for .32 of an hour. Wednesday was rainy and cold, a great day for Mandy to spend 2.25 hours reading. On Thursday, she spent .50 of an hour. On Friday, she read for 1.36 of an hour. On Saturday, she had two reading sessions which totaled 3.55 hours. On Sunday, she squeezed in .25 hours. How many total hours did Mandy read in a week?

9.68 hrs.

Page 168

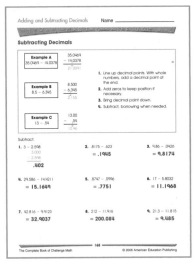

Adding and Subtracting Decimals **Name** _____

Subtracting Decimals

Example A
$$35.0469 - 14.0378$$
35.0469 − 14.0378 = 21.0091

Example B
8.500 − 6.345 = 2.155

Example C
13.00 − .54 = 12.46

1. Line up decimal points. With whole numbers, add a decimal point at the end.
2. Add zeros to keep position if necessary.
3. Bring decimal point down.
4. Subtract, borrowing when needed.

Subtract.

1. 3 − 2.598 = .402
2. .8175 − .623 = .1945
3. 9.86 − .0426 = 9.8174
4. 29.586 − 14.4211 = 15.1649
5. .8747 − .0996 = .7751
6. 17 − 5.8032 = 11.1968
7. 42.816 − 9.9123 = 32.9037
8. 212 − 11.916 = 200.084
9. 21.3 − 11.815 = 9.485

Page 169

Name _____ *Adding and Subtracting Decimals*

Subtracting Decimals from Whole Numbers

Example A
3.00 − .26 = 2.74

1. Put decimal point after whole number.
2. Line up decimals.
3. Add zero(s) after decimal.
4. Bring decimal point down.
5. Subtract, borrowing when needed.

Example B
58.00 − 12.09 = 45.91

Subtract.

1. 79.00 − .84 = 78.16
2. 25.0 − 24.3 = .7
3. 16.00 − 11.04 = 4.96
4. 5 − .112 = 4.888
5. 57 − 1.08 = 55.92
6. 98 − 58.36 = 39.64
7. 123 − 12.91 = 110.09
8. 85 − 6.07 = 78.93
9. 29 − 19.456 = 9.544

Page 170

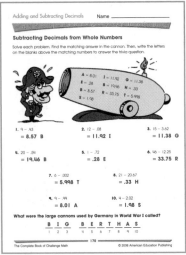

Adding and Subtracting Decimals **Name** _____

Subtracting Decimals from Whole Numbers

Solve each problem. Find the matching answer. Then, write the letters on the blanks above the matching numbers to answer the trivia question.

A = 8.01   I = 11.92   G = 11.38
B = .28   B = 19.46   H = .33
B = 8.57   R = 33.75   T = 5.998
E = 1.98

1. 9 − .43 = 8.57 B
2. 12 − .08 = 11.92 I
3. 15 − 3.62 = 11.38 G
4. 20 − .54 = 19.46 B
5. 1 − .72 = .28 E
6. 46 − 12.25 = 33.75 R
7. 6 − .002 = 5.998 T
8. 21 − 20.67 = .33 H
9. 9 − .99 = 8.01 A
10. 4 − 2.02 = 1.98 S

What were the large cannons used by Germany in World War I called?

B I G   B E R T H A S
1 2 3   4 5 6 7 8 9 10

Page 171

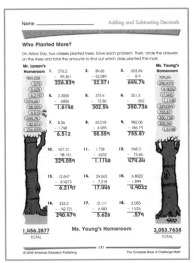

Name _____ *Adding and Subtracting Decimals*

Who Planted More?

On Arbor Day, two classes planted trees. Solve each problem. Then, circle the answers on the trees and total the amounts to find out which class planted the most.

Mr. Larson's Homeroom

1. 276.2 − 49.361 = 226.839
2. 84.66 − 52.089 = 32.571
3. 653.64 − 8.9 = 644.74
4. 2.3004 − .6856 = 1.6148
5. 375.4 − 72.86 = 302.54
6. 351.3 − .562 = 350.738
7. 8.26 − 1.748 = 6.512
8. 66.018 − 6.459 = 58.559
9. 942.06 − 186.19 = 755.87
10. 427.21 − 98.151 = 329.059
11. 1.738 − .6232 = 1.1148
12. 548.3 − 73.66 = 474.64
13. 12.647 − 6.4273 = 6.2197
14. 24.663 − 7.218 = 17.445
15. 6.8022 − 1.899 = 4.9032
16. 333.2 − 42.721 = 290.479
17. 12.111 − 6.483 = 5.628
18. 2.055 − 1.476 = .579

1,456.2877
TOTAL

Ms. Young's Homeroom

2,053.7638
TOTAL

Page 172

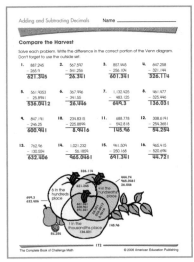

Adding and Subtracting Decimals **Name** _____

Compare the Harvest

Solve each problem. Write the difference in the correct portion of the Venn diagram. Don't forget to use the outside set.

1. 887.245 − 265.9 = 621.345
2. 567.597 − 541.256 = 26.341
3. 857.445 − 256.104 = 601.341
4. 647.258 − 321.144 = 326.114
5. 561.9353 − 25.8941 = 536.0412
6. 367.996 − 341.55 = 26.446
7. 1,132.425 − 483.125 = 649.3
8. 461.477 − 325.446 = 136.031
9. 847.191 − 246.25 = 600.941
10. 234.8315 − 225.8899 = 8.9416
11. 688.778 − 542.818 = 145.96
12. 308.6191 − 254.3651 = 54.254
13. 762.96 − 130.554 = 632.406
14. 1,021.232 − 56.1859 = 965.0461
15. 941.509 − 250.168 = 691.341
16. 965.415 − 520.694 = 44.721

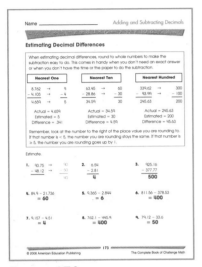

Page 173

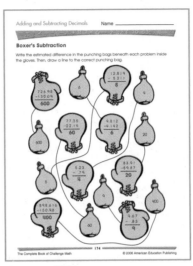

Page 174

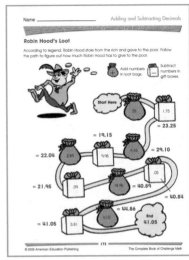

Page 175

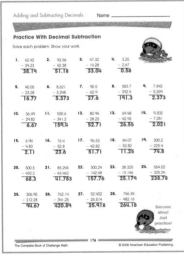

Page 176

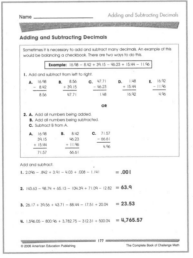

Page 177

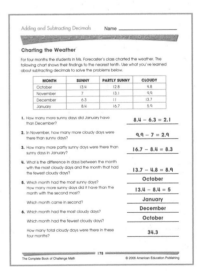

Page 178

The Complete Book of Challenge Math

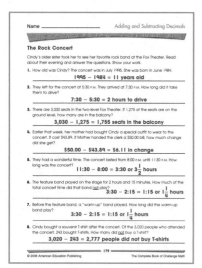

Page 179

Page 180

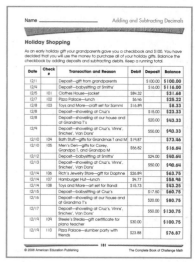

Page 181

Page 182

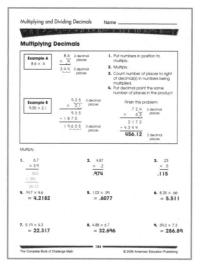

Page 184

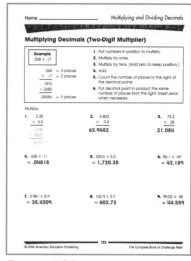

Page 185

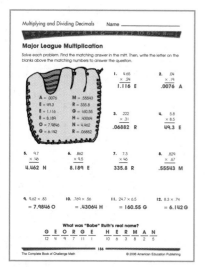

Page 186

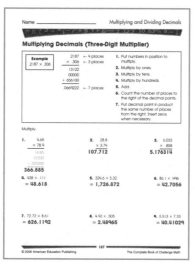

Page 187

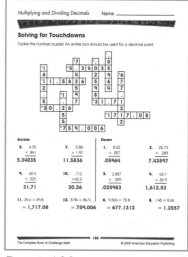

Page 188

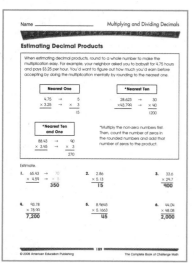

Page 189

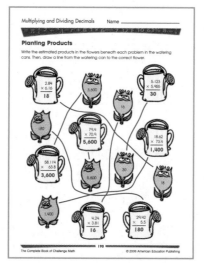

Page 190

Page 191

The Complete Book of Challenge Math

Answer Key

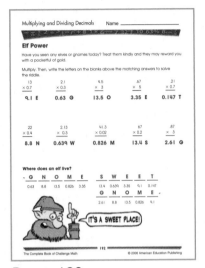

Page 192

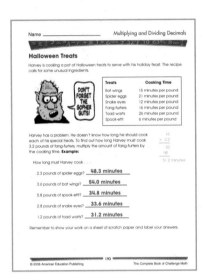

Page 193

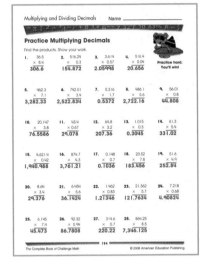

Page 194

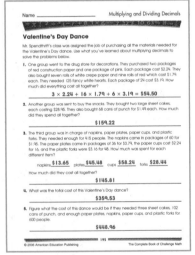

Page 195

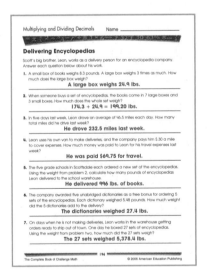

Page 196

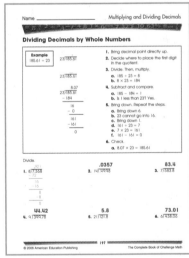

Page 197

Page 198

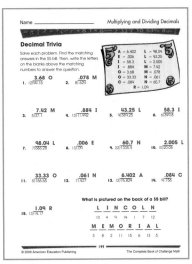

Page 199

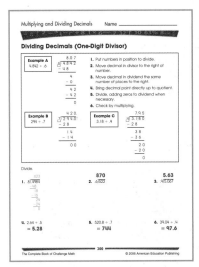

Page 200

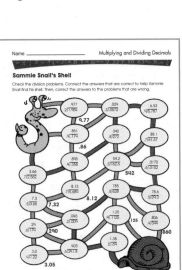

Page 201

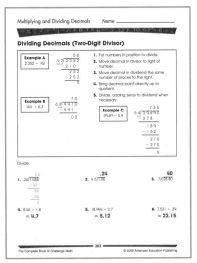

Page 202

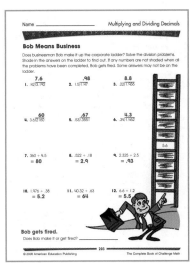

Page 203

The Complete Book of Challenge Math

Answer Key

Page 204

Multiplying and Dividing Decimals — Name _____

Fill That Basket

Solve each problem. Shade in the answers in the produce baskets to determine which has the largest amount of produce.

1. **2.31** 6)13.86	2. **46.3** 8)370.4	3. **5.316** 4)21.264	4. **.35** 24)8.4
5. **1.68** 36)60.48	6. **4.66** 87)405.42	7. **.36** 49)17.64	8. **69.24** 3)207.72
9. **7.69** 8)61.52	10. **342.1** 4)1368.4	11. **7.33** 52)381.16	12. **3.225** 8)27.735
13. **61.4** 6.2)380.68	14. **1.02** 3.4)3.468	15. **32.01** .06)1.9206	16. **56.2** 2.1)118.02
17. **62.3** 4.2)261.66	18. **13.8** .14)1.932	19. **7.35** 2.9)21.315	20. **28.68** .013).37284

B has the most produce.

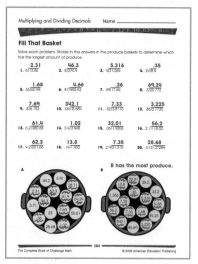

A

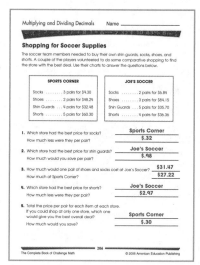

B

Page 205

Name _____ — **Multiplying and Dividing Decimals**

To Market, to Market

At the local grocery store, prices vary greatly. Most items come in a variety of package sizes. A wise shopper finds the unit rate or unit price, then bases purchasing decisions on the best prices. Find the unit rate of each item. Circle the best deal.

Potato Chips—14-oz. package of Brand A for $2.66 **$0.19 per oz.**	14-oz. package of store brand for $1.96 **($0.14 per oz.)**
8-oz. package of cream cheese for $1.84 **$0.23 per oz.**	8-oz. package of store brand for $1.36 **($0.17 per oz.)**
Ice cream—2 quarts of Brand B for $5.00 **$1.25 per pint**	2 quarts of Brand C for $3.20 **($0.80 per pint)**
Apple Juice—64 ounces of Brand M for $2.56 **$0.04 per oz.**	64 ounces of Brand T for $1.92 **($0.03 per oz.)**
32 ounces of taco chips for $1.76 **$0.055 or $0.06 per oz.**	32 ounces of Brand T for $1.12 **($0.035 or $0.04 per oz.)**
Microwave Popcorn—3 packages of Brand P for $3.36 **$1.12 per package**	4 packages of Brand S for $1.47 **($0.37 per package)**
3 packages of snack crackers for $2.07 **($0.69 per package)**	6 packages of Brand P for $5.76 **$0.96 per package**

Page 206

Multiplying and Dividing Decimals — Name _____

Shopping for Soccer Supplies

The soccer team members needed to buy their own shin guards, socks, shoes, and shorts. A couple of the players volunteered to do some comparative shopping to find the store with the best deal. Use their charts to answer the questions below.

SPORTS CORNER	JOE'S SOCCER
Socks . . . . 3 pairs for $9.30	Socks . . . . 2 pairs for $6.84
Shoes . . . . 2 pairs for $48.24	Shoes . . . . 3 pairs for $84.15
Shin Guards . . . 4 pairs for $32.48	Shin Guards . . 5 pairs for $35.70
Shorts . . . . 5 pairs for $60.30	Shorts . . . . 4 pairs for $36.36

1. Which store had the best price for socks? — **Sports Corner**
   How much less were they per pair? — **$.32**

2. Which store had the best price for shin guards? — **Joe's Soccer**
   How much would you save per pair? — **$.98**

3. How much would one pair of shoes and socks cost at Joe's Soccer? — **$31.47**
   How much at Sports Corner? — **$27.22**

4. Which store had the best price for shorts? — **Joe's Soccer**
   How much less were they per pair? — **$2.97**

5. Total the price per pair for each item at each store. If you could shop at only one store, which one would give you the best overall price? — **Sports Corner**
   How much would you save? — **$.30**

Page 207

Name _____ — **Multiplying and Dividing Decimals**

Eating at Earl's

Lindsey invited six friends to have lunch with her at Earl's Sandwich Shoppe. Each girl ordered a sandwich and a soft drink. When the bill came Lindsey noticed that someone had smeared the lunch check with big blobs of mustard.

Help Lindsey find out what was written under those dried blobs of mustard. Use your problem-solving skills to write the correct numbers or words in the mustard blobs.

Earl's Sandwich Shoppe Menu

Sandwiches		Soft drinks	Large	Small
Earl's Club $2.79		Fruit Juices	$1.25	$1.05
Mort's Meatball $3.29		Lemonade	$0.96	$0.65
Tony's Tuna $2.49		Spring Water	$0.85	$0.55
Chuck's Chicken $2.29				
Vick's Veggie $2.97				
Frank's Frank $1.49				

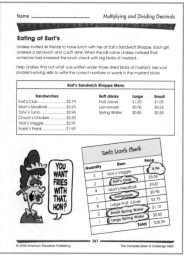

YOU WANT FRIES WITH THAT, HON?

Earl's Lunch Check

Quantity	Item	Price
2	Vick's Veggie	$5.94
2	Earl's Club	$5.58
3	Mort's Meatball	$9.87
1	Lemonade	$0.96
1	Large Fruit Juices	$3.75
2	Small Spring Water	$1.10
1	Large Spring Water	$0.85
	Total	$28.04

Page 208

Multiplying and Dividing Decimals — Name _____

Estimating Decimal Quotients

When estimating decimal quotients, round to a whole number to make the division easy. For example, if you had 17.8 milliliters of medicine left and took 3.12 milliliters each day, how many days of medicine would you have left?

Example A

$17.8 \div 3.12 \approx 18 \div 3 = 6$

1. Round the numbers at a place value that makes the division easy.
2. Divide the rounded non-zero numbers.
3. Cancel all zeros in the divisor and the same number of zeros in the dividend.
4. Bring up any remaining zeros.

Example B

$629.48 \div 88.23 \approx 630 \div 90$

7
90)630

Example C

$4,489.56 \div 52.6 \approx 4,500 \div 50$

90
50)4500

Estimate.

1. 14.97 ÷ 2.73
   ≈ 5 5)15

2. 476.92 ÷ 62.8
   = 8

3. 3,589.662 ÷ 88.74
   = 40

4. 36.43 ÷ 5.782
   = 6

5. 419,551 ÷ 72.21
   = 6

6. 6,389.75 ÷ 78.57
   = 80

Page 209

Name _____ — **Multiplying and Dividing Decimals**

Put Your Best Foot Forward

Write the estimated quotients shown on the feet beneath each problem inside the socks. Then, draw a line from the sock to the correct foot.

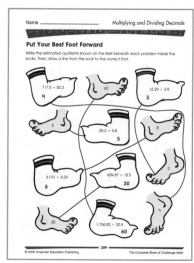

Problem	Answer
717.5 ÷ 82.3	9
12.24 ÷ 3.9	3
25.2 ÷ 4.8	5
31.91 ÷ 4.24	8
604.87 ÷ 18.5	30
1,756.82 ÷ 32.4	30 (feet: 60, 5, 8, 3, 4)

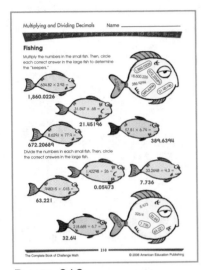

Page 210

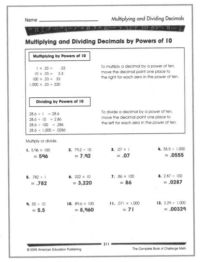

Page 211

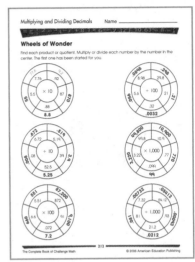

Page 212

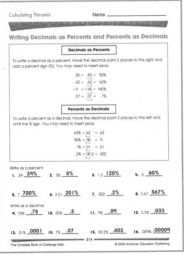

Page 214

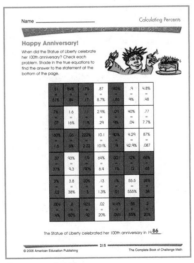

Page 215

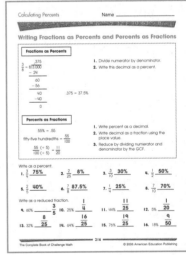

Page 216

The Complete Book of Challenge Math

Answer Key

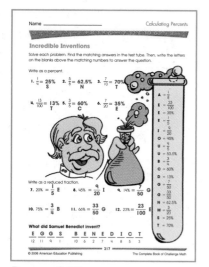

Page 217

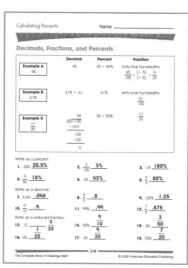

Page 218

Page 219

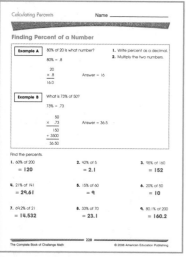

Page 220

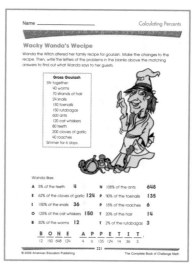

Page 221

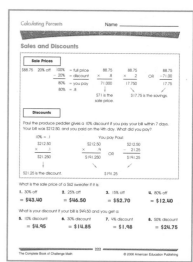

Page 222

The Complete Book of Challenge Math

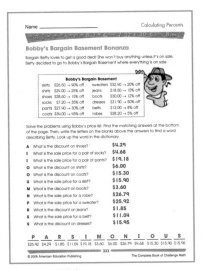

Page 223

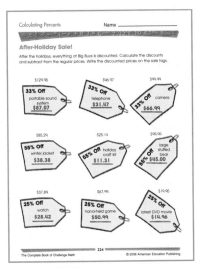

Page 224

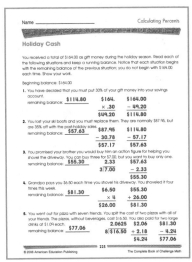

Page 225

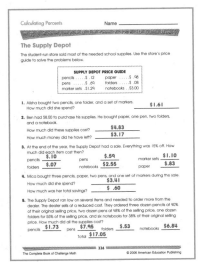

Page 226

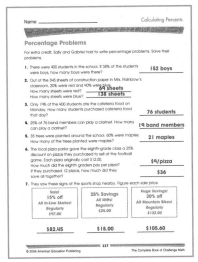

Page 227

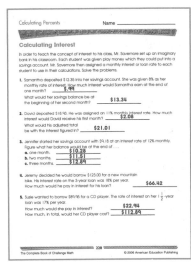

Page 228

The Complete Book of Challenge Math

Answer Key

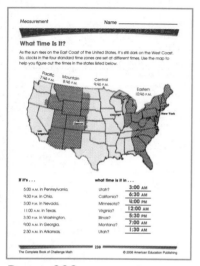

Page 230

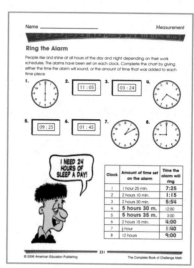

Page 231

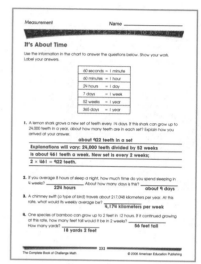

Page 232

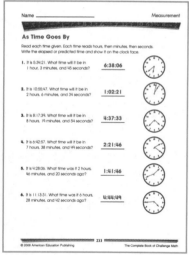

Page 233

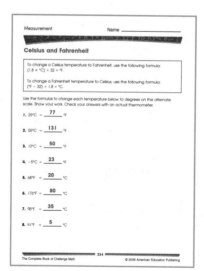

Page 234

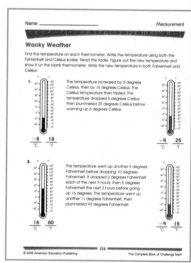

Page 235

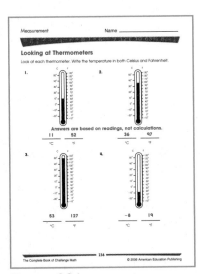

Page 236

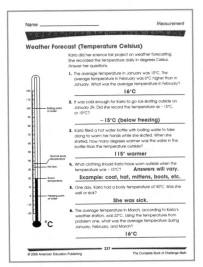

Page 237

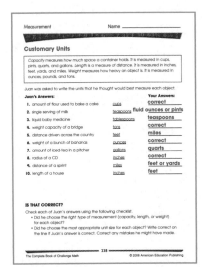

Page 238

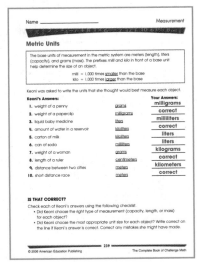

Page 239

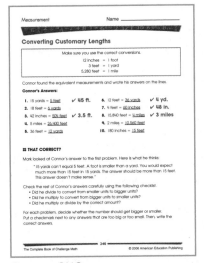

Page 240

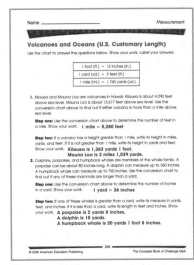

Page 241

The Complete Book of Challenge Math

Answer Key

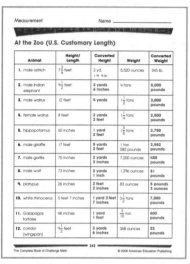

Page 242

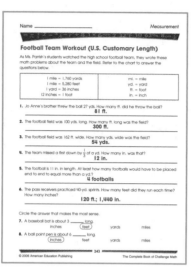

Page 243

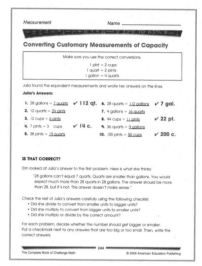

Page 244

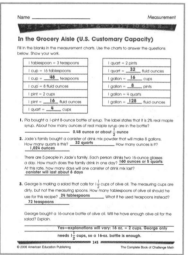

Page 245

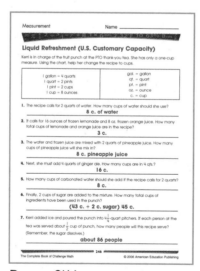

Page 246

Page 247

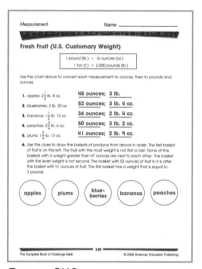

Page 248

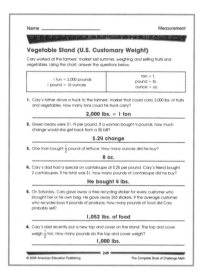

Page 249

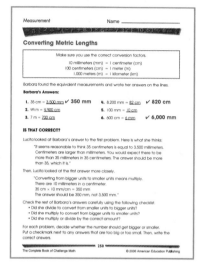

Page 250

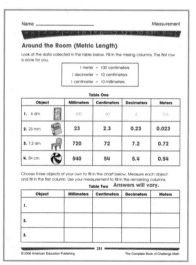

Page 251

Page 252

Page 253

The Complete Book of Challenge Math

Answer Key

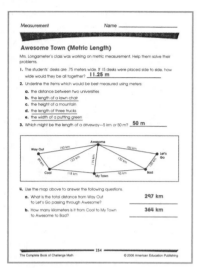

Page 254

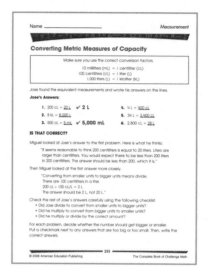

Page 255

Page 256

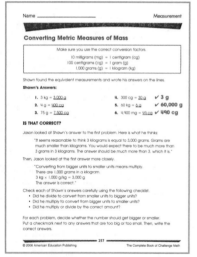

Page 257

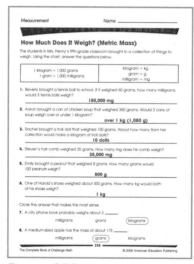

Page 258

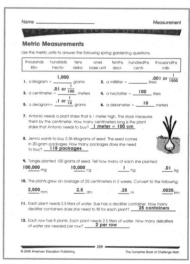

Page 259

The Complete Book of Challenge Math

© 2006 American Education Publishing

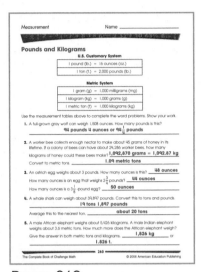

Page 260

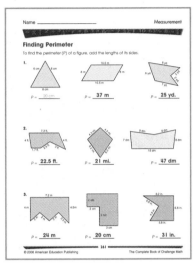

Page 261

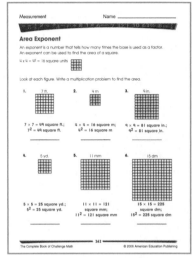

Page 262

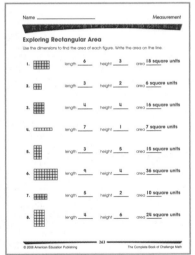

Page 263

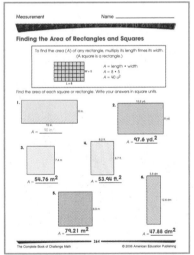

Page 264

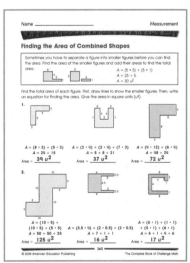

Page 265

The Complete Book of Challenge Math

Answer Key

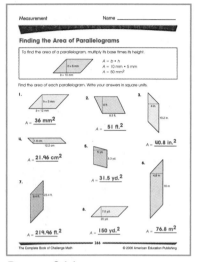

Page 266

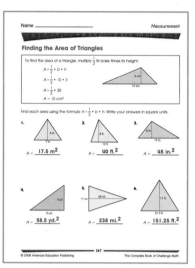

Page 267

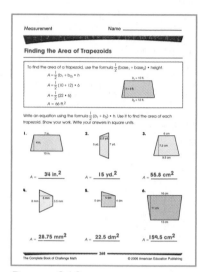

Page 268

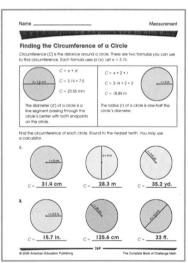

Page 269

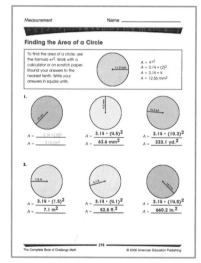

Page 270

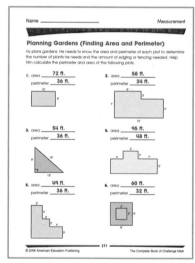

Page 271

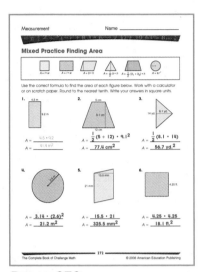

Page 272

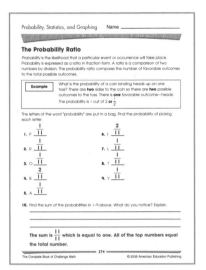

Page 274

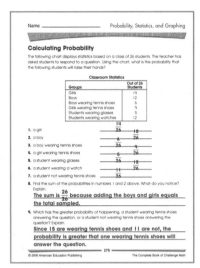

Page 275

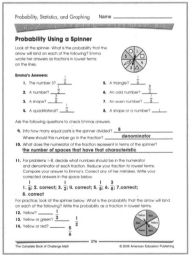

Page 276

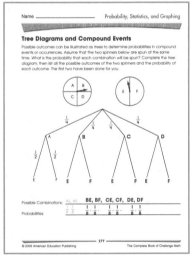

Page 277

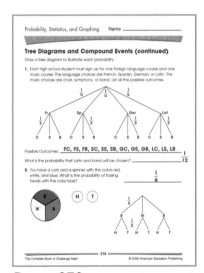

Page 278

The Complete Book of Challenge Math

Answer Key

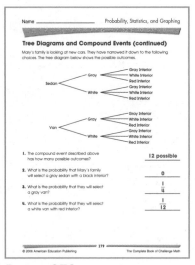

Page 279

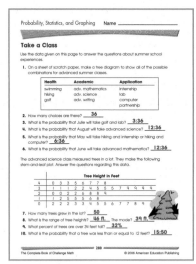

Page 280

Page 281

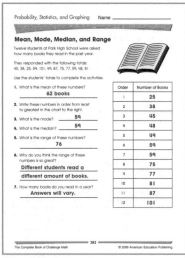

Page 282

Page 283

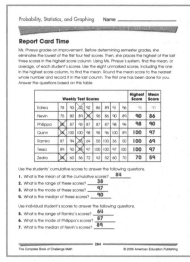

Page 284

Page 285

Name _____ Probability, Statistics, and Graphing

Interpreting Statistics

Find the mean, mode, median, and range of the information in each graph below. Round the answer to the hundredths place.

Mile Relay Practice Times	
DAY	TIMES
Monday	3.29 minutes
Tuesday	3.24 minutes
Wednesday	3.48 minutes
Thursday	3.24 minutes
Friday	3.89 minutes

mean: 3.43
mode: 3.24
median: 3.29
range: .65

Candy Bars Sold	
DAY	NUMBER OF BARS
Monday	127
Tuesday	225
Wednesday	93
Thursday	82
Friday	111
Saturday	137
Sunday	82

mean: 122.43
mode: 82
median: 111
range: 143

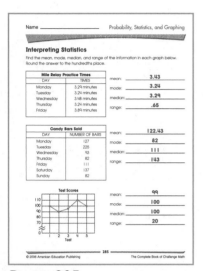

Test Scores

mean: 99
mode: 100
median: 100
range: 20

Page 285

Page 286

Probability, Statistics, and Graphing   Name _____

Working With Frequency Tables

A *frequency table* is a good way to show information. Frequency tables show how often something has occurred.

Answer the following questions using the frequency table below.

Books Checked Out by Students					
Type	Monday	Tuesday	Wednesday	Thursday	Friday
Nonfiction	23	20	26	18	12
Fairy Tales	11	14	8	15	7
Adventure	29	21	32	24	16
Mystery	20	20	26	36	30

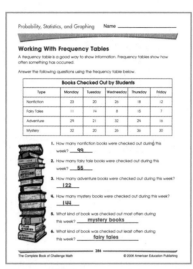

1. How many nonfiction books were checked out during this week? **99**

2. How many fairy tale books were checked out during this week? **55**

3. How many adventure books were checked out during this week? **122**

4. How many mystery books were checked out during this week? **144**

5. What kind of book was checked out most often during this week? **mystery books**

6. What kind of book was checked out least often during this week? **fairy tales**

Page 286

Page 287

Name _____ Probability, Statistics, and Graphing

Hair Colors

Relative frequency states the actual frequency of an event related to the total number possible.

The following chart shows the results of a classroom survey that a teacher took.

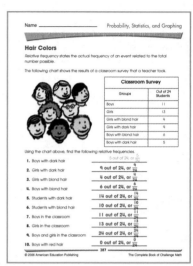

Classroom Survey	
Groups	Out of 24 Students
Boys	11
Girls	13
Girls with blond hair	4
Girls with dark hair	9
Boys with blond hair	6
Boys with dark hair	5

Using the chart above, find the following relative frequencies.

1. Boys with dark hair — 5 out of 24, or $\frac{5}{24}$
2. Girls with dark hair — 9 out of 24, or $\frac{9}{24}$
3. Girls with blond hair — 4 out of 24, or $\frac{4}{24}$
4. Boys with blond hair — 6 out of 24, or $\frac{6}{24}$
5. Students with dark hair — 14 out of 24, or $\frac{14}{24}$
6. Students with blond hair — 10 out of 24, or $\frac{10}{24}$
7. Boys in the classroom — 11 out of 24, or $\frac{11}{24}$
8. Girls in the classroom — 13 out of 24, or $\frac{13}{24}$
9. Boys and girls in the classroom — 24 out of 24, or $\frac{24}{24}$
10. Boys with red hair — 0 out of 24, or $\frac{0}{24}$

Page 287

Page 288

Probability, Statistics, and Graphing   Name _____

Probability and Relative Frequency

The relative frequency of an outcome is the ratio:

$$\frac{\text{frequency of the outcome}}{\text{total frequencies of outcomes}}$$

1. Make a table to show the relative frequencies from the following car survey.

A car dealer surveyed 200 recent car buyers. Seventy-six of his customers bought red cars, fifty-two customers bought blue cars, forty customers bought gray cars, and the rest purchased white cars.

Color of Cars Purchased	
Color	Relative Frequency
red	$\frac{76}{200}$
blue	$\frac{52}{200}$
gray	$\frac{40}{200}$
white	$\frac{32}{200}$

2. Using the table you made, find the probability (P) that each car will be chosen in the future.
   a. P (red) $\frac{19}{50}$ c. P (blue) $\frac{13}{50}$
   b. P (grey) $\frac{1}{5}$ d. P (white) $\frac{4}{25}$

3. Based on the relative frequency shown on the table, what color cars should his business buy the most of next year? Explain.
   Red, because it was purchased most frequently this year.

4. What color cars should he buy the least of next year? Explain.
   White, because the fewest customers showed interest in white cars.

Page 288

Page 289

Name _____ Probability, Statistics, and Graphing

Calculating Relative Frequency

Solve the following.

1. Mike is an excellent offensive soccer player. On any given scoring attempt, the probability that Mike will score a soccer goal is $\frac{4}{5}$. He has attempted to score 20 times. How many goals has he probably scored? **16 goals**

2. The probability that Mary will run the mile in under 5 minutes is $\frac{6}{10}$. During the season, she has run the mile 150 times. How many times has she probably run the mile in under 5 minutes? **90 times**

3. The probability that Sue's dog will catch a ball when thrown is $\frac{8}{12}$. One evening, the ball was thrown 204 times. How many times did the dog probably catch the ball? **136 times**

4. At the movie theater, the probability that a ticket will be purchased for an action-thriller is $\frac{5}{6}$. If 360 people go to the movie theater, how many will probably see an action-thriller? **300 people**

5. The probability that a cardinal will land at the bird feeder is $\frac{2}{12}$. Ninety-six birds have landed at the feeder today. Probably how many were cardinals? **16 cardinals**

6. The probability that a band member will play a cornet is $\frac{5}{8}$. There are 128 band members. How many probably play a cornet? **80 band members**

Page 289

Page 290

Probability, Statistics, and Graphing   Name _____

Working With Picture Graphs

The school newspaper editors at Bluebird Lane School encouraged students to take part in after-school activities. They published this picture graph. Refer to the graph to answer each question.

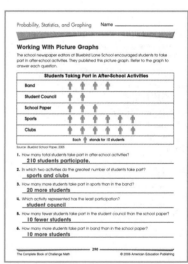

Students Taking Part in After-School Activities

Each stands for 10 students.

1. How many total students take part in after-school activities? **210 students participate.**

2. In which two activities do the greatest number of students take part? **sports and clubs**

3. How many more students take part in sports than in the band? **20 more students**

4. Which activity represented has the least participation? **student council**

5. How many fewer students take part in the student council than the school paper? **10 fewer students**

6. How many more students take part in band than in the school paper? **10 more students**

Page 290

Answer Key

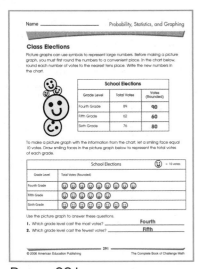

Page 291

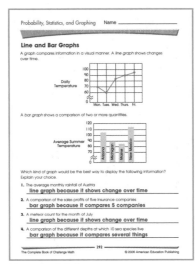

Page 292

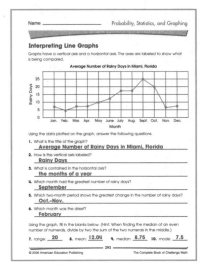

Page 293

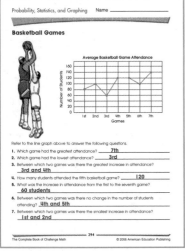

Page 294

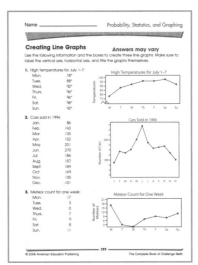

Page 295

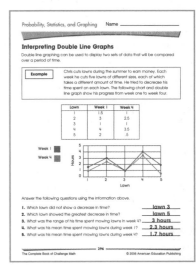

Page 296

Answer Key

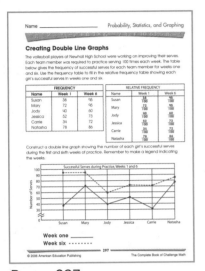

Page 297

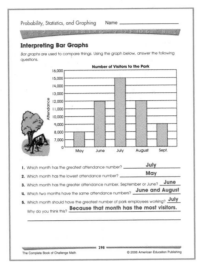

Page 298

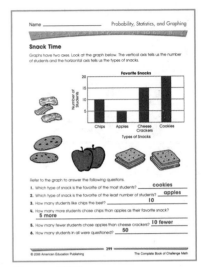

Page 299

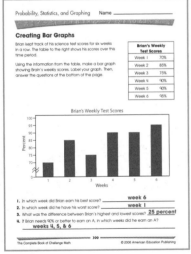

Page 300

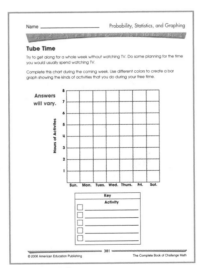

Page 301

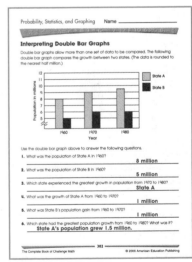

Page 302

The Complete Book of Challenge Math

Answer Key

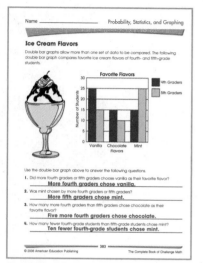

Page 303

Ice Cream Flavors

Double bar graphs allow more than one set of data to be compared. The following double bar graph compares favorite ice cream flavors of fourth- and fifth-grade students.

Favorite Flavors
(4th Graders / 5th Graders)

Use the double bar graph above to answer the following questions.

1. Did more fourth graders or fifth graders choose vanilla as their favorite flavor?
   More fourth graders chose vanilla.

2. Was mint chosen by more fourth graders or fifth graders?
   More fifth graders chose mint.

3. How many more fourth graders than fifth graders chose chocolate as their favorite flavor?
   Five more fourth graders chose chocolate.

4. How many fewer fourth-grade students than fifth-grade students chose mint?
   Ten fewer fourth-grade students chose mint.

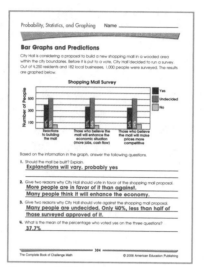

Page 304

Bar Graphs and Predictions

City Hall is considering a proposal to build a new shopping mall in a wooded area within the city boundaries. Before it is put to a vote, City Hall decided to run a survey. Out of 4,250 residents and 182 local businesses, 1,000 people were surveyed. The results are graphed below.

Shopping Mall Survey
(Yes / Undecided / No)

Based on the information in the graph, answer the following questions.

1. Should the mall be built? Explain.
   Explanations will vary. probably yes

2. Give two reasons why City Hall should vote in favor of the shopping mall proposal.
   More people are in favor of it than against.
   Many people think it will enhance the economy.

3. Give two reasons why City Hall should vote against the shopping mall proposal.
   Many people are undecided. Only 40%, less than half of those surveyed approved of it.

4. What is the mean of the percentage who voted yes on the three questions?
   37.7%

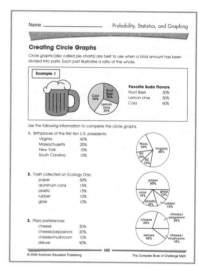

Page 305

Creating Circle Graphs

Circle graphs (also called pie charts) are best to use when a total amount has been divided into parts. Each part illustrates a ratio of the whole.

Example 1

Favorite Soda Flavors
Root Beer   30%
Lemon Lime   30%
Cola   40%

Use the following information to complete the circle graphs.

1. Birthplaces of the first ten U.S. presidents:
   Virginia   60%
   Massachusetts   20%
   New York   10%
   South Carolina   10%

2. Trash collected on Ecology Day:
   paper   50%
   aluminum cans 15%
   plastic   15%
   rubber   10%
   glass   10%

3. Pizza preferences:
   cheese   30%
   cheese/pepperoni 20%
   cheese/mushroom 10%
   deluxe   40%

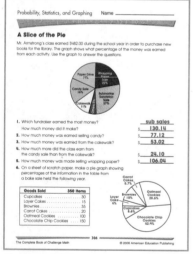

Page 306

A Slice of the Pie

Mr. Armstrong's class earned $482.00 during the school year in order to purchase new books for the library. The graph shows what percentage of the money was earned from each activity. Use the graph to answer the questions.

1. Which fundraiser earned the most money? **sub sales**
   How much money did it make? $ **130.14**
2. How much money was earned selling candy? $ **77.12**
3. How much money was earned from the cakewalk? $ **53.02**
4. How much more did the class earn from the candy sale than from the cakewalk? $ **24.10**
5. How much money was made selling wrapping paper? $ **106.04**
6. On a sheet of scratch paper, make a pie graph showing percentages of the information in the table from a bake sale held the following year.

Goods Sold	350 items
Cupcakes	30
Layer Cakes	15
Brownies	35
Carrot Cakes	20
Oatmeal Cookies	100
Chocolate Chip Cookies	150

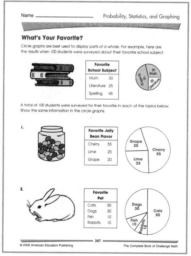

Page 307

What's Your Favorite?

Circle graphs are best used to display parts of a whole. For example, here are the results when 100 students were surveyed about their favorite school subject.

Favorite School Subject	
Math	30
Literature	25
Spelling	45

A total of 100 students were surveyed for their favorite in each of the topics below. Show the same information in the circle graphs.

1.
Favorite Jelly Bean Flavor	
Cherry	55
Lime	25
Grape	20

2.
Favorite Pet	
Cats	50
Dogs	30
Fish	10
Rabbits	10

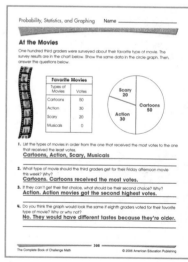

Page 308

At the Movies

One hundred third graders were surveyed about their favorite type of movie. The survey results are in the chart below. Show the same data in the circle graph. Then, answer the questions below.

Favorite Movies	
Types of Movies	Votes
Cartoons	50
Action	30
Scary	20
Musicals	0

1. List the types of movies in order from the one that received the most votes to the one that received the least votes.
   Cartoons, Action, Scary, Musicals

2. What type of movie should the third graders get for their Friday afternoon movie this week? Why?
   Cartoons. Cartoons received the most votes.

3. If they can't get their first choice, what should be their second choice? Why?
   Action. Action movies got the second highest votes.

4. Do you think the graph would look the same if eighth graders voted for their favorite type of movie? Why or why not?
   No. They would have different tastes because they're older.

The Complete Book of Challenge Math

© 2006 American Education Publishing